ON FILMS

1976 - 1998

YANN BEAUVAIS

Edited by
SCOTT HAMMEN

Eyewash
Books

CONTENTS

EDITOR'S NOTE

As its title indicates, the subject of this collection covers the work of the artist yann beauvais during almost exactly the last quarter of the 20th century. But the calendrical precision is purely coincidental. The years just happened to correspond both to the period he worked primarily in the medium of photochemical film and his most active role in the larger history of experimental film in Paris. And it was for entirely different reasons that both ended just before 2000.

NOR IS the choice of this period meant to diminish in any way the importance of his subsequent activity. In the new century yann beauvais moved on both geographically from Paris and artistically into electronic media. But the importance of his work when he was based in Paris both as an artist in Super 8 and 16mm film and as a champion of other filmmakers through his work as a critic, curator, distributor, and exhibitor, deserves specific attention. He recalled this period with characteristic modesty:

.   .   .

THERE HAVE ALWAYS BEEN MUSICIANS' musicians so I thought maybe I was a filmmakers' filmmaker. I might never have public recognition but other filmmakers might recognize me and realize that, had I not been there, something would have been lacking.

SOMETHING INDEED WOULD HAVE BEEN LACKING and the ambition of this book is to suggest just how significant this void would have been.

SCOTT HAMMEN
    Paris, October 2021

A NOTE ON THE TEXT

Making Films (1976 - 1997) is a transcription of yann beauvais's spontaneous spoken commentary recorded in 2017 while viewing his film work. It was transcribed and then edited for coherence with his approval.

Articles on Film (1979 - 1998) is a translation of the complete text of *Poussière d'image: articles de film (1979-1998)* published in 1998 by Paris Expérimental. Certain chapters were originally published separately in English and, in those cases, the original translator is credited. All of the others have been translated for the first time by this book's editor.

The images in **Making Films** are taken from some of the films discussed. The cover image as well as those introducing the six sections of **Articles on Film** are taken from beauvais's 1994 film *New York Long Distance.*

PART I

MAKING FILMS (1976 - 1997)

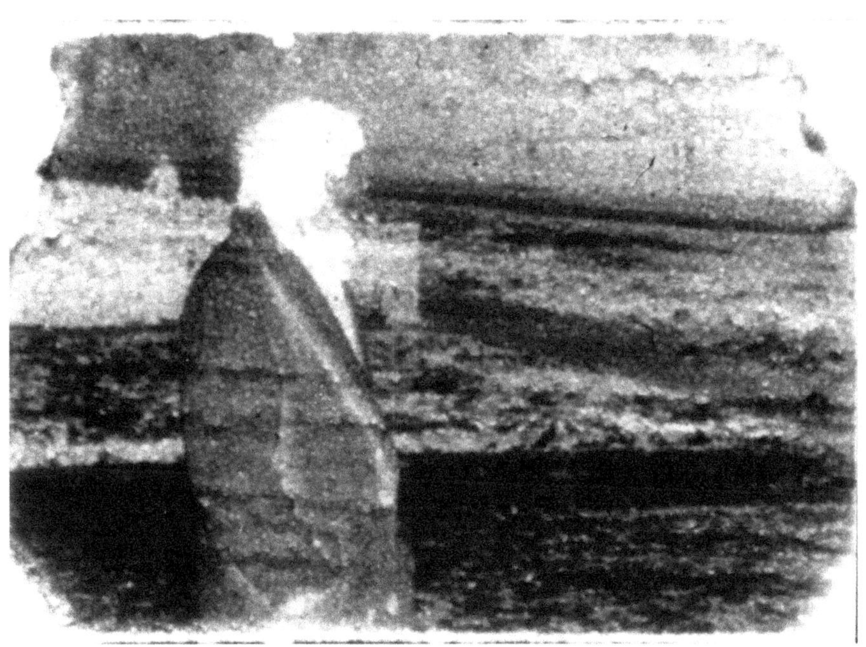

Disjet, 1979-1982 / 16mm / color / silent / single screen / 40' 00

PROLOGUE

My involvement with film started early. When I was very young, I remember projecting images with a 19th-century magic lantern in the basement of my grandfather's house in Cannes when I was there on vacation. Later, around the age of seven, I went to see a film at the theater Normandie on the Champs-Élysées, a big movie theater in Paris. It gave me a splitting headache and I vowed I would never go back. The headache came from being in a dark space with a huge image and noise that was too loud.

But this problem didn't last long and, just a few years later, I was already going to the movies two or three times a week.

When I was 14, I travelled with my mother and younger brother from Paris to Sicily by car. And when I spoke of my interest in movies to a friend of the family in Rome, he said, "I've got a camera I can lend you." He gave me a Paillard Bolex Double 8mm and one roll of film. So I decided to do a film of our entire vacation on only one roll. I knew that to make it last for the whole trip, I had to be economical so I shot everything in very short sequences.

I didn't have the roll processed until seven years later when I had started to think about making films and remembered that it existed. I asked my mother to help me find it, had it developed, and was surprised first that there was still an image at all and then that there was no shot longer than one second. At the time I had had no idea what this would look like when projected; I had just needed to economize on film. So when we went to the volcano on Mount Etna or the ruins at Paestum, I had shot in very short takes and everything went really fast. I obviously had no idea at the time that diary films would be an important form for me and that my childhood roll would be uncannily similar in style to one of the originators of that form, Jonas Mekas.

Anyway, from the age of 14 until I started making my own films, I was going to the cinema almost every day. Movie-going became almost a physical addiction - I didn't feel well if I couldn't get to a cinema frequently and would always rather be watching a film than sitting in a classroom. I went mostly to "art et essai" cinemas, what in the US would be called an "art house," that showed films of directors such as Antonioni, Fellini, or Bergman. I found these European films more interesting than big Hollywood productions I guess because they had a less predictable visual style and there was sometimes a certain plasticity to the camera motion.

Eventually I realized that I wanted to make films but not narrative films because I had no talent for telling stories. I started getting interested in early Russian cinema and thinking that there was a relation between cinema and philosophy. In particular the experience of seeing Kubrick's *2001: A Space Odyssey* (1969) made me think that a film could deal with philosophical issues, that there was something more intriguing than just a story, that you could express thought with moving images as well as words.

When I got to the Nanterre campus of the Université de Paris, it was the beginning of the semiological approach to film. Personally I found it quite boring but you had to accept semiology if you wanted to take a film course. Fortunately, the great ethnological filmmaker Jean Rouch was teaching a class at the Cinémathèque Française on Saturday mornings that did not conform to the prevailing fashion.

Even if most of the films he showed were not exactly my cup of tea, it was one of the rare places where you could see a wide variety of films, including some experimental work, and I found the diversity of styles stimulating.

I was studying philosophy but it was never my intention to become a philosophy teacher. I already knew that I was going to make films – and that they would not be films based on stories. We were studying Nietzsche, Deleuze, and Heidegger and the philosopher François Laruelle was my thesis supervisor. He was open to my doing something on film and I began by writing my thesis on film as a device for reproducing ideology. I think I was the first student at Nanterre to do a master's thesis in philosophy about film.

But actually I ended up not following any of the academic rules and what I did turned out to be more of a manifesto than a master's thesis. Fortunately, in the years following the 1968 upheaval, the university faculty were extremely tolerant and would support you even if you didn't do what they expected or hoped you would do. I eventually realized that my written thesis was of little interest to read and I started to wonder whether it would be possible to condense it into a film.

I started with some footage that I had found at the flea market in St. Ouen and began to scrape off the emulsion and draw on it with a felt tip pen. I wanted to reduce my thesis down to certain visual concepts with each concept appearing for three to five frames on the film. Watching the film would then take the place of reading the thesis. What interested me was whether it was possible to portray an abstract concept as an image and try to make the viewer think through rhythmical patterns rather than words. It turned out to be very tedious to do and I didn't succeed in making a full minute of film with the concept but for thirty seconds or so, it worked.

So even though I was surrounded primarily by other philosophy students, I already knew that I wanted to explore how film could function in the same abstract way as music. And it was at just this time that I discovered the films of Jonas Mekas and others at the university ciné-club in Nanterre. One day they showed Mekas' *Diaries, Notes, and Sketches* (1969) and I couldn't watch it all because I had a job as a messenger but I was able to see a couple hours of it before I had to leave for work.

I think I also saw films by Fernand Léger and Dziga Vertov in Jean Rouch's class at the Cinémathèque, or was it somewhere else? Rouch wasn't yet as open to experimental film as he was to become later but he at least knew that the people who were coming to his screenings were looking for something beyond the prevalent academic approach to film at the time, the semiology which I found suffocating. So in Rouch's class I first discovered that there was a history of ethnological film and experimental film which I was then able to explore even further in a class taught by Claudine Eizykman and Guy Fihman at the Paris university campus at Vincennes.

I gave my master's thesis film to Eizykman and Fihman for them to read and they were quite surprised to discover that, even though I was coming from the philosophy program at Nanterre and had not yet taken their class, I was aware of experimental films and had begun making them myself.

At Vincennes Eizykman and Fihman were showing a mixture of things, sometimes historical films, sometimes contemporary, their own or their students' or a visiting filmmaker. I remember Werner Nekes coming to show his work at the Maison des Beaux Arts, a place devoted to experimental film run by Dominique Willoughby, a student of theirs. The mixture depended on the students' particular interests. Sometimes it was related to Eizykman's text, *La jouissance-cinéma*, which analyzed issues in traditional cinema and showed how experimental film dealt with them differently.

I enrolled at the university at Vincennes in order to take this class but I soon encountered problems which had less to do with film than with being openly gay. Gay sexuality was problematic somehow for Eizykman and Fihman but at the time I was as interested in boys as in film and Vincennes at the time was an extraordinary place to meet people. But it was difficult for some people to accept that I was not in the closet.

On the academic side, I had started to write a doctoral thesis in the field of aesthetics under the direction of Daniel Charles, the philosopher and musician who had founded the Music Department at Vincennes and was a specialist in John Cage. My PhD was going to be in philosophy but I was not looking forward at all to writing chapters about such things as the philosophical conception of time. So it was a great relief, when I came back from the summer break, to learn that Michel Guy, the Minister of Education and Culture, had cancelled funding for the program in aesthetics I was enrolled in.

This liberated me from thesis-writing and, although I was still officially enrolled in the university, I no longer had any formal academic requirements and was just able to enjoy being at a place where I could discover the type of films that interested me. At the time sexual politics were just as important to me as artistic concerns and I felt that I needed to prepare to fight for recognition on both fronts. It helped that as I learned more about the history of experimental film, I discovered how many had been made by gay men.

Meanwhile I continued my exploration of how film could be used to play with rhythmical patterns analogous to music and how concepts and text could be used as images and vice versa. I knew that I wanted to make films composed on musical, not narrative, structure.

Students in the film class were allowed one roll of film per year, a roll of black-and-white film stock. Another advantage of being officially enrolled was that it gave me access to a projector. So I was able to shoot and project my first film: it was *R* (1976).

At the time I was working nights at a music store and at around eleven one night Eizykman and Fihman came to the store and asked me if they could include *R* in the Paris Film Coop which they had established to promote and distribute experimental film. I was surprised by their request as I had not yet really understood that making work of this sort meant that you had also to think about how the work was going to be seen.

Eizykman and Fihman had succeeded in getting a program of experimental films shown in a few conventional cinemas in Paris. But it was an anomaly due to the fact that Eizykman's film *V. W. – Vitesse*

Women (1974) had received a bit of publicity when it won a prize at the Knokke-le-Zoute International Festival of Experimental Film in Belgium. But I never believed that traditional cinemas were the appropriate place to show these kinds of films.

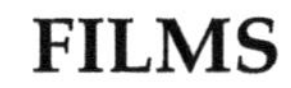

FILMS

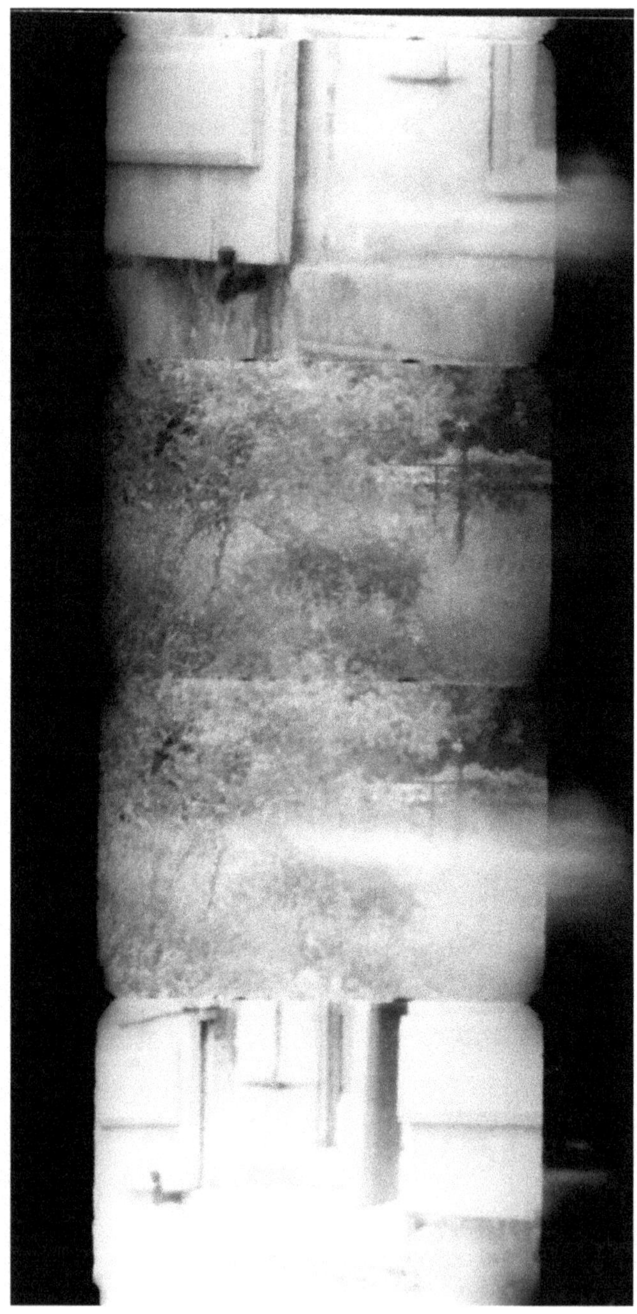

R, 1975 / 16mm /b&w/ silent/ 02:50

R

So for *R* my project was to do something with the one roll provided by the university. I knew I wanted to do a kind of transcription of music.

I had gone to the Charente region to shoot it because that particular place was important to me: the house of my aunt and uncle was near the town of Saintes where there was a festival of Baroque music. And in Royan, not far away, in the late winter of that year there was a festival of contemporary music. Even though the principal activity in the countryside was to grow grapes for cognac, you could still hear a lot of music.

And since my cousin was a co-director of the festival in Saintes, some of the participating musicians were living in my aunt and uncle's house and from my room I could hear them rehearsing, one playing a harpsichord, another a cello. I had memories of playing Bach on the piano as a child and so I used this experience to construct a graphic representation that I could execute with my camera, constructing a sort of landscape from the configuration of piano keys.

I wanted to use landscape as if it was a piano keyboard, with each note being a shot of the landscape so I could "play" the landscape with my camera. I didn't want the viewer to "hear" the music but rather to use the structure of the relation between each note in order to reconstitute the landscape.

My goal was not to make a realistic panoramic shot of the landscape but an artificial one, one that showed how cinema is a succession of artificial movements, using black frames to emphasize the discontinuity.

Although I was not aware of it while I was shooting, I had put my hand in front of the camera at times and it appeared as a sort of white cone in the frame. At first it looked like a mistake but then I realized that this cone was really interesting because it introduced another element into the image which I ended up emphasizing rather than eliminating.

So I started with a core visual transcription of music but, since I was basing it on baroque forms, I wanted to perform variations around this core. These variations were an expression of total freedom but always within boundaries of the fixed rules I had set myself.

At this point I had seen the experiments that Walter Ruttmann, Hans Richter, and Viking Eggeling had done with the visual portrayal of music in the 1920s. Ruttmann and Eggeling were primarily thinking about finding visual equivalents for melody through lines whereas Richter was thinking more about rhythm. And I felt that there was something both satisfying and unsatisfying in both approaches. I liked what they were doing very much but I still felt something was lacking. I felt it was somehow not quite stimulating enough so *R* was my attempt to address this frustration.

But when Eizykman and Fihman included *R* in their 1975 program of films, it seemed premature for me. It was only my first film, a very fragile beginning, and yet it was suddenly being shown publicly in many places. I felt like it was too soon, like they were taking my film away from me too quickly after its birth. I understood why it was strategically good for them because it added one more name to the list of filmmakers in France that they got credit for encouraging. But their objectives had nothing to do with me and it didn't feel right that they were using my tentative first film for their own purposes.

After *R*, I tried to do a film which I called *F* and which was just on windows. It was closer to the approach of Viking Eggeling than *R* but it didn't work. It was based on the idea of taking a shape and producing a line which was then repeated and developed based only on some images of a window. But unlike Richter and Eggeling who worked with drawings, I started with filmed images. Where in *R* I was dealing with rhythm, with *F* I was trying to see if I could work with the idea of a line. But I wasn't happy with it and I took it out of distribution rapidly.

Then I made a film which I called *Prélude au Carré* which also grew out of *R*. It was based on *Red Square*, the 1915 painting by Malevitch, and involved a square which takes on a certain thickness and volume and moves in four different directions. I first composed a sort of score consisting of 40 or 50 pages of painted red squares which I then filmed frame-by-frame. Watching the result was a lot less interesting than the experience of making it but I learned a lot.

At this time I wanted to make films but was moving very slowly as I needed to prepare them with detailed drawings. I did a whole series of films after *R* based on these studies which were very useful as learning experiences but total failures as films. They enabled me to learn about duration, the dynamics of shot versus counter-shot, proportional relationships and, above all, the simple fact that just because something worked in a painting didn't necessarily mean it would work in a film.

These were all very important things to discover because I was still convinced that I could compose music in the form of film by using elements from painting. I had seen some of Oskar Fischinger's work in this domain and, even though it was not at all what I wanted to do, had found it very inspiring. What I specifically wanted to know was whether there was another way I could shape and construct forms and control how they related to a background. So for several years after *R*, I continued to test different possibilities.

I went quite far with my formal experiments but not many of them are visible today. Partly this is because I never made prints and only have an unprojectable original but it is also partly because, however interesting they were to do, I never felt they were worth showing.

From the time I first started making films, I knew that I was always going to work on different but parallel tracks and would need to jump from one to the other. Just as in music there is Bach, which is quite formal and sometimes considered too structured to be sensual and then there is jazz which is often improvised and more sensual, so within my filmmaking I tend to periodically step back from difficulties of formal inquiry to seek refreshment in a more relaxed domain. After concentrating very intensely on purely formal concerns, I realized that I risked exhausting myself if I could not escape to something informal as a way to catch my breath.

This eventually took the form of diary films and, while this offered relief to me creatively, it also produced a major problem in the way my work was perceived by others since I was defying categorization as an artist.

I had known from the beginning that I was never going to make a living from my work and I thought that at least that gave me the freedom to move from one style of film to another, recharging my batteries by using the energy I got from working one way to working in another way.

But I hadn't realized that jumping from one track to another was also going to be held against me as an artist because it meant for many people that I had no characterized style. I was always being asked why I didn't stick to one track. While I saw it as the freedom to break down the rules which define a particular style, others saw it as a lack of seriousness.

It seemed that I was on my way to becoming a kind of ugly duckling in the small French experimental film world. I wasn't exactly ignored - I was cited in books and articles, such as Dominique Noguez's survey book *Thirty Years of Experimental Film in France* (1975), but critics and programmers did not really know what to do with me.

No one seemed to understand that I didn't see my goal as simply perfecting a certain style but rather as questioning the nature of cinema. I was more interested in the infinite varieties of the process of making films than in one particular style. And, as I was leaping from one track to another, I saw a lot of connections which those looking at my work didn't see.

I had problems around this issue with other filmmakers as well as with critics. I would get impatient with their trying to conform to the same patterns as the artist in the contemporary art market where one is rewarded for staying within the bounds of a defined style. I don't want to be acceptable to galleries and please collectors by working in a predictable style. As an artist my role is not to please.

And I can't cut myself up into categories - at some moments I am most concerned with gay issues, at others with radical politics, at others with the formal material of film. It's like a mosaic that together makes up who I am. Unfortunately, it seems most critics do not like the difficulty of dealing with an artist who is multi-faceted and does not have a single obsession.

But the reason I have not gone crazy is that I have always felt that I could go down many different roads and that if I hit a dead end on one of them, I could go down another, find another private garden.

At this time I was no longer involved with any academic institution, but was just surviving, going from one place to another. I was getting to know some people who were involved with the Collectif Jeune Cinéma and we would gather in the evenings to screen our films. But I was trying to see all kinds of films, not just the work of one small group. There were a lot of films focusing on the body at the time; most were not extraordinary but I did find some of them interesting. And some of the people who were making them were fascinating. There was no institutional structure for all this; it was just a loose network of filmmakers sharing their work.

But there were already intense rivalries developing in this small world. The fights - particularly between the Collectif Jeune Cinéma founded by Marcel Mazé and the Paris Films Coop led by Claudine Eizykman and Guy Fihman, were becoming increasingly bitter and I found myself in the middle, questioning both sides. My film *R* was in distribution at Paris Film Coop so I was associated with them and that inevitably meant that those allied with Collectif Jeune Cinéma considered me an enemy. It was awful.

So I tried to stay out of it on a daily basis and ended up spending a lot of time in London. It was at this time that I started putting my films into distribution at the London Filmmakers Coop. I was attracted to a movement of musicians in London at the time called Rock Against Racism and to the work of English filmmakers like Derek Jarman. And it was easy to see films that mattered to me there. In addition to the London Filmmakers Coop, there was the Other Cinema, and the ICA (Institute of Contemporary Arts) Cinema. Sometimes there were programs at the Tate Gallery.

Experimental filmmaking in London was also connected to the Punk movement and that is how I met Miles McKane. He had been involved in radical politics as a graphic designer first in New Zealand and then in London.

I knew that I was going to devote my life to filmmaking but I never had the illusion that I would ever be able to support myself from my films. So I continued working in a music store to earn enough to buy film and make prints. A lot of filmmakers around me hoped that they would one day earn their living in the film industry but I thought that they were missing the whole point about what an experimental filmmaker does and were looking for recognition in the wrong place.

Eventually, back in Paris from London, I was asked by the filmmakers Unglee and Philip Dubuquoy to join them in a programming initiative called Adicinex which was showing films at midnight at L'Entrepôt cinema in Paris.

I was now convinced that there was no separation between making a film, organizing a space to show a film, and distributing films. I saw it as a creative continuum. Being an experimental filmmaker for me meant a commitment not just to making films but also solving the problems of how to create awareness about them. The issues raised in making a film are inevitably connected to how it is going to be seen. You can put your head in the sand and ignore them but they will not disappear.

It was unacceptable to me that a younger generation of filmmakers were being forced to continue the fights of an older generation, forced to take sides in disputes that were not their own. I felt it was as if their freedom was being confiscated and that they were being forced to follow a single established trend at a time when in fact there were multiple choices open to them.

When Miles and I decided to found Light Cone, I asked Paul Sharits and Malcolm Le Grice whom I knew from my time in the US and the UK, as well as a number of French filmmakers - there were probably around ten of us altogether - to deposit prints of their films.

From the beginning, we were engaged on multiple fronts - distribution, screenings, publication. I organized events where we invited filmmakers - among them Michel Nedjar, Teo Hernandez, Jakobois,

Rose Lowder to screen their work. And we mounted an exhibition of what we called "frozen film frames," single frames from films printed and displayed as photographs.

We were widely mocked by French academics because Light Cone was an English name and it got even worse when we started publishing our magazine Scratch because both Miles and I were dyslexic and it was filled with spelling mistakes. So they made fun of us even though they bought the magazine anyway because it was the only place where they could read interviews with certain important film artists such as Sharits.

Some filmmakers were at first angry because they thought Light Cone was further undermining the two organizations that were fighting with each other but then more and more of them began to come to us from both sides. This made me happy because it meant that my analysis of the situation had not been wrong. Something WAS necessary to break the existing patterns.

I had realized very early on that my films were never going to please a wide public but did attract and encourage other filmmakers, sometimes strengthening their own will to make films. There have always been musicians' musicians so I thought maybe I was a film-makers' filmmaker. I might never have public recognition but other filmmakers might recognize me and realize that, had I not been there, something would have been lacking. And doing things like creating a distribution channel through Light Cone and showing films through Scratch was part of this.

Très rare film (1975-78)

Très rare film was my first diary film and it opened the possibility for me to explore new areas that were outside the predominant structural film tendencies of the time. It has only been shown publicly once or twice.

Most of it was shot frame-by-frame except for one sequence that lasts around 3 minutes of the stump of a tree which was quite peculiar because of its color. It was brown up to a certain height but then turned to red. I decided to stop moving the camera after each frame and to shoot the stomp in a continuous sequence, hoping that the viewer would perceive the movement in the sawdust. But instead it drove people mad because after all the single frame shooting, they couldn't make any sense out of a fixed image. I'm not sure I could make sense out of it either but, to me, it was very necessary.

The stump was quite near the place I had made *R* so I think I must have shot it around the same time and was probably the first roll of color film I ever shot.

Anyway, *Très rare film* was a sort of compilation of all of my diary films up to that time and I showed it mostly just to the friends who appeared in it – most of whom didn't like it because it moved too fast. The title was a reference to a 1915 painting by Francis Picabia *Très rare tableau sur la terre*. What I loved in Picabia's work was his sense of bad taste, the fact that he had no respect for the rules, his love of non-accomplishment - not following through and not finishing things. I felt that described very well what I was doing. It seemed to me that in experimental film there were a lot of people celebrating themselves and their own lives so I was trying to NOT celebrate my life. With my film diaries, I wanted to share my life but without turning it into a dramatic spectacle.

Mis en Pièces (1976-1978)

It started with one of my cousins, a little older than me, who was working with a theater group at the university at Vincennes dealing with feminist and lesbian issues and she was interested in exploring connections between theater and experimental film. She asked me if I was interested in seeing one of their plays and possibly doing something with it. So I went to see the play and was surprised to see how artificially theatrical it was.

I shot two or three rolls of the performance on negative film, had a print made, and then started cutting it into one or two frames at a time. I felt that I was really starting to learn a lot about the technique of editing. I never actually finished cutting it – I had underestimated the difficulty of editing a long sequence two frames at a time. And projecting the film or making a print of it proved impossible as it stood so I had to intersperse longer sequences in between the two frames just to get the lab to accept to print it.

When my cousin finally saw the film, she didn't really know what to make of it. She had hoped it might result in something that could be integrated into the performances of her play but obviously it wasn't. I had thought theater people would be interested but after just one projection, I realized that they clearly were not.

The film did circulate a bit – it was shown on a few programs at universities and festivals. For me it was a very good learning experience even if I ultimately failed at what I had originally wanted to do. I learned about the technical limits of frame-by-frame editing, how to create rhythmical patterns, how to perceive multiple events simultaneously, and how musical patterns could be created by changing just one frame in a repeated sequence. But, in the end, the theatrical subject was probably too distracting for viewers to notice these things.

Wanderer (1978)

Wanderer was extracted from *Très Rare Film* and consists of some diary film sections I shot on a trip to the US, mostly in New York, in and around Manhattan. I liked these sequences on their own. It had a certain autonomy from *Très Rare Film* in that it was all shot in a short time in a specific place.

But it was not just to extract something of more manageable length from the longer film as I have never been concerned with duration as an obstacle to exhibiting my work. Nor has the film gauge or number of screens been an issue for me. I consider that the viewer's problem.

The New York footage had emotional meaning for me as well – shooting it was a way of recovering from an unhappy love affair. Not that it was therapeutic in the emotional sense but filming certain places forced me to dissociate them from sentimental memories and find other interesting things about them. So it helped me to recover emotionally although this is not at all visible in the film. There's no way that the viewer could realize this but it was important to me.

I was staying with my father and brother who were living in a New Jersey suburb at the time and was able to get into Manhattan easily and see films and discover the city on my own. I saw a lot of experimental films, at Anthology Film Archives, at MoMA, at Collective for Living Cinema. I remember a very rare screening there of Warhol's *Vinyl* presented by its star, Ondine. At the time I didn't make any connection to what I was doing and Jonas Mekas's film diaries but realized later how close what I was doing was to his work.

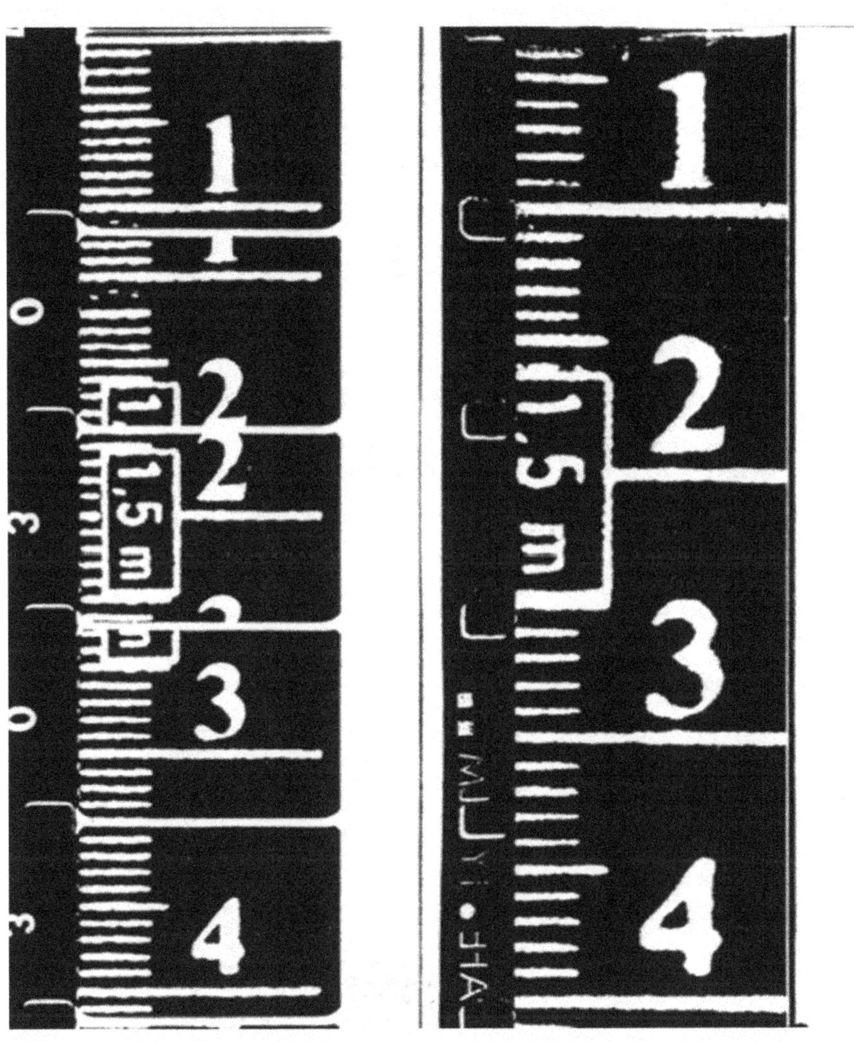

Temps de mètre, 1980 / 16mm / color / silent / 17' 00

Temps de mètre (1980)

So far my formal experiments *R*, and *Mise en Pièces,* had been very satisfying as learning experiences but completely unsatisfying as viewing experiences for both me and others. I was beginning to conclude that I just wasn't capable of expressing myself through film and this feeling was exacerbated by my innate lack of self-confidence. But, at the same time, I felt compelled to continue this work so it was somewhat paradoxical. It seemed that the work was of no interest but I kept thinking about it and trying to figure out what I was really after.

I began to realize that the world of experimental film was inherently conservative and that I had a fundamental need to break the rules. While, by definition, the form of experimental film was supposed to be totally open, it seemed to me that many of the films I saw were very strictly formatted. Beneath the appearance of complete freedom, there seemed to me to be some rules that were very authoritarian. I realize now that *Temps de mètre* was a radical reaction to that.

I had been working with the composer Martin Davorin-Jagodic on a performance piece which we called *According to...* It was made from a paper printout of articles I had written for the magazine *GaiPied* that I cut into perforated strips of the same dimensions as 16mm film and gave to Davorin to use as a musical score by running it through a projector. While I was doing that, I realized it was going to be how I was going to work with *Temps de mètre* – to make a paper print of a dressmaker's measuring tape and make a film of it.

I knew it was quite ambitious – the question of the measuring stick as an object had been raised by Marcel Duchamp and I wanted to have a kind of dialogue with him. I know it was totally presumptuous. Duchamp had made *3 stoppages étalon* in 1913 as an inquiry into how we perceive the notion of length and what constitutes a work of art.

So I copied the paper print of the measuring tape three times, as had Duchamp, but then turned it into a film that could be projected as a loop. I realized that the original loop was going to deteriorate as it was projected and I wanted it to last longer so I went to a lab to make a film of each gradation of the one meter length. Then I added a text which was a sort of manifesto in which I defined the relationship between the measure of a meter and notions of authority. And finally, to acknowledge my gay identity, I tinted the whole thing slightly pink.

I decided – somewhat arbitrarily – that the final film of the loop would run for 17 minutes. I was sure that it was not going to satisfy those who viewed it but I needed to do it for myself. *R* had been well received since it was safely within the current trend of "structural film" – the accepted norm at the time for experimental film and conceptual art. So I knew that *Temps de mètre* would disappoint viewers' expectations and, since it was going to annoy people anyway, I made the text extremely authoritarian in tone.

Since then *Temps de mètre* has probably been more talked about than actually seen but it was now been acquired by a few museum collections and been shown at times. So it continues to infuriate people.

ACCORDING TO... (1980)

I had met the Croatian composer Martin Davorin-Jagodic a few years earlier. He was teaching at the École Nationale des Arts Décoratifs in Paris and had seen *R* and *Mise en pièces* and, to my great surprise, wanted to meet me. I was quite interested in some of the concepts he was using in music, particularly the idea of chance. He introduced me to John Cage and how Cage incorporated the element of chance in his works and how that can transform the way things are perceived.

Davorin's work was among the most radical on the contemporary music scene. He was part of a group of musicians, mostly immigrants from Eastern Europe, who dealt with questions of improvisation and its relation to traditional performance practices. Exploring their work was just as stimulating for me as my discovery of experimental film because it taught me that everything was possible.

I brought my images to his concerts and agreed to stop and start the projection in any way he wanted. He made me understand that it was good at times to not be too attached to my images, to not always insist that they be displayed perfectly, but to have a certain detachment and allow my images to be appropriated for other purposes. I could not have articulated this at the time but it corresponded to what I already felt. So we worked together on a number of occasions with me incorporating my work into his performances.

I gave the images of *According to...* to Davorin for him to transform into a musical score. I had constructed a system of big dots flickering and small dots in a line alternating every seven seconds in a loop. And, completely unintentionally, the rhythm ended up corresponding to that of human respiration.

The idea was to "perform" the film by projecting the moving images through the film's frames printed on transparent paper while Davorin played the score. It wasn't possible to do it this way at every location but we did it when we could. The important thing though is that we made no distinction between a film event and a musical event – the two elements were autonomous and could be combined in any way that circumstances permitted.

In any case, the experience of making both *Temps de mètre* and *According to...* were extremely satisfying to me because I had a constant sense of anticipation and expectation. I have always felt that if you already know exactly how a given work is going to turn out, there really isn't much point in making it. In our performances we felt simultaneously both totally free from and deeply respectful of the other's work. And the disparities between what I expected and what actually happened were always fascinating.

But these works were also extremely demanding on me personally and left me so exhausted that I occasionally needed to take a break and work on something lighter and more spontaneous that did not need such intense reflection. One way of doing this was to do public programming of the films of others that I wanted to see.

I have never really made a distinction between my different forms of engagement with film - whether it is making them, showing them, or publishing about them. They were all attempts to open up new ways of looking at film.

In 1977 or 1978, I programmed films for a couple of months in a space in the north of Paris near the Gare du Nord, renting films with my own money from the Paris Films Coop. And then in 1979 I started programming screenings at the cinema L'Entrepôt in Montparnasse with Unglee and Philip Dubuquoy. I often organized thematic programs rather than one-person retrospectives in order to see the films in a new way. My first programming efforts were a way of doing homework to prepare myself to propose a new way of looking at film. And they would eventually culminate in programming to accompany the exhibition *Alibis* at the Centre Pompidou in July 1984.

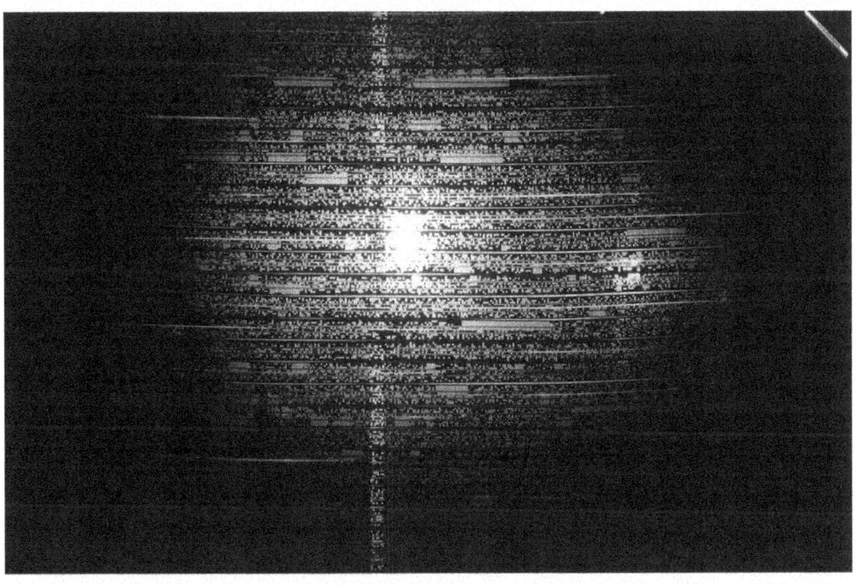

According To..., 1980, 16mm projection for music by Martin Davorin-Jagodić

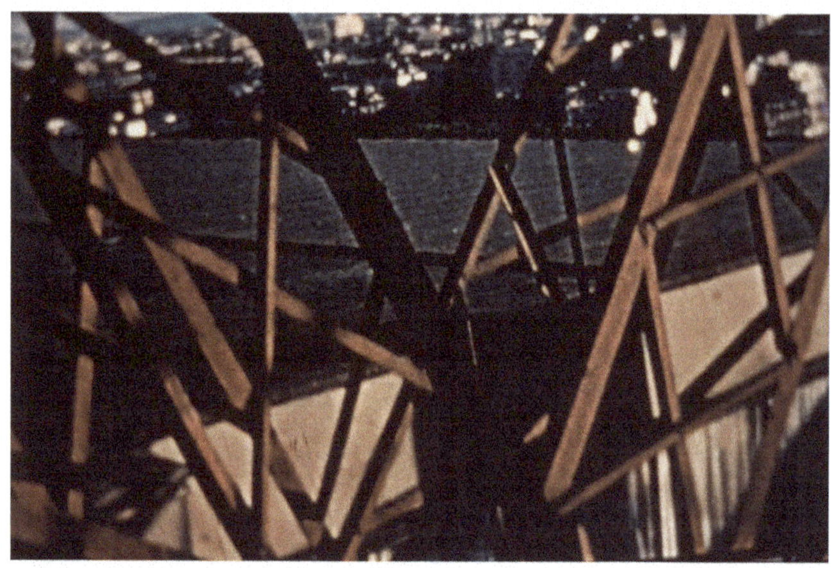

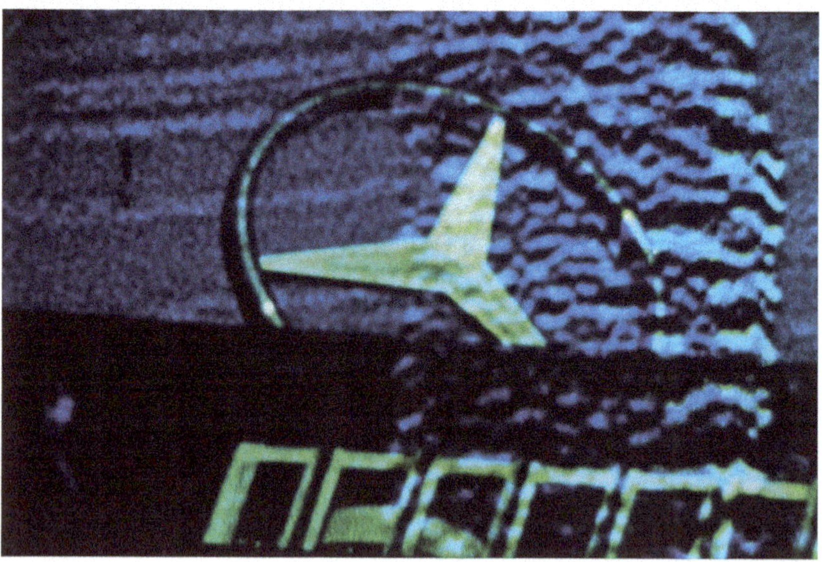

Disjet, 1979-1982 / 16mm / color / silent / single screen / 40' 00

Disjet **(1979 - 1982)**

Disjet can be seen as a way of escaping into a more spontaneous diary form after the intensity of the work on *Temps de mètre* and *According to...* but, compared to *Très Rare Film*, the diary elements are much more controlled. I paid more attention to the composition and editing, opposing positive and negative images and precisely calculating the frames of each sequence. I was trying to add a new dimension to the diary format by introducing some formal concerns into a context which was fundamentally lyrical.

Colors appear in film negative in a way I really like because they are more schematic. The negative image changes the way things are seen because pure form is perceived before an image's content is recognized. The image has a more musical dimension when it loses its purely representational quality.

So the film is a mixture of formal concerns with the nature of film with the more straightforward diaristic goal of recording moments in my personal life. There are events – such as one of the most important gay rights demonstrations of the time – which are clearly recognizable. But leaving most of the footage in negative keeps the representational dimension from dominating. I didn't want it to be just about my personal memories. The places where much of the footage was shot – both my own and found footage - were near where I was born so it has a very personal meaning for me but that was not something I wanted to share explicitly with the viewer.

I never actually made a positive print of all the negative images I was working with so I didn't even know what it was going to look like projected in a "normal" way. And, since my editing process involved repeated screenings of the negative original, it eventually became so damaged I could never have had a suitable positive print made even if I had wanted to.

But I can honestly say that the reaction of the audience has never entered into my thinking when I am making a film and many of my concerns are not even necessarily perceptible to the viewer. And since the duration of my work is extremely variable, it is sometimes almost impossible to program. For example, I recently made a performance piece that lasts for thirteen hours.

But for me the very fact that experimental film does not need to be a linear narrative means there should be no constraints on duration one way or another. An experimental filmmaker has total freedom to investigate the notion of time and I want to take advantage of that. *Disjet* may be difficult for viewers because of its length but I can't let that be a problem for me.

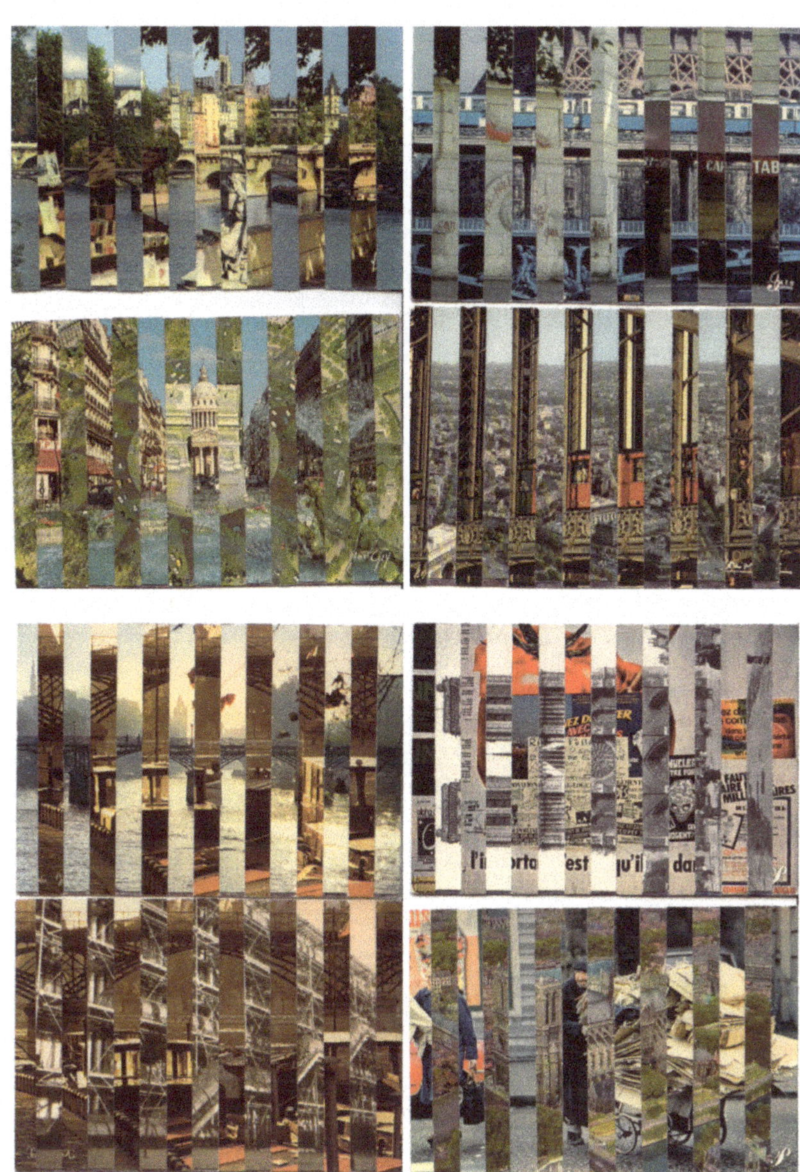

Éliclipse, 1982 / 16mm / color / silent / 31' 00

Éliclipse (1982)

There are glimpses in *Disjet* of places in Paris that are also visible in *Éliclipse* which is a film about postcard clichés of Paris, inspired in a way by Marcel Duchamp. For a while I had been collecting the most clichéd postcards I could find; I found views of Paris from the 1950s and 1960s which I mixed in with contemporary views, all showing what were considered typical scenes from Parisian life. I chose post-cards with a variety of themes, sometimes purely visual, sometimes architectural, sometimes socio-political.

It was a lot of work to cut up the postcards and mix the pieces but I got some help from Miles McKane and some other friends. After-wards, playing with the pieces to reassemble them in different ways was like an enjoyable game, a visual editing process. For a while, when I was very young, I had wanted to be an architect. So working with these fragments of postcards became a way of playing out my childhood dream of building something.

But then came the frame-by-frame shooting which was absolutely tedious.

I made a lot of scores to figure out how to proceed and then shot a lot. Finally I had everything I shot developed and printed. It pretty much worked in the way I wanted it to but I realized that the duration – 31 minutes – was wrong. I knew it was too long as soon as I saw it but I didn't have to courage to have another print made.

Still, it taught me a lot about the differences between what we perceive directly by looking at something and how it appears when captured in an image. I realized, for example, how little information is needed in an image to produce the perception of a movement or a shape. And that was really useful. It also made me realize for the first time that there was a lot I wanted to express with single images. Some, not all, but some, of the images in the film work quite well on their own.

Of course all of the months of work that went into physically cutting up the postcards into strips and reassembling them could probably be done digitally today in a matter of minutes. But if I had been working with digital images, I think it would have had a completely different meaning because the important thing in *Éliclipse* is that they were actual postcards, material objects that were manually sent through the mail and received by individuals. A postcard is a way of formally communicating to someone else that you have actually been someplace and I wanted to play with that.

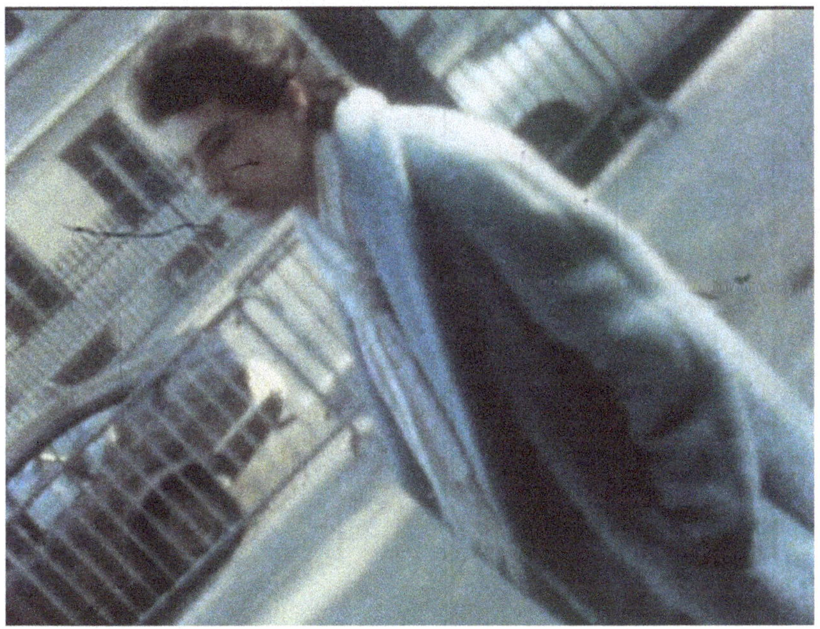

Miles, 1983 / Super 8mm / color / silent / single screen / 3' 00

MILES (1983)

I met Miles in 1980 and we became lovers. He had immigrated from New Zealand to live in the punk world of London and we figured out a way to live together between London and Paris, either my going to London or his coming to Paris. I was programming for Adicinex and, since Miles was a designer, I asked him to design things for the program. At that point, he had been involved with design, politics, and performance art, but not so much with experimental film.

In 1981 we did a major program in Avignon at the invitation of Rose Lowder; we had two programs a day over two weeks. I programmed the films and Miles designed the catalogue. He was becoming more and more involved with film at this point which meant that we could work on making them together. And I made a film portrait of him in Super 8.

I didn't do any actual editing for the film except removing the exposed frames you get when you change Super 8 cartridges in the middle of the roll. I was switching back and forth between color and black-and-white cartridges so there were a number of frames exposed in the middle of the roll.

The film was a small gesture, close in spirit, I think, to Derek Jarman's Super 8 film portraits.

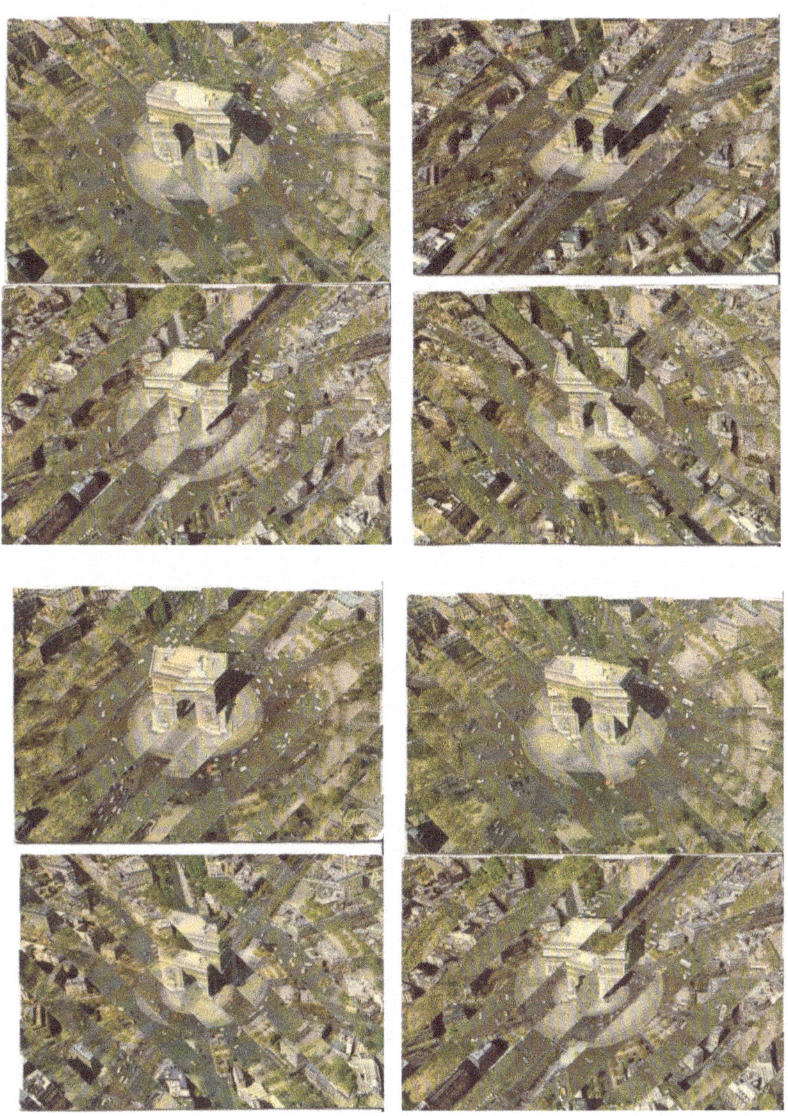

Enjeux, 1984 / 16mm / color / silent / single screen / 5' 30

ENJEUX **(1984)**

I realized while making *Éliclipse* that there were so many perceptual possibilities in the process of deconstructing images that, if I just concentrated on a single object, maybe I could explore them better. There had been black-and-white flicker effects in *Éliclipse*, but now I decided to add color to play tricks with our perception of the Arc de Triomphe, to transform it from a celebration of war into something else.

In the process, I learned something quite interesting about the movement of diagonal lines – although it would not be until 13 years later when I made *Des Rives* that I actually succeeded in achieving what I was striving for.

Since childhood I had been fascinated by the movement of windshield wipers and *Enjeux* was my first attempt to do something with these forms. I thought by using the diagonal forms I had developed for *Éliclipse*, I could simulate a panoramic motion in a different way than *R* but still giving an impression of displacement. Like *R*, the film investigated how displacing static forms can create a sensation of movement. So both *Enjeux* and *Sans Titre 84* share the objective of *R* which was to investigate ways to evoke a sensation of motion from immobile forms.

Sans Titre 84 (1984)

My original idea in using the Arc de Triomphe and the Place de l'Étoile was to play with the relation between the geometry of its location – a star sitting at the exact center of twelve equally-spaced avenues radiating outwards. A view from each side of each avenue would thus result in 24 images, the standard number of frames projected per second in film projection.

I started by trying to find an existing postcard view of the Arc de Triomphe from each of the 24 angles but this proved impossible so I ended up using my own images. Once I'd had them printed in the 10cm x 15cm postcard format, I then cut them into strips and reassembled them into several hundred combinations, verifying at each step that the combinations worked visually exactly as I wanted. Obviously, in the pre-digital era this was extremely time-consuming.

Some of the combinations I had already sketched but there were others which suggested themselves once I started working. And those I needed to explore. I had a collection of sketches of the overall structure which I used as a point of departure and then responded to opportunities in an improvisational way as I proceeded. It was by being in an intense state of concentration on the forms that I was able to discover these possibilities.

The sketches were a combination of initial ideas and a record of what I had already done. I kept a notebook in which I made observations on things that inspired me – for example the double screen work of Paul Sharits. I tried to analyze what worked and why and, when I felt it was something that could work for me, I made sketches to indicate what I could do. Then as I was actually shooting I also made notes in order to be able to keep track of my process and, if something did not turn out the way I wanted, to be able to back up to the exact step where I went wrong.

In a sense, these notebooks could be considered as a score in the musical sense although, of course, they do not reflect the sequences which were spontaneously improvised.

From the beginning, I had conceived it as a double screen work. I think there may have been a print for single screen but it was always intended for two. There were two prints edited in very slightly different ways but when projected simultaneously, these differences become increasingly visible.

From very early on, I had worked with multiple screen projection – occasionally projecting *R* on two screens, often in concert performances with Davorin. For me the multiple screen format relates closely to musical performance where multiple instruments play together. I have always wanted to explore how film projection can function in ways analogous to ways music is performed.

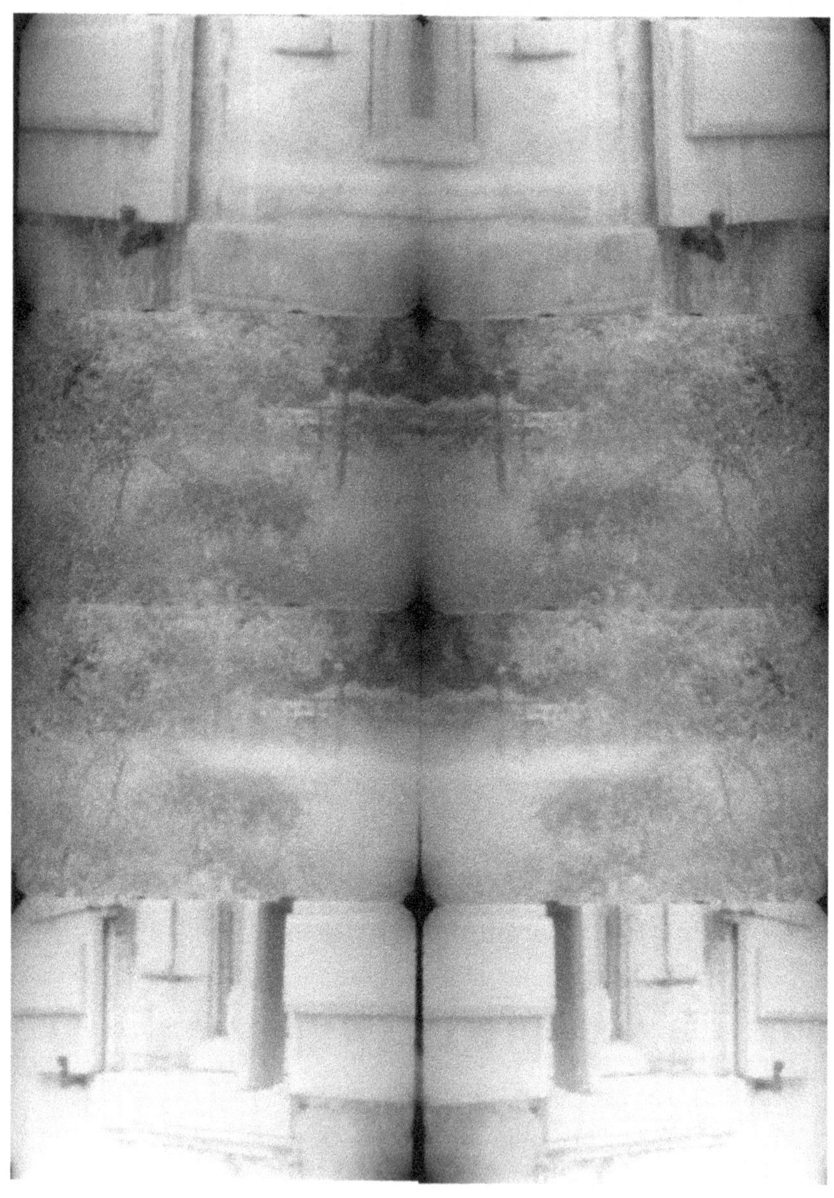

RR (double screen) 1976-1985 / 16mm / b&w / silent / double screen / 6' 00

RR (double screen) (1976-1985)

As I was working with Davorin and exploring the musical dimension of projected film, I eventually realized that the structure of *R* was well suited to double screen projection but it took quite a while to actually do it because of the financial challenge of preparing a new high quality negative from which to print and then to pay for multiple prints.

The original prints of *R* were "double perf" – in other words with the sprocket holes on both sides so that they could be projected with the emulsion side of the film facing either in or out. And I never gave instructions as to which was the correct way or whether it should be projected backwards or forwards. But when finally I was able to afford to make multiple prints in order to project it in a double screen format, I had to decide in what position and in what direction to project it.

But showing *R* in a double screen format was something I had always wanted to do; the fact that I finally succeeded in making the prints in 1985 had more to do with my financial situation than any evolution in my thinking.

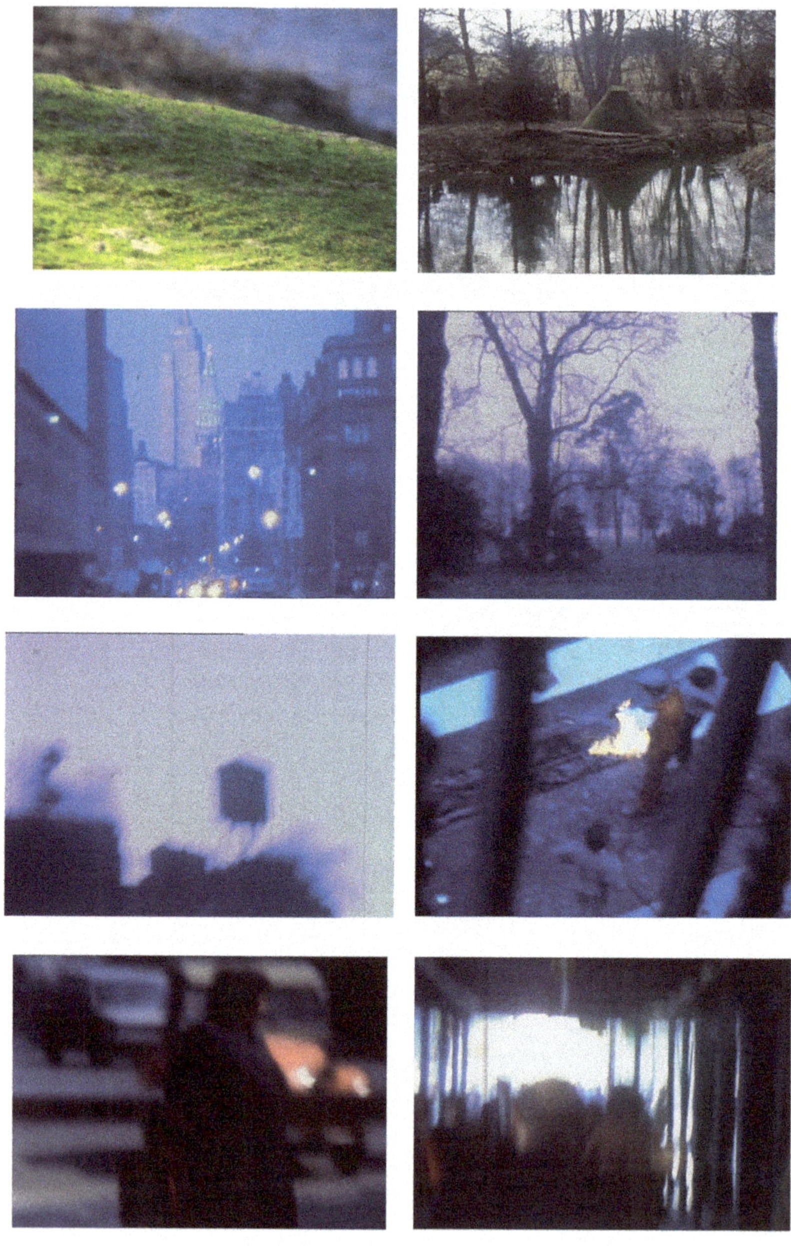

Journaux 1983-1985 / Super 8mm / color / silent / 13' 00

Journaux 1983-1985

Journaux is a compilation of my diaries starting about the same time as I shot *Miles* and covers our life in a series of Paris apartments. The first is the one on rue de Maubeuge where I had first organized screenings and you can see the frozen film frame installation of *According To... which* I put in front of a window.

It was a huge space which we were sharing with some others and we had room to store the collection of prints we had assembled to distribute through Light Cone. Before we moved there, we had stored everything in a 9 square-meter maid's room but now we had space and were able to organize screenings there. We showed Paul Sharits' films for small groups of friends and different people who had asked Paul to view his work.

The diaries cover a time when I was frequently in New York and Paul helped me to get some screenings of my work there. So there are scenes from these in the film. The loft where I stayed in New York was on the Bowery and eventually became the home of Millenium Film Workshop. At this time I also organized screenings around the East Village with the filmmaker and gay activist Lionel Soukaz.

Journaux also contains original footage that I was to rework 25 years later in digital video. One was *Meeting Paul in Buffalo* (2010), a trip to see Paul Sharits and another was *Entre Deux Mondes* (2010), a visit to the Château de Versailles gardens in the winter of 1983, that I had always wanted to do more with.

If I now had the financial means to digitalize all of my Super 8, I could make a lot of films because Super 8 allowed me to film much more easily than 16mm and have a kind of sketchbook that was a wonderful source of ideas. There were things that I wanted to do that would have required an optical printer – to which I didn't have access at the time, that could now be done digitally. It's something that I'll probably never be able to do but I know that there are a number of potential films in that Super 8 footage.

But at the time I enjoyed the easy spontaneity of these diary sequences because it was great to do something very close to life that did not require a lot of thought and was a relief from the painstaking planning and editing of my formal work.

During the period I was shooting *Journaux*, I had the opportunity to meet and see the work of a number of American filmmakers and artists active at the time. When I went to Buffalo to see Paul Sharits, I also met Hollis Frampton, Tony Conrad, Barbara Broughel, and then in New York, at Millenium Film Workshop and Collective for Living Cinema. There is a scene where I am filming from a car coming back into Manhattan with Robert Breer after visiting him at his home outside the city.

My own diary style I think falls somewhere in between the style of Jonas Mekas and that of Howard Guttenplan who spoke about his film diaries as "shooting in stride." But my work differs from theirs fundamentally in that I avoided shooting other filmmakers; I didn't want to report on the film scene. I filmed artists with whom I had a particular bond of friendship but I never sought to create "Anthropological Sketches" – as Mekas described his own portraits of the New York art scene.

At the time I projected the original Super 8 of *Journaux* and, by the time I eventually made a print, it was already quite damaged. But it felt right at that time to start showing this as a film because a lot of things felt like they had been resolved. I finally had an adequate space to run Light Cone, a space to live with Miles, and a space to show my films. So it seemed logical to connect all these events with the film I had been shooting as a sort of affirmation of all these activities.

From about 1985, it was clear that Light Cone was going to have an important role. I was also asked to organize programs of experimental film at the Cinémathèque Française – the first was based on the collection at MoMA done with Jon Gartenberg who was a curator there at the time. Another was a two-week series called "Cinéma des plasticiens" for which we also published a small book. It became obvious that we were starting to have an impact and succeeding at getting some major institutions – MoMA, the Cinémathèque, the Centre Pompidou to work together to help us.

Journaux was a way to commemorate these milestones.

AMOROSO (1983-1986)

Amoroso was shot in 16mm mostly in one summer when a friend loaned us his apartment in Rome. It was shot in the same way I had been shooting in Super 8. Despite the fact that the camera weighed 5 kilos, I tried to handle it as if it was a Super 8 camera. One of things I wanted to do was to evoke *Eaux d'Artifice* (1953), the film Kenneth Anger shot outside Rome at the Villa d'Este in Tivoli. Anger had tinted his entire film in blue, so I tinted mine as well but in red.

The first time I had visited the Villa d'Este in Tivoli was when I was 12 or 13 and was really enchanted by the place. I knew that, if I ever could get back, I wanted to film there. When I saw Anger's *Eaux d'Artifice*, I was actually angry because I thought he had somehow confiscated the place from me. So when I finally got there with Miles, I felt I had to affirm my presence.

And there was another important point of reference: I also wanted to evoke Franz Liszt's suite for solo piano, *Les jeux d'eau à la Villa d'Este*. I felt Liszt's music reflected the same sort of fascination with Italian gardens that I felt. But this didn't mean that I literally wanted to put his music on the film. I was actually quite surprised by the garish way Anger used Vivaldi on *Eaux d'Artifice*. I thought that, far from paying homage to the spirit of Baroque, it gave it a kind of perverse pop culture quality, certainly not something I was striving for. I was looking more to explore the theme of memory.

I chose to shoot on 16mm because the design of the Bolex camera offered the possibility of playing with a variety of color filters. I had a collection of filters and was fascinated with how they could change the feeling of the images. In general I kept the sequences in chrono-logical order as I did in my diaries but I did do some editing. For example, at the end I reversed the motion of the water at Tivoli in order to form a sort of loop connecting the end to the beginning.

Although the approach in *Amoroso* is quite close to *Journaux,* it was quite deliberate that the title is far more expressive. For one thing, I wanted to make it clear that it was very much about love and I liked what happens when "Roma" is spelled backwards. The film was a way to share the experience of being in love in a city that I love.

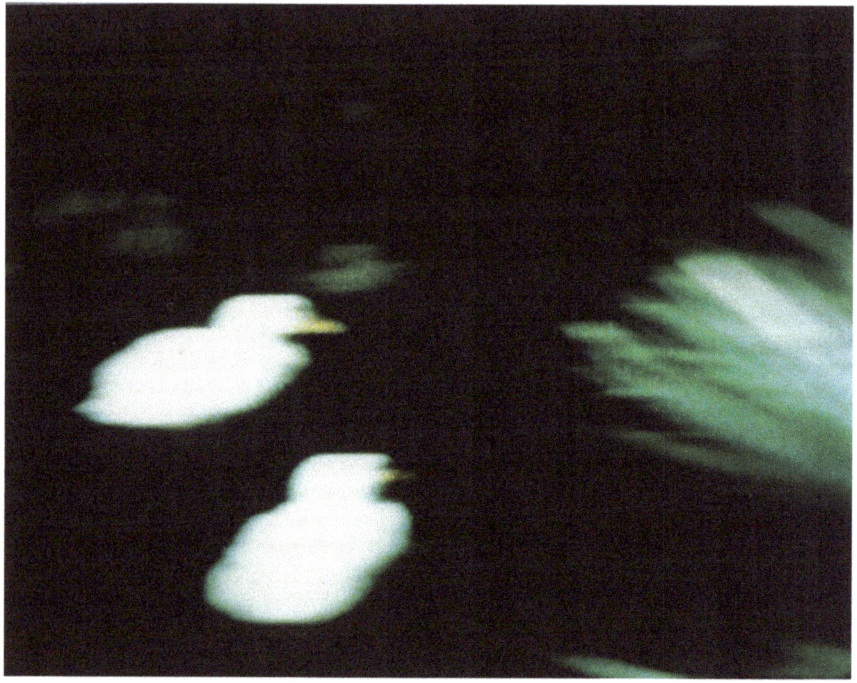

Amoroso, 1983-1986 / 16mm / color / silent / 14' 00

VO/ID 1985-1986

There are two components in the soundtrack of *VO/ID*. One is Gilles Deleuze reading a text of Nietzsche. When I was studying philosophy as a university student, I got very involved in Nietzsche. The other is Mick Jagger singing a song called *Cocksucker Blues*, a song about being gay.

The Jagger song was totally censored but at my night job in a music store, we received promotional records from music companies and some of them were recordings that ended up being censored and never publicly released. It was one of two Mick Jagger songs that could only be found on this black market of never-released music.

I wanted to use *Cocksucker Blues* not because it was censored but because it was an expression of my gay identity, a way of asserting my own personality that went against the prevailing bias in experimental film toward very impersonal and academic "structural" work. I wanted to raise other issues, including political ones regarding the relation of experimental film to institutions and the established art world.

Even in my title, I wanted to signal my intention to address these issues. "VO" is the French abbreviation for "Version originale," in other words, a film in its original language. "ID" is of course the term for an official document proving identity but there is also the psychological definition of "id."

I conceived *VO/ID* from the beginning as being for two screens and wrote the text so that the meaning of the words on one screen would play off those on the other. I worked from a sort of score and counted the number of black frames between each exposed frame. With the combination of Mick Jagger's transgressive lyrics, Deleuze's reading of Nietzsche, the juxtaposition of opposing words on two screens, in two different languages, I knew that the effect was going to be disorienting and disturbing and that viewers were going to be angry that I wasn't following the rules for what was expected in the current practice of experimental film.

Working with multiple layers of information and combining formal visual elements with text has been a constant concern for me. But at this moment I felt that films that dealt with the relation of text to image in a formal way – such as Michael Snow's work - were starting to be considered as just another hygienic art market commodity and that people around me were avoiding political responsibility for what they were doing. So I needed to make a statement both as a curator and an artist and I wanted to use this film as my weapon to strike a blow for more direct political discourse.

It was at the same time that I curated the exhibition *Alibis* at the Centre Pompidou and proposed an alternative vision of the history of experimental film in the 1970s and 1980s, attacking what I considered the imperialism of the structural film movement. I was trying to bring back an element of real world content that had been completely excluded from structural film.

Maybe if I had been aware at the time of the work of Beth B and Scott B who were assaulting the academic formalism of gallery art in New York with their punk "B-Movies," I would have felt this need less urgently. But, since nothing like it was being done in Europe, I felt it was a necessity to make this kind of film.

In running Light Cone I considered I had a responsibility to show work of all kinds, but personally I felt I had to also remain politically engaged. It was not that I wanted people to take my side but I wanted filmmakers to at least think about their political position both within the art world and the world as a whole.

In any case, *VO/ID* ended up being screened quite a bit and purchased by a number of institutions but it also frustrated people because they could not understand why I could not decide exactly what kind of film I wanted to make. They thought I should choose between the different kinds of films I had made.

But it was impossible; I had to keep all of the ways. For me it was like the human body: a conglomeration of different cells, no one of which has a higher value than another. What I do in my formal work – playing with alternations of black and white and the exact duration of text on the screen – is nourished by the rhythmical patterns that emerge in my more spontaneous diary films. They may seem very different visually but I see close connections at the level of the process. In both of these kinds of works, the process involves increasingly complex layers of images and how they relate to each other and to sound.

The very nature of the experience of viewing an experimental film should be one of opening your mind to different ways of processing image and sound. We have to be more open. The fact that critics and curators would have preferred to put my work into a single distinct category is not my problem and, as I have always had difficulty accepting authority, the more I am pushed to do this, the more I resist.

In *VO/ID* I wanted to revisit some of the issues that such artists as Paul Sharits and Tony Conrad were addressing with the flicker effect. I wanted to move it beyond just the visual phenomenon of words randomly pulsating on the screen but to enable the viewer to make a connection to the words' meanings. I deliberately made sure that the words do not move too fast so that the viewer also has the time to think about their meaning. I calculated on paper the exact number of frames that each word would be displayed before shooting. It's a method of working I would return to later in *SID A IDS* (1992) and in my first video work, *Still Life* (1997).

At this time I was continuing my publishing activity along with programming and making my own films. I had first done the book *musique film* (1986) with the Cinémathèque Française which was a continuation of my interest in how film can be the visual equivalent of musical notation. It also drew from my unfinished PhD thesis.

My research and experiments have always spanned a multitude of activities and I've never tried to attach a relative order of importance to them. Sometimes it has been my filmmaking activity which has led me into doing research for a book or program, sometimes it works in the other direction but for me work in one domain has always informed and stimulated work in another. I've never seen any difference between being a filmmaker, a curator, a distributor, or a writer.

In the case of working with text it started first with making the film *VO/ID* and then the same line of inquiry led me to write *Mots: Dites, Image* which was published to accompany twenty programs at the Cinéma du Musée at the Centre Pompidou in 1988. It surveyed the history of the use of words in experimental film starting with the very first films at the beginning of the 20th century.

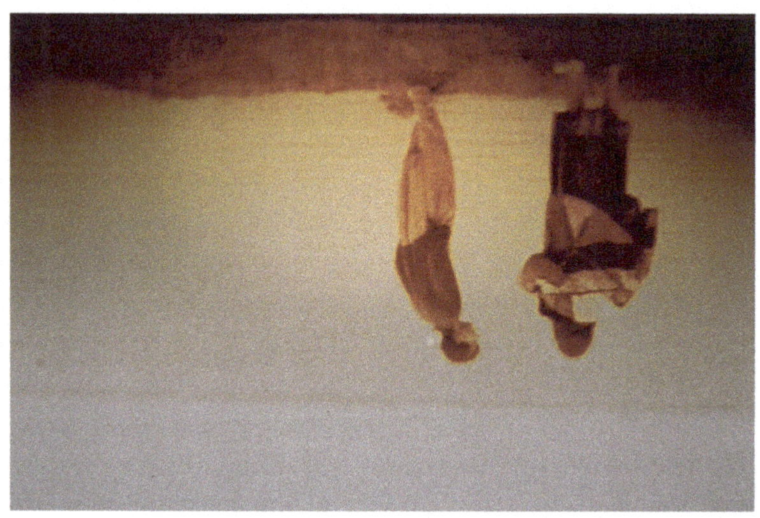

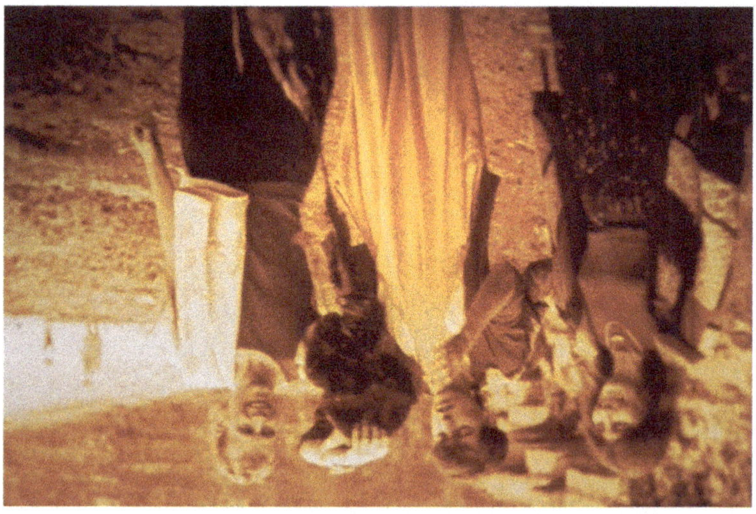

Divers-Épars, 1987 / 16mm / color / sound / 12' 00

Divers-Épars (1987)

These different experiences seemed to indicate that it might be possible to merge the different tendencies in my work – the structural concerns and diary films. It struck me that the introduction of found footage could give me a level of control over the structure of a film that was not possible with totally improvised diary footage.

I found some shots from the beginning of the 1960s of a fashion model walking on a red carpet and some others of a boat going under the Pont Neuf in Paris. I felt a personal connection to both of these sequences because my mother had worked as a model for Dior at this period and the boat footage was quite similar to what I had shot spontaneously for my diary at the same place. But, at the same time, the fact that it was anonymous found footage and not my own images seemed to give another layer of meaning to the film.

There were twelve sequences in all, arranged in a way that for me recalled the structure of serial music and I instructed the lab to tint each sequence differently, to turn the positive images red and the negative images blue. But I also gave them deliberately erroneous information about what parts were negative or positive so that there would be an element of unpredictability in the result.

I edited the film entirely without sound but when I finished I chose a piece of music from the Alban Berg opera *Lulu* which was both highly lyrical and rigorously based on the twelve tone serial technique invented by Arnold Schoenberg.

A few years earlier I had been able to see two complete performances of Alban Berg's opera, *Lulu*. Berg had not finished it at the time of his death in 1935 and his widow had forbidden anyone else to complete it. But when she died in 1976, it was completed by Friedrich Cerha and performed for the first time at the Opéra Garnier in Paris under the direction of Pierre Boulez. I was totally enthralled by it and lucky enough to get to see it twice.

Since then I had felt that my ideas had been nurtured by Berg and the opera *Lulu* had been haunting me. I was quite amazed at how he succeeded at disguising the formal structure of the twelve-tone technique with a joyful lyricism. It was exactly what I was striving for visually by masking my methodical concern for structure with the apparent spontaneity of diary films. Using part of Berg's opera as the soundtrack for *Divers-Épars* was my way of acknowledging this.

I was not aiming for an exact correspondence between the crescendos in the opera and specific sequences in the film but I wanted to suggest the parallel in the tension between lyricism and formal structure. However, viewers always seemed to experience the soundtrack as being perfectly synchronized with the images.

Interestingly there were two American filmmakers who were dealing with similar issues at the same time, Vincent Grenier and Larry Gottheim. The three of us were all seeking ways to somehow loosen the formal constraints of structural film and expand into other areas. In my case, I felt I was able in *Divers-Épars* to finally reconcile the disparate concerns of *Amoroso* and *VO/ID* and integrate them into a single work. And it also allowed me to bring together the two aspects of musicality in my earlier work: the use of music directly on the soundtrack and the application of musical structure to a visual medium.

29 10 88 (1988)

The title *29 10 88* is simply the date of an installation/performance that Miles had made at the Café de la Danse in Paris. Miles created a series of white plaster cones which were conceived to be displayed together in the open space that we were using for screenings at the time. People could take a cone if they wanted as a gift and then put a candle in its place. The intent of the film was simply to capture the feeling of the expansion and transformation of the space as the event evolved. It was a document/film in the spirit of Actionist films that sought not so much to provide a record of an event as to suggest other ways of visually experiencing it.

It was conceived from the beginning as a double screen work with the second screen mirroring the first and synchronized with it. It relates back to the strategy I had started working with in *R* but also plays with the idea of a cone of light as the projector beam forms two conical shapes in the air. It added another dimension to the performance event that Miles had created with his physical cones and it seemed to me essential that there be two screens to establish a sculptural dimension.

I still like this film a lot as it evokes a whole tradition of film-makers interacting with sculpture such as Gordon Matta-Clark's *Conical Intersect* (1975) which in turn paid homage to Anthony McCall's *Line Describing A Cone* (1973), or Richard Serra's *Steelmill/Stahlwerk* (1979). Of course I'm not suggesting that I'm in the same league as those sculptors but I definitely see a connection to what I was trying to do with Miles's piece.

It was shot over the course of the event which lasted a day; one can see that there are very few candles and a lot of cones at the beginning and then progressively more candles and fewer cones as the day progresses. The instructions given the participants were perhaps a bit too restrictive to totally succeed as a concept but this worked in favor of its visual depiction in the film.

Tas De Beaux Gosses (1989)

This film grew out of my friendship with fashion designer François Xavier with whom I had travelled across the US some years before. He had an interest in experimental film and in the 1980s, as he started to be recognized as a designer, I would see him frequently at our screenings and he would ask Miles and me to help him with his shows. So I decided one year to film a number of different shows that he did.

One of the original aspects of his work was to question the traditional ideas about models. Instead of the standard tall, highly muscular men, he chose men who were skinny and often short. Another curious sign of the times was that almost all of the models were men – I think there is only one woman. So François Xavier was breaking a lot of rules. Later on, similar things were done by a number of English designers but at the time he was challenging the accepted ways of dressing men.

I filmed his shows in the style of my diaries, mixing together footage from a number of different occasions. One was at a huge fashion show at the Porte de Versailles exposition center, another in a night club, another at the Pompidou Centre. There was certainly some kind of punk music accompanying all these events and I regret now that I didn't include any of it because it would have been very evocative of that particular time. Most of the film was edited in-camera and then I just mixed the different sequences for more impact.

Even though fashion is a field that is far removed from experimental film and music, I think Francois Xavier had some similar concerns. It was a moment in many fields when there was an anarchical spirit and young artists and designers were willing to break with traditional structures, violate accepted rules, and think about the body in new ways.

Anyway, Francois Xavier knew that I was not going to do a straightforward fashion documentary because he knew my work. And, in the end, he quite liked what I did. To thank me for the film he gave me an amazing coat he had created which I still have.

Spetsai (1989)

Spetsai began as a diary film shot on the island of the same name in southern Greece. It was shot in a mixture of Super 8 and 16mm; then the Super 8 was blown up to 16. The words come from a Guy Debord text about ecology that had just been published. It occurred to me that this beautiful place, in a country that was the birthplace of western philosophy might, in fact, be totally polluted by radiation.

I was getting uncomfortable with the idea of a film diary and had started to challenge it in *Divers-Épars* and was now looking for another way to take its traditional elements – the rhythms of daily life, beautiful landscapes – and turn them towards a way of thinking about larger things. I didn't have this in mind specifically when I was shooting the footage but, once I looked at the footage, I knew that it would not be enough for it just to be beautiful. I really wanted to find a way to transform how the viewer would relate to the content of the image.

So I set up a series of images of text that, every seven seconds, would interrupt the seductive color of the Greek landscapes in the photographic images. And the viewer would have to stay alert enough to relate the text to what preceded or followed it. In this sense, *Spetsai* is closer to a structural film like Hollis Frampton's *Nostalgia* (1971) than to a diary film.

I was looking for an element that would in fact do the opposite of focusing attention on the diary content – as Jonas Mekas does with his voice-over commentary in his diaries. I wanted to do something crude and disturbing that would interfere with the viewer's natural impulse to relate to the subject and force the viewer to engage on two separate levels simultaneously – one on the level of the images, the other on the label of the text.

First I selected the Guy Debord text that I wanted to use – a number of short extracts from his book whose length I calculated exactly in relation to where I wanted to insert it into the images. I didn't want the text to function as subtitles but to appear as it does in the book, two lines at a time, respecting the line break as printed. I wanted to juxtapose two very different fields, film and text, which, when combined would create a new way to "read" the image as opposed to the way in which one normally reads a text.

I deliberately allowed the viewers time to read the text, knowing full well that they would not read it because at times it was washed out by the image behind it or because I knew the image's subject would distract from the text. But I was not expecting the viewers to comprehend the text word-for-word, I wanted to challenge the way image and text are perceived simultaneously in order to create new perceptions that would differ from one viewer to another.

Unlike subtitles which are clearly secondary to the image and expected to simply explain what is happening in a film, I placed the text in the middle of the screen to suggest that perhaps it was the principal element and the film behind it was secondary.

And I chose a specific extract in which Debord is speaking about the nuclear disaster at the Windscale reactor in the UK where the gravity of the disaster was covered up by simply changing the name of the nuclear facility to Sellafield. I put this information from Debord on top of the images of the island in a way that would raise doubts about whether the same thing happened at Spetsai.

Of course I couldn't be sure that the viewer would have this response but all of the elements are there for it to happen – the text provokes an alternative way to digest the visual information offered by the image. There were similarities here to what Paul Sharits did in his earlier films using flicker effects and texts.

At first I thought of having the text read as a voice-over but then I realized that that would make it too easy for the viewer to follow the text and image as parallel elements because we are very used to listening and watching simultaneously when watching films. Instead I wanted there to be a constant perceptual challenge to sort the two out visually, to question how we perceive and think about images.

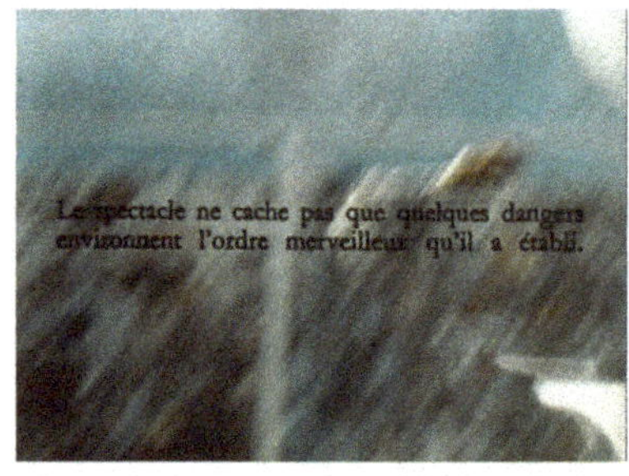
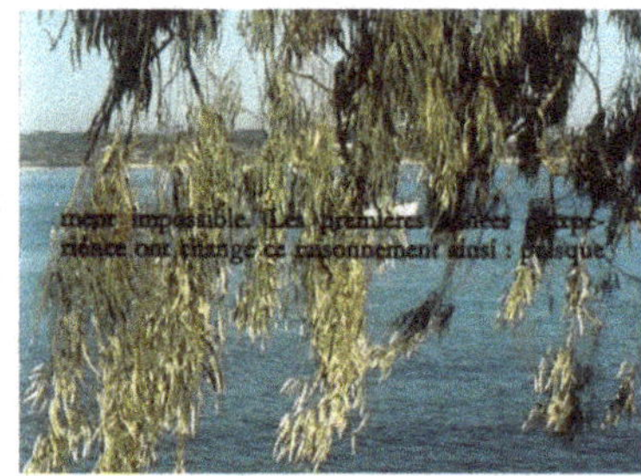
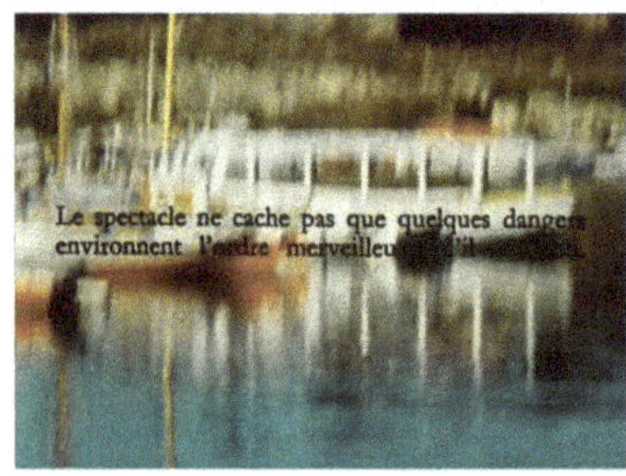
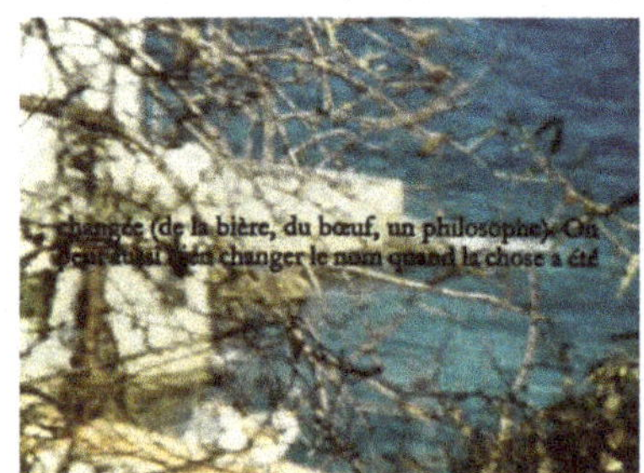

Spetsai, 1989 / 16mm & Super 8mm / color / silent / 15' 00

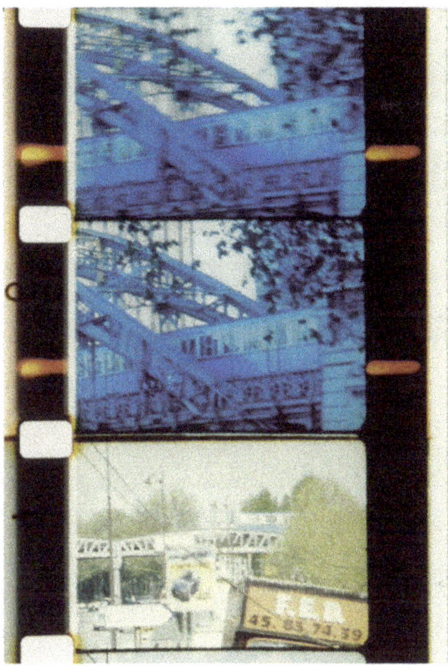

Ligne d'eau (1989)

Ligne d'eau consisted of pan shots of places in Paris where a sort of choreography is created by the crossing of metro cars over canal barges. It grew out of a series of experiments with installations which I had done at La Zonmée, an artists cooperative in the Paris suburb of Montreuil where I was later to organize a series of expanded cinema programs. The organizers of La Zonmée were interested in my double screen work and asked me to create an installation in their space. They had a big room with a shop window directly on the street which had Venetian blinds.

So I set up the projector to project on the window with the blinds sometimes open, sometimes closed, and I realized that there was a slight spatial displacement between the images on the blinds and those on the window. Then, when I added a second projector showing the same film with a slight delay, there was a double displacement.

Obviously the film could not have been distributed in this way so

I made two identical prints and provided instructions for projecting the second with a slight delay and for the projectionist to vary the projector speed. This was just one of a series of experiments in my expanded cinema events dealing with how the same film can reveal unexpected things when several prints are projected simultaneously with a slight delay between them.

The exact running time of the version in distribution is listed as 8 minutes but this was somewhat arbitrary since, when installed as a loop in a performance situation, it could have gone on forever. What's interesting in a performance is how viewers supply their own synchronicity as they watch, perceiving, for example, a continuity between the movement of the metro train and the movement of boats on the canal which could never have been predicted in the original film. Unfortunately I never made any video recordings of these events so they are lost but the lessons I learned by doing them were absolutely essential for installations that I was going to do later such as *des rives* (1998).

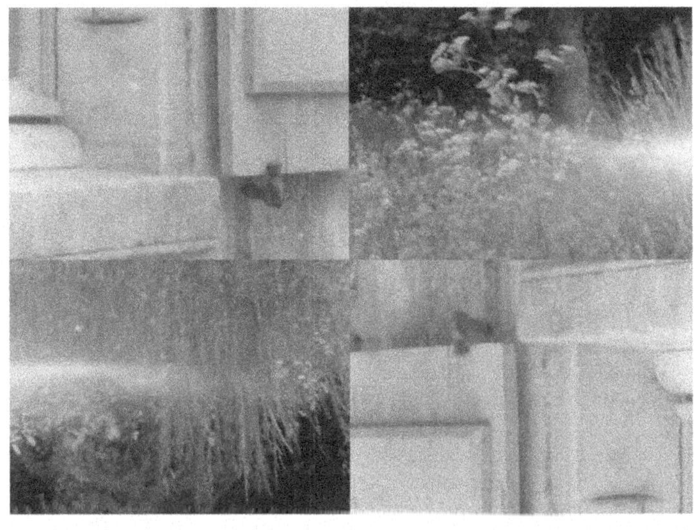

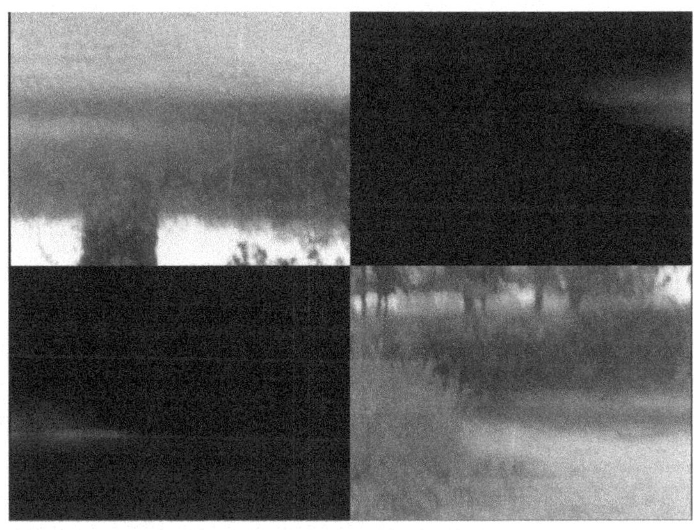

Quatr'un, 1975-1991 / 16mm / b&w / silent / four screens / 15' 04

Quatr'un (1975-1991)

Quatr'un was originally conceived not as a film but as an installation which, as its name indicates, consists of four variants of one film sequence. The first time I installed it was at La Zonmée in Montreuil. The room was about 20m square and I put a 6m by 4m screen in the middle of the room and each of the four projectors were about 11 meters from the screen, two on each side.

Each projector was running the same loop but the loops were of slightly different duration so that, as the performance progressed, they became more and more out-of-sync. The loop consisted of my first film *R* and continued my exploration of the potential of Baroque music to be expressed in visual terms.

I intended for the viewer to move around the room to view the four images from different perspectives. The nature of the projection – with the images side-by-side yet originating from opposite sides of the screen – draws attention to the fact that a projected image is two-dimensional and has no depth. One passes from one frontal perception of the screen to the other with nothing in-between. I was also interested in how the shadows of the viewers themselves established a sort of dialogue.

As it turns out, *R*, my very first film, has had a long life, starting with its original form in 1976 when I was still at the university at Vincennes, then becoming the double screen version *RR* in 1985 and then the four-screen *Quatr'un* starting in 1991. And, although it would be too complicated to put them into distribution, there have been other versions too – several triple-screen versions, and a six-screen version. Although the original sequence was very simple and technically quite primitive, I feel like I could continue to explore the variations forever. I guess this is because, at its core, my work is concerned with the process not content.

After its installation at La Zonmée, I had the opportunity to recreate the two-sided four projector configuration at several other places, once in Italy and another time at a church in Nantes which was absolutely marvelous. It was quite an experience for the spectator to be able to switch from one side of the screen to another, creating a cubic dimension.

I have made more recent prints for one video projector so that the film can continue to be shown today but still simulate the effect of a multiple projector installation. It lasts 15 minutes but, of course, since it is designed as a loop, this duration is somewhat arbitrary.

I now realize that I was dealing with some of the basic issues of optical perception that the filmmaker Ken Jacobs has examined in his work based on very early films, although the starting point for my inquiries has always been music not cinema.

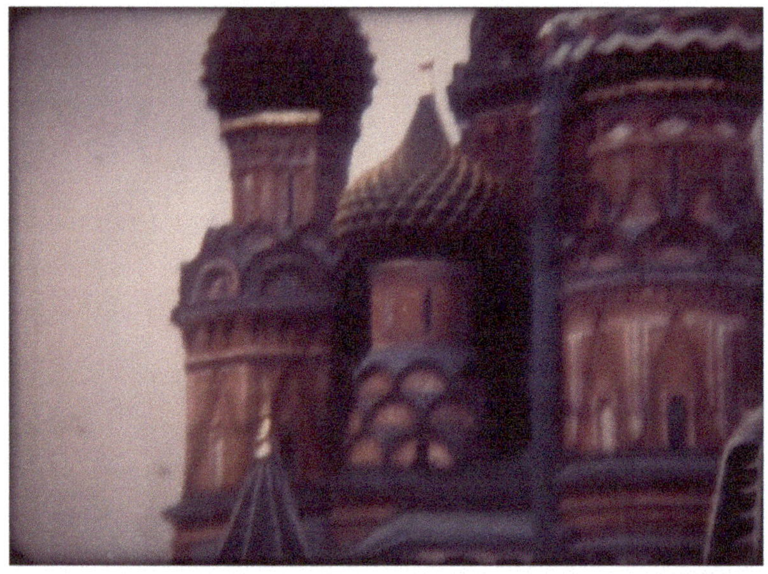

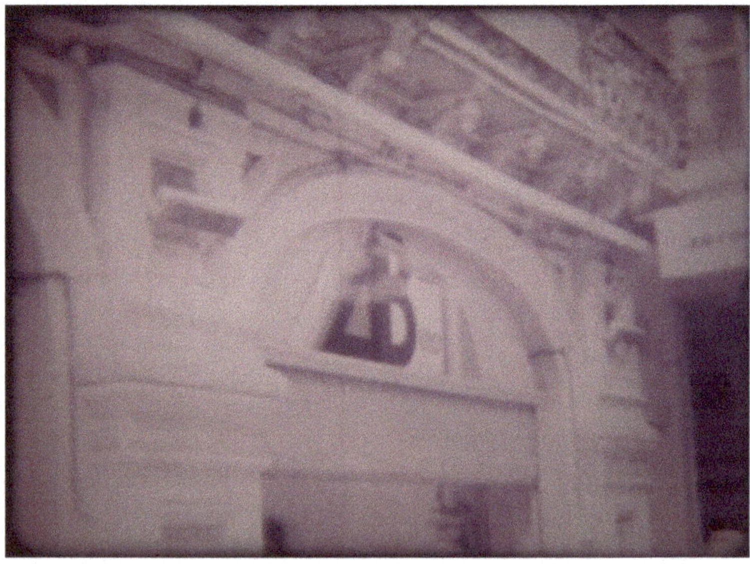

We've Got the Red Blues, 1991 / 16mm / color / sound / 15' 00

We've Got the Red Blues (1991)

In 1990 I went to Riga and later to Moscow with Vivian Ostrovsky and shot diary footage in Super 8. Back in Paris, I helped Vivian prepare the footage to be reworked on an optical printer and we got the idea of doing a version that combined both our footage on two screens and it became *Work and Progress* (1999). Because of the difficulty of distributing double screen work, Vivian eventually had the two 16mm screens printed together in 35mm so it could be screened with a single projector.

But I also worked on a version containing just my own footage combined with found footage and sequences from Dziga Vertov and Eisenstein films, eventually calling it *We've Got the Red Blues* (1991).

When I was shooting I wasn't thinking about a soundtrack but I finally decided to add sound to some sections and leave other sections silent. For the sound sections I chose Olivier Messiaen's *Quatuor pour la fin du temps* which Messiaen composed when he was in a concentration camp.

I used the two movements from Messiaen's quartet which were the slowest and the most reflective, almost nostalgic, and which did not at all fit with the original diaristic spirit in which the images had been shot. So they offer a completely different way to think about them. And the fact that the sound is intermittent is also intended to perturb the viewer because it is impossible to definitively classify the film as either sound or silent.

The relation between image and sound is intended to be destabilizing. Conceptually what I wanted to do definitely had affinities with *Spetsai* and *Divers-Épars* but *We've Got the Red Blues* is simpler and it is really the use of sound and its coming and going which dominates the viewer's perceptions.

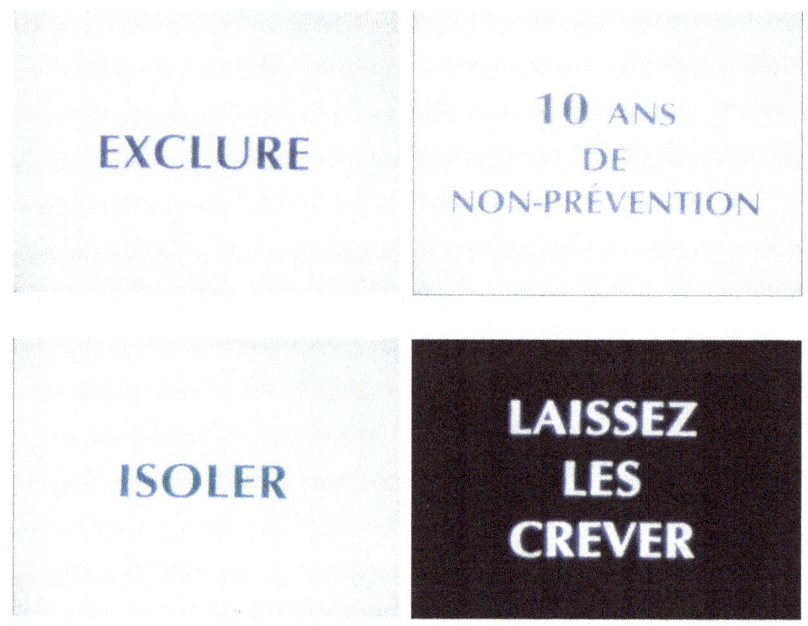

SID A IDS, 1992 / 16mm / color / silent / single screen / 5' 30

SID A IDS (1992)

In the early 1990s it seemed to me that French film and video makers were pretty much ignoring the issue of AIDS. A lot of artists were dying but it was as if no one thought the subject should have anything to do with art. So I appealed to a number of film and video makers to contribute to a film about AIDS, the entire proceeds of which would then be given to the group *Positif* which was dedicated to helping AIDS victims. My goal was to gather together enough material for a 70 minute program and my contribution to it was *SID A IDS.*

I decided to go back to working with pure text as I had in *VO/ID* using a French text I wrote which would appear word-by-word in white against a black background with occasional pink frames. It was militant in tone addressing how AIDS was being represented in public discourse and how it was being dealt with politically.

I eventually sold the compilation to the French-German television network ARTE and gave all of the money they paid me to *Act Up,* the group which had succeeded *Positif.* I had wanted them to give the money directly to *Act Up* but they refused because they did not want to be perceived as having supported a highly political organization.

I was facing issues I had already confronted in *Spetsai* and *VO/ID* about how to address political and social content. As an experimental filmmaker trying to work simultaneously on a political and esthetic level, I wanted *SID A IDS* to be a response to the AIDS crisis that benefitted from everything I had learned as a filmmaker up to then.

For me the schism between those interested in esthetic inquiry and those interested in political discourse is analogous to the lack of mutual comprehension between musicians and filmmakers. It has always seemed strange to me that so few of those interested in experimental music or dance can cope with experimental film and vice versa. By the same token, it seems that if you are involved in experimental work in the arts, you should be able to apply your approach to other domains as well.

I remember when the critic and theoretician Annette Michelson saw my video *Still Life* (1997). She was furious and asked me why I hadn't just given her a pamphlet to read. I replied that my intention was not to get her to read but to get her to think and that as a filmmaker the only way I knew how to do that was to provoke her both on a political and aesthetic level, challenging the way form shapes content and the way content shapes form.

This of course can be frustrating, even painful, in the way any new experience can be – like hearing contemporary music for the first time or trying to read a written musical score if you have never done it before. But if you keep trying, the pain disappears. I know that political people do not like formal aesthetic concerns interfering with a political message and that those involved in art dislike the intrusion of political elements but the fact that it is painful does not mean it should not be done.

Maybe what I was doing was unconventional in the context of experimental film, but it was hardly unprecedented in the larger art world. Mayakovsky and the Russian futurists were doing it in poetry and theater in the early years of the century and the Canadian artists collective General Idea were doing it in all sorts of media starting in the late 1960s. Particularly in the US, a lot of new forms of performance art were a direct response to the AIDS crisis. Politics and art cross paths all the time.

As early as 1984 when I made *Enjeux*, I transferred film to VHS in order to create a video installation at Scratch Video, a pioneering alternative video series that was running in a small club in Brixton, South London at the time. I liked the way that video allowed me to investigate looping and other new ways of looking at moving images.

I was working with a lot of musicians in the 1980s and for them, even though images were usually on 16mm film and sound on magnetic tape, it was always the process that mattered, not the specific physical support for it. Video was not my medium of choice for shooting because of the difficulty of editing it but because of its flexibility as a projection medium, it was useful as a bridge for the integration of my film images into installations.

But the advent of digital media changed that. By the late 1990s it was clear that, given the way I wanted to use text and create installations, digital tools were necessary. When I wanted to make *Still Life* in 1997, it was obvious I could not do it in film. And then there was the purely logistical side; I no longer had the physical strength to travel with 16mm projectors and looping systems to show my work. I remember that, in 2000, to do a series of six programs in New Zealand, I had to carry 80 kilos of film equipment with me. If I had presented the same thing digitally, I would probably have needed only a laptop.

There was also the problem of disappearing film stocks. Since I had never wanted to limit myself to one particular film gauge – 16mm or Super 8 – or one type of film – color, black-and-white, negative or reversal, I was used to a variety to choose from. But gradually there were fewer and fewer choices of film stock and fewer and fewer labs to process and print them. And it was all getting more and more expensive.

There wasn't a precise moment when I suddenly decided that I would switch to working entirely digitally but the availability of the Final Cut video editing software in the early 2000s and the huge improvement in the quality of video projection finally convinced me.

It also changed what I was doing because the miniDV format cameras at the time did not permit shooting single frames or short bursts of frames in the way I did for my diary films. So I simply stopped making diary films.

But in the larger sense, I never felt that my filmmaking was based on specific tools for recording images. I have always been concerned less with concrete questions of process than with what viewers can experience in real time in different performance environments.

I have always shared with the British artist Malcolm Le Grice the belief that it is not the technical quality of the image that matters. Le Grice has always moved freely from film to video to computer and back, adapting them to create a certain type of image. There's no reason to expect video and digital tools to simulate a film image; they can be used for other things that are also stimulating. At first I didn't think that I could use video but I gradually realized that this was due to narrow-mindedness on my part and not some inherent limitation of the medium.

I felt that, over the years, I had done my best to explore the innate qualities of Super 8 and 16 film and to push them to their limits. So that by the early 2000s I was ready to move on. The fact that at this time I was traveling more and more frequently to Brazil where there was no access at all to film confirmed my decision. I still remember my last trip across Brazil in 2002 with a 5-kilo 16mm camera; it has just physically too much. And in addition it was impossible to work discreetly since the sight of a large 16mm camera was so unusual by this time that it attracted too much attention when people saw me filming.

I always loved the physical process of editing 16mm film so I must admit that I miss it sometimes. And I would also love to have digital versions of all of the Super 8 diary footage I shot over the years in order to be able to explore the new ways of editing that digital tools offer.

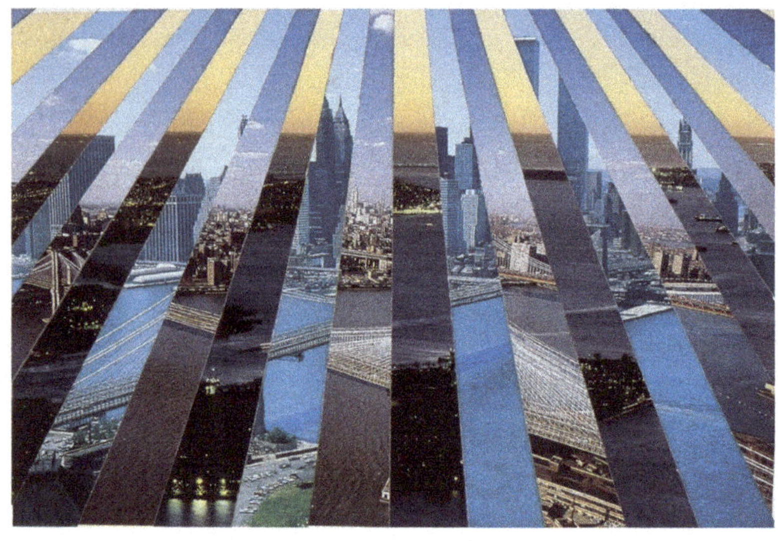

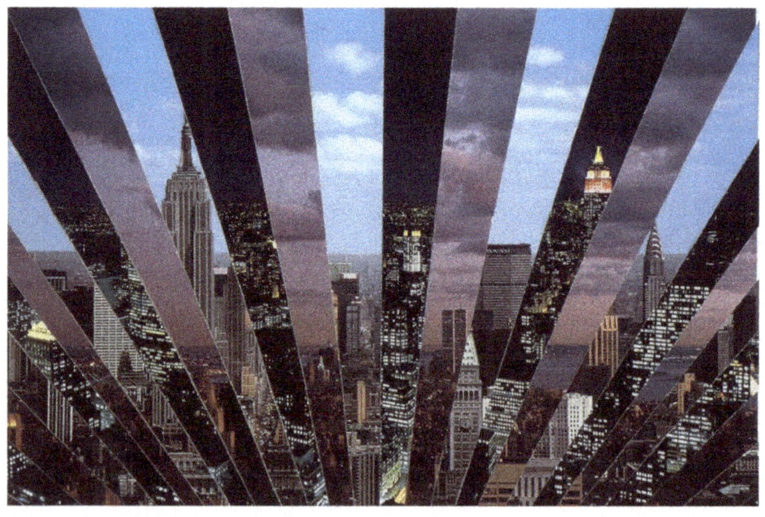

New York Long Distance, 1994 / 16mm / color / sound / 9' 00

New York Long Distance (1994)

A number of my on-going concerns seemed to coalesce in New York Long Distance; one is a formal inquiry into how to deal with multiple, simultaneous images of a city, an extension of explorations that I had early conducted in Éliclipse, *Sans Titre 1984*, and *Enjeux*. And there was the autobiographical concern – how to portray moments of my personal life publicly. This struggle to find some way of reconciling the rigorously formal and impersonal elements of a "structural" film with the lyrical, intimate qualities of the "diary" film had always been a major concern for me; with *New York Long Distance* I confronted the challenge directly.

I realize now that Paul Sharits had been trying to address similar concerns with *Dream Displacement* (1976), his installation, originally exhibited at the Albright-Knox Art Gallery in Buffalo in 1976. I see now that he too was trying to express a very personal angst with formal abstract forms. I had exhibited it at Scratch in the early 1980s but hadn't made the connection to my own work.

My concern was how to handle two parallel tracks in my own work in a manner that would both connect them and keep them separate, trying to use autobiographical content in the same way I was using pure sound and image. I keep thinking of something the Canadian animator Norman McLaren once said: "Emotion is motion and motion is emotion."

On the visual side I wanted to play off 2D and 3D, the two-dimensionality of graphic elements with the perception of depth in photographic images, three-dimensionality. But then on the aural side, with the soundtrack, I opened another field.

Another element was playing visually with the fascination that Americans have with the city of New York. I see a relation between the visible architectural verticality of New York and the hierarchical distribution of power in American society and I thought I could have some fun with that. I was also conscious of the history of American painting, particularly how artists such as Frank Stella and John Chamberlain used areas of pure color.

When I accepted the post of film curator at the American Center, they sent me to New York to meet the members of their board and have my appointment confirmed. And then, after I started the job, they would send me every two months or so. But New York had always been a point of reference in my life starting with my first visit at the age of eight or nine and it was the place where I had interacted with film both as a source of inspiration as a filmmaker and of information and documentation as a curator. So I had a very close connection to the place on many different tracks - personally, artistically, professionally, politically.

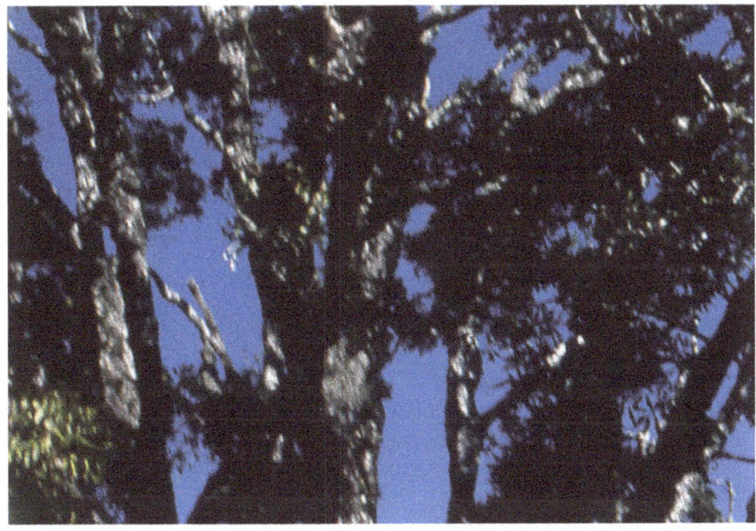

SANS TITRE 96, 1996-1997 / 16mm / b&w / silent / 3' 00

SANS TITRE 96 (1996-1997)

SANS TITRE 96 was shot on a single 16mm roll that I had hand-developed. It is a study of fog penetrating a forest and was shot near Sydney, Australia. It was strange because the forest seemed tropical but I had always associated fog with northern, wintry climates. It was only possible to see fragments of the landscape, not details, and it reminded me of the black-and-white Japanese film *KIRI* (1972) by Sakumi Hagiwara in which a fixed view of a mountain landscape is totally obscured by fog and details slowly become invisible.

EPILOGUE

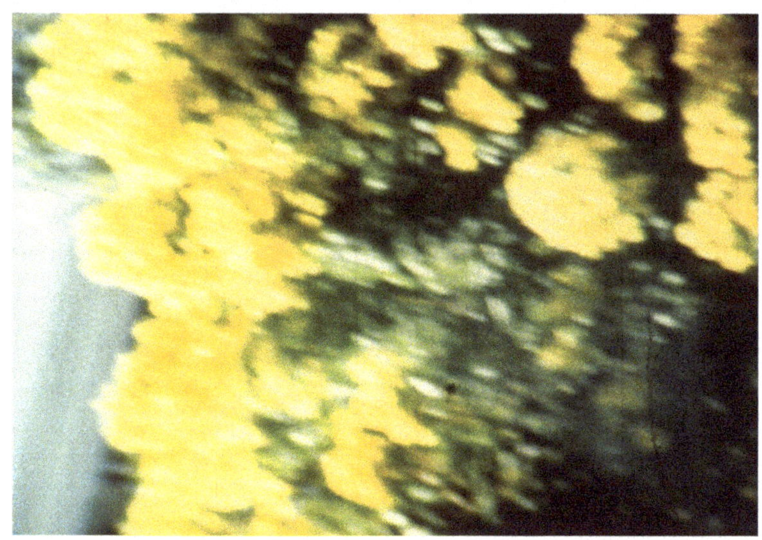

A Drift, 2002 / 16mm / color / sound / 9' 00

A DRIFT was shot in New Zealand. When I went there to show several programs of work in 2001, I made up my mind to finally finish a film from footage I had shot there on previous trips. But apart from these last short works, I had stopped dealing with film as film and begun having my Super 8 and 16mm footage transferred to video so that I could edit it digitally.

In New Zealand I had been travelling with two 16mm film projectors, a looping device, and camera equipment to film, altogether over 80 kilos of equipment. Transporting it all was just too much and I finally decided to stop working with film. I had never become involved in doing my own film processing by hand and, for some reason, I was never able to develop a good relationship with film labs – something that had become essential for the few artists determined to continue to work with 16mm film.

Cost was a factor as well since, after the American Center closed and my job there ended, I had very little money available for buying and processing film. But perhaps the most critical factor was that, since a lot of my work was for multiple screens, I had to carry the necessary configuration of projectors with me when I was travelling to show my work. Along with my normal luggage, this was just too physically exhausting.

This was the period when, for a multitude of reasons, I decided to withdraw from the experimental film scene. On a personal artistic level I was devoting more time to live multiple-screen installations and that meant I was doing less curating and programming. After my first installation at La Zonmée in 1993, I had a lot of requests from alternative spaces to exhibit live film installations and it was time-consuming to travel and set everything up. But I thought it was even more important than the work I had been doing showing films in the conventional way because it was like opening up another history of experimental film.

The German musician Thomas Köner had been working with the filmmaker Jürgen Reble on live sound to accompany his films. When he saw *Still Life*, he said he really wanted to do something with me because it was entirely different from what he was doing with Jürgen.

He was interested in how my work addressed politics and textual information – areas that were completely outside Jürgen's work – and he thought he could work with me.

I liked Thomas as a person and admired him as a musician. I would make a point to see him when I was in Germany. But it wasn't until later on that I realized that there were elements in my work that were completely new for him – things like working with text and voice which he had never done and which became important elements in his own work. He was involved with the installations *Quatr'un* (1975-91) and *Des Rives* (1998), and the video *Tu, sempre (2001)*. Jürgen, Thomas, and I also did performances together a few times, even though Jürgen and I did not really share the same aesthetic.

I felt if I succeeded in getting recognition for this tradition of film-as-installation, it would open up the museum world to experimental film and it could be something they could display in their galleries. It was a way of expanding experimental film practice into another domain, a critical moment when a number of French and British artists were beginning to get involved in this field of "exhibition cinema." I was also happy to be a source of information for artists such as Pierre Huyghe who were exploring these practices.

My performance work meant that I could not be as physically present for daily work at Light Cone. When I accepted the post at the American Center in 1995, I already knew that it would be necessary to see if Light Cone would be able to survive without my direct personal involvement on a daily basis. But that year ended up being the heaviest institutional involvement I had ever experienced. I helped on the series *Poétique de la couleur* at the Louvre, did a major Gregory Markopoulos retrospective at the American Center, programmed *Plus Dure Sera la Chute* at le Jeu de Paume, and *Le je filmé* at the Centre Pompidou.

So I started worrying that it was getting out of control and that I was going to burn myself out. I had to take a hard look at my priorities.

I had separated from Miles and started doing more teaching. I felt that teaching experimental film in the art school context might help to fight the appropriation of the history of experimental film by academic institutions. In addition, because my film *SID A IDS* had had a sizable impact on awareness about AIDS, I wanted to continue to work on the issue of connecting the broader domain of gay activism and gay artists' work.

After 2000, although I was still living part of the time in Paris, I was really no longer a part of the Paris experimental film scene. About half of my time was actually in Mulhouse where I was teaching at the École supérieure d'art de Mulhouse. And then, outside the academic year, I would be in Brazil to be with my partner Edson Barrus.

While I was working at the American Center, I was still seen primarily as the founder of Light Cone and I was tired of this and felt the organization needed to become more distinct from me personally. It was true that I still had the title of director but from the beginning of 2001 when I started teaching in Mulhouse, I was not really a Parisian anymore and I needed to make a break.

When I stepped back and looked at all my Paris institutional connections in 1995 – the Louvre, the American Center, the Jeu de Paume, the Centre Pompidou, I realized that I had become exactly the kind of domineering institutional presence that I had so rebelled against when I was younger. And I sensed that people were increasingly reducing me to simply the embodiment of an institution. This meant that when I became engaged in other areas, when, for example, I would show my own work in a gallery or museum, people thought I was betraying my official role in the experimental film world. So there was something wrong and I made a decision to end this chapter in my life.

ARTICLES ON FILM (1979-1998)

PREFACE

Experimental cinema has always been considered as a minor form. To borrow a term that Jonas Mekas was fond of, I would call it invisible cinema, invisible yet nevertheless essential for those who would understand what it means to film. It is an art form which must constantly redefine, reposition itself, and make itself heard. To make experimental films is to put oneself at its service. Experimental film is not an established art form, with experimental film nothing can ever be assumed. It is in constant evolution, it is struggle and resistance. It must always start from scratch. To be a filmmaker is to fight for the existence of this cinema against its burial, its denial, its disappearance, and to fight for this cinema is to promote it by as many means as possible. The promotion and defense of experimental film also means writing about it and to do so in addition to creating, distributing, showing, and teaching film: activities I have pursued like so many before me and so many since. I belong to a generation of filmmakers here in France who have actively championed this cinema: Jean-Michel Bouhours, Maria Klonaris, Christian Lebrat, Rose Lowder, Miles McKane, Dominique Noguez, Alain-Alcide Sudre and Katerina Thomadaki.

So when Christian Lebrat proposed the idea of this book to me, I accepted it in the spirit of what this cinema is to me: a passion, a genuine commitment. In re-reading everything I have written over the last almost twenty years, I have been struck as much by my determination as by my awkwardness, the enthusiasm of my writing. I had to choose from my articles according to different criteria: the inherent interest of certain texts, the availability of certain others. In fact, I have written a lot for catalogues and periodicals outside France and not only on French experimental film. I have included only one text of this nature, even though the temptation was great to include one that I wrote last summer for an exhibition in Stuttgart. In this text I had in fact dealt with the impossibility of a national history of cinema that did not take into account external influences.

It is surely far easier for me to write in the knowledge that my text will be translated than it is to respect the decorum of a language in which - for a number of reasons - I find myself increasingly ill at ease.

Being forced to make choices has suddenly forced me to be aware of the number of articles I have written. And it has given me the occasion to exclude those whose only interest was their topicality and others which were simply not very good. Others have been excluded which are available elsewhere (in the catalogues *Le Je filmé, Mot: dites , images,* etc.) and those which will subsequently be published elsewhere (*Hommage à Scratch, Les Gais savoirs...*) I have strictly excluded all articles and interviews devoted to my own work. I have given priority to essays on filmmakers. Except for Andy Warhol, many of the filmmakers who interested me have been relatively little discussed in France.

I have taken advantage of the opportunity that this book offers me to correct, bring up-to-date, and expand certain articles such as *The Film noir, First-person Cinema, Homage to Mario Montez.* At the end of each article will be found a list of its previous publications as well as the language it appeared in. Its version will be indicated as well. One of the peculiarities of my writing (what I guess could be called my style?) comes from the fact that I like to go back to an older article and rework it in the light of more recent films I have discovered since its original publication: an art of variation.

This book does not claim to cover the entire field of experimental cinema. It reflects my activism, hence its sub-title: articles on film. I regret that I have not been able to include certain filmmakers about whom I have written detailed articles or whom I have interviewed - I won't list them - but that unfortunately is inevitable in such a book.

The book is divided into five chapters organized - except for the first one - in chronological order. The emphasis is on contemporary film - meaning experimental film since the end of the 1950s and beginning of the 1960. But that hasn't prevented me, in order to make my case, from drawing on "pre-history." There is a single exception to this rule: the article comparing László Moholy-Nagy and Len Lye. Here I followed the lead of my editor who had pointed out the absence of writing in France on the film work of these two artists. In regard to the chapter on gay film, it is intended to be understood in a restricted sense. It is not a chapter on queer cinema - which by definition includes gay, lesbian, trans-gender and bisexual - on which I have written a number of to-be-published articles. Gay and lesbian cinema can in no way be summed up only by the pages in this chapter.

That publication would never have been possible were it not for the generosity of the A.F.A.A (Association française d'action artistique) which, when I was awarded a Villa Medicis Hors les Murs fellowship in New York, allowed me to devote part of my time to the rewriting of some of the texts of this book. I would like to thank Jean-Michel Bouhours whose steadfast support led me to think that it was possible to accomplish a critical study of experimental film. I am grateful for the patience of all the filmmakers who on occasion had to submit to my fastidious interrogations. Finally, I would like to thank my editor for his suggestions and perseverance.

My commitment to experimental film would not have been the same had I not shared it with Miles McKane. His presence, his advice were invaluable to me - and not only for the actual writing of the text. This book is dedicated to him.

1

ON CONTEMPORARY CINEMA

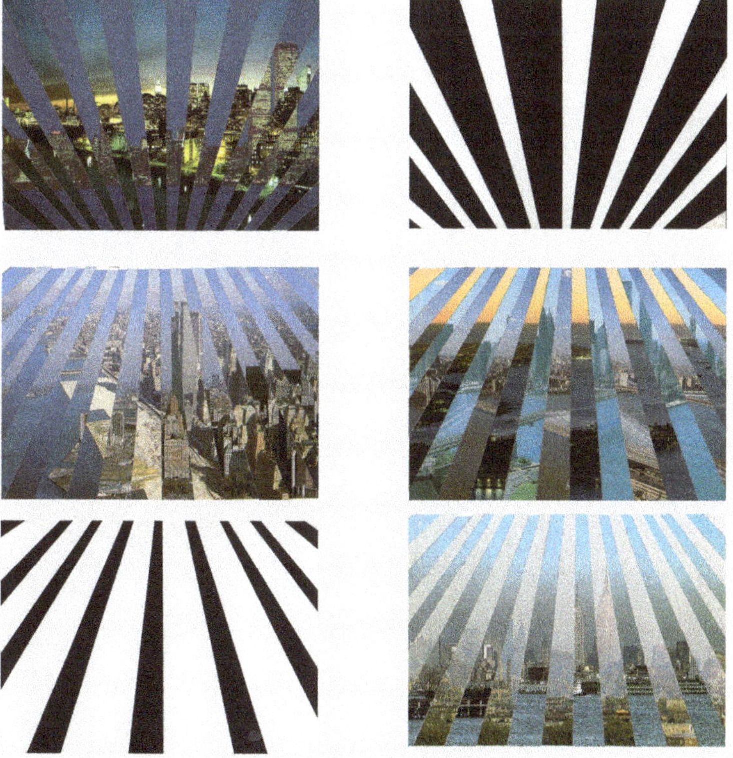

RESISTANCE CINEMA

Contemporary experimental cinema is characterized by a multiplicity of approaches. True to the path of other fields of art, it is not united by any central theme with the exception of a few passing trends which sporadically dominate a few domains in particular; such a fashion today is the notion of intimacy, another is role-playing in the manner of karaoke.

Based on some examples, I would like to point out the pertinence of certain approaches which have been applied in or on the edges of experimental film.

Exhibitions devoted to film or its effects are numerous. Film has become the paradigm of art: it functions as the ultimate point of reference. Artists' installations borrow from experimental film some of the analytical strategies that it has engendered in the course of its history and converts them, through video projection, into endless projection. In the use of fundamentally inflationistic video-film installation, the frontality of projection is rarely called into question. What seems to be fascinating about film is that it needs to be projected in a dark room. This fact alone seems to suffice - any image will do as long as it is projected. This attitude prevails; the image matters little, the nature of its projection even less![1]

But if the use of film as a moment of nostalgia is utilized with extraordinary vigor in many art exhibitions,[2] it is nevertheless evident that installations are once again present in the domain of experimental film. This development appears to derive its force from a resurgence today of performance art and "expanded cinema."

The use of film in these two cases is not the same. For visual artists what matters is the reference to film itself. Film is thus understood in its classic sense: a cinema of fiction where the installation will consist of recycling the space where film is experienced, incarnated by the projection in a room. The reference is to film and its particularities. Different aspects of cinema are recycled: the travelling shots in the work of Claude Closky, Hollywood classics of the 1950s and 1960s in the work of Mark Dean, different versions of the same film in the work of Pierre Huyghe. The processes of film are celebrated or, to put it another way, a superficial recycling of standardized effects is executed. A fascination with *Psycho* (1960) is acknowledged in the case of Douglas Gordon, with *Le Mépris* (1963) in the case of Ange Leccia. In this way adoration is bestowed on the accoutrements of cinema: the voice of Snow White, the black frame, the disaster film, intertitles....

In the case of experimental filmmakers, or those who admit to this label, there can be found a different use of film from that of visual artists. These filmmakers question above all the modalities of the filmic apparatus and break it down. In this way *Leap Frog* (1993) by Miles McKane uses three loops of different lengths projected side-by-side in the form of a horizontal triptych. He stages an amphibian ballet featuring frogs jumping out of the frame sometimes re-entering the same screen, other times the adjoining one in chaotic sepia-toned iridescence. The filmic apparatus is an integral part of the work. Nothing is hidden. The noise of the projector is only varied when splices pass through it. The flight of insects is captured in slow motion.[3] The animal's occupation of the screen is minimal at its very least; it only appears to better jump out of it or to throw itself into the water. The surface of the water blends into that of the physical filmic image, its grain, as much as that of the image itself is different at each projection. The extreme stretching out of the action underlines the fragility of the proposition which is distorted by randomness and at every moment risks dissolving entirely into the emptiness of the screen. A plentitude of nothingness is achieved. Synchronicity does not have the upper hand because it remains just a potentiality, an anachronism which makes each viewing a unique experience by simultaneously confronting the reproduction of a recording with the differences between each version depending on the space in which it is projected rather than its sequential continuity. The artists impose a random simultaneity onto the multiplicity of simultaneous views presented successively. They apply to the sequence what other film-makers have questioned through the serialization of individual frames. I am thinking here primarily of the work of Ernie Gehr or of Rose Lowder. The latter, in a remarkable way, reveals the gap between direct and filmic perception. What is recorded on film results in specific effects which have little to do with their actual recording. Films such as *Rue des Teinturiers* (1978) or the *Bouquets* series (1995-1996) are perfect examples in this respect. They share with *Serene Velocity* (1970) by Ernie Gehr the elaboration of a perspective which questions the very possibility of its existence by working on the juxtaposition of vanishing points. In contrast to these film-makers, Miles McKane organizes the filmic process around the use of chance; he does it in *Leap Frog* as he also does in the installation *Maison ardente* (1994). On the other hand, this is not the case with *Little Girl* (1997) which concentrates on loss, disappearance and incandescence based on the deterioration of a film sequence. In this installation, a little girl is caught up in the relentless tickling of the emulsion. Film devours its objects by the very instability of its physical material. It is this instability itself which Jürgen Reble uses in one of his latest films *Instable Materie* (1995). Since this film, he has gravitated toward performances and installations where there are no longer any prints of the film but only duplicates (a series of originals) which are destroyed during each performance. The physical material of the filmstrip, its grain and its textures are altered by chemical agents and become the unique preoccupation of his work. It is most often executed with the accompaniment of live sound created by Thomas Köner. The latter incorporates sound elements captured during the presentation which he associates and processes according to the stretching out of layers of sound reflecting the movement of suspended blocks of sound. These layers of sound evoke but do not repeat the process of dissolution visible on the screen.[4] In *Chicago* (1996), Jürgen Reble, working from a sequence shot on the elevated railway in Chicago, creates a sense of the loss and disintegration of film emulsion. By bleaching out the original film, rendering it fragile, he reduces the representation of the city to a dusty muddle. For this film Thomas Köner records the dust on the optical soundtrack and from it creates a sound composition, a veritable journey into the abyss of a blast of air. The film portrays the obliteration of a city by the means of sound and image.

These questions of disappearance, of dissolution are preponderant in contemporary film. Each filmmaker adapts them according to their own aesthetic proclivities.

If one can speak of a cinema of recycling,[5] it clearly grows out of a dissolution that results from an intensive use of manipulated found footage. *Tuning the Sleeping Machine* (1996) by David Sherman could be the archetypical example in the sense that the film plays on the idea of visual interference. In this sort of recycling, the notion of noise and parasitic echoes are essential to understand the eruption of representation. In the manner of Jürgen Reble, David Sherman or the Orgone Cinema and Metamkine collectives provokes the emergence of figurative motifs aimed at the inexorable dissolution of the chaotic bustle of the film material. These filmmakers all work with artisanal development and chemical manipulation of the film itself, creating a dynamic tension with the film material's inherent photographic and chemical aspects. Such processes permit the transformation (almost sliding towards although not quite morphing into) of one state into another, while always based on pure chance. It has affinities to the spirit of Stan Brakhage's project when he was making *Dog Star Man* (1961-1964). In this elegy, the application of colors, Chinese inks, combined with different emulsions is carried out with the masterful gestures of an artist at the height of his expressive power. Today films that work with the material of film itself do not promote a vision of a subject but question the very capacity of film to still produce images. What counts is above all the movement of masses of color even before they can even be assigned to a particular category. The films of Julie Murray are a further example. Her latest film *If You Stand With Your Back to the Slowing of the Speed of Light in Water* (1997) is notable for its constant dissolution of found or filmed photographic sequences into the backwash of its visual or aural raw material. Nothing is fixed, everything is in transit, between abstraction and figuration, between what is recognizable and the unknown, between images and sounds. We are faced with a cinema which advances by inhumation and revelation. *Dervish Machine* (1992) by Bradley Eros and Jeanne Liotta or *Macumba* (1995) and *Party* (1995) by Dietmar Brehm belong to this tendency. We are also faced with a cinema of hypnosis of which one of the primary expressions is *The Secret Garden* (1988) by Phil Solomon. In addition, the importance and the quality of the soundtracks in contemporary cinema deserves note. These seem to come directly out of the experiments of the Super 8 movement of the 1980s, inaugurated in Great Britain by Derek Jarman and the New Romantics in Germany by Michael Brynntrup, Alte Kinder, and Schmezldahin. In France, this Super 8 movement has been perpetuated above all thanks to Teo Hernandez, Jakobois, and Stéphane Marti. These highly elaborated soundtracks often emphasize parasitic noises, scratches, tears, sighs, and hisses. The use of this raw sound evokes the textures of the image. This materiality must be understood as the revenge of the gesture. It is a question of appropriation of a diversion of the means offered by digital technology. This last would favor a clean, antiseptic sound. This material, these traces are often perceived as the sudden intrusion and affirmation of a subject, of a body; at other times they are the trace of a memory or nostalgia: *The Film of Her* (1996) by Bill Morrison.

The reprocessing of sequences facilitates distancing in relation to the material employed as in certain parts of *Chronic* (1996) by Jennifer Reeves. The filmmaker here paints a portrait of a woman who has practiced self-mutilation since adolescence. The use of documentary images that have been optically re-worked is evocative of Nina Fonoroff's film, *The Accused Mazurka* (1994), which looks at a woman undergoing a crisis of depersonalization. In these two films, in spite of the disparity of the sequences used, it is the accumulation of layers of images flowing one into another which marks the distance and the rupture; they are the signs of loss, of our loss. We are in fact put into a paradoxical situation: even while outside the character's view, we nevertheless feel her full force. In *Chronic*, this separation creates an indecisiveness in its expression relative to the richness in the way the image is treated. This richness detaches us from the surface of the screen, plunging us into an abyss of forms and color which undermine in a way the original document.

In a similar manner in *De Profundis* (1997) by Lawrence Brose a richness of texture and intervention on the surface of the film in this ode to the male body. The film offers a critical reading of the contemporary gay world as if through the eyes of Oscar Wilde. This criticism is expressed through the chemical transformation of numerous disparate cinematographic elements ranging from home movies of the 1920s through gay pornography including documentary shots of the Radical Fairies, etc. We are plunged into a torrent of reworked images, submerged by the richness and intensity of images and sounds which sweep away any pre-established vision one might have about homosexuality. We disappear before these images; our glance follows the images' surface searching for a coherence that has been removed. The same aesthetic of disappearance can be glimpsed in the film *Frank's Cock* (1994) and *Letters from Home* (1996) by Mike Hoolboom, even if these last two films do not strive to overwhelm. These films are concerned with the fact of being HIV positive and being diagnosed with AIDS; they seek to recover the memory of a time, of a being, of a feeling. This recovery at times takes on a nostalgic quality, manifested in a few superimpositions such as a sunset over a man's face in *Letters from Home*.[6] The film examines in this way the melancholy manifest in the space featuring bodies transformed in one way or another - whether with age, sickness, or death.

The trace of this transformation can be found in the alternation between their physical or filmic representation. In *Letters from Home* it is a reprise from expected death which unsettles everything. Possessed by this anticipation of death, suddenly images must be imagined of a future which had previously seemed to have no relevance. This double movement is portrayed on the screen by superimpositions and on the soundtrack by multiple voices.

If to share a past that has never ended has nothing to do with dissolution, to no longer be able to share a past proves unacceptable and places the loss as a way to live in a world in which film offers a probable charade, an almost virtual sharing based on images of the beyond and the positioning of the filmmakers. In *The Fallen World* (1983) by Marjorie Keller, is it the music which convokes the melancholy about this submerged world or is it the vision of Shelley's tomb? With *Momento Mori* (1995) by Jim Hubbard or with *Zefiro Torna* (1992) by Jonas Mekas, it is the loyalty of a deceased friend which inevitably convokes this emotion. In this case, the loss is not the result of the film's work but its motivation. This difference of intention is the distinctive mark of these films, but it is not their only meaning. The films can also be thought of as an act of resistance. Resistance to the past, to the present, to powers of every sort: political, cinematographic, etc. It is in this sense that the films of William Jones and primarily *Massillon* (1992) can be understood, a journey through a homophobic America. *Birth of a Nation* by Jonas Mekas (1997), a celebration of the activists of invisible cinema, can also be understood in this way.

It is necessary to state that the scope of experimental cinema cannot be summed up by these few films. The practice of recycling images from all sorts of sources is still current today and takes many different approaches. We have noted a few films that favor ways of reworking to endow themselves with an unprecedented otherness. For other filmmakers, it is the editing process which takes precedence. By an expanded way of assembling short sequences and animated optical illusions, Takashi Ito paints the portrait of a renowned Japanese transvestite in *Gi-Souchi-M* (1996). His editing makes it possible to distribute and fracture sequences through an alternation and weaving together which reveals previously unseen forms of the story. In the same way, two admirable montage films, *Mechanics of the Brain* (1997) by Henry Hills and *Shangaied Text* by Ken Kobland, draw on films about the history of cinema in order to offer new ways of looking at film. The former uses Pudovkin's film on Pavlov and offers a frantic choreography of corporal reactions to different types of stimulation. Masterful editing alternates with, among other things, extracts from Pudovkin's films, dance sequences in a laboratory and a polar bear taking a swim. There is fascination in the sequence of the bear's delicacy in the movement of his front paw as he swims on his back. This sequence pays homage to that of the washerwoman climbing a stairway in *Ballet mécanique* (Fernand Léger, 1924). Both are repeated multiple times. This makes for a montage film that excels at covering its tracks and whose soundtrack adds a supplementary playful dimension. Faced with so much information, we become like a dog faced with so many different sorts of stimuli that it no longer knows how to react. Disoriented, we no longer know how to read the messages. Only images of revolution remain to us, their spectacularization, as in Ken Kobland's film which made use of a video mixing studio for its editing and which was distributed and projected on both film and video.

In contrast to these forms of montage is the limpidity of films consisting of a single shot or a variation on a single initial shot such as those of Karl Kels which display precise framing and an economical use of effects at the service of a direct approach to light. Whether in *Stars* (1991) or *Untiled* (1995), the composition of the image is the primordial concern. Karl Kels' poetic vision is shared by Scott Hammen in *Seven Landscapes* (1995) and *Field Studies* (1996) and Marcelle Thirache in *Clair de pluie* (1986). Their poetry grows out of the quality of the framing, the architecture of their light.

The expression of dissolution allows us to envisage one aspect of contemporary cinema. Nevertheless, it is not the only domain that filmmakers draw from. Other attitudes can be discovered which explore intimacy found in seemingly insignificant daily events which often go unnoticed. Paradoxically, the recent work of Malcolm Le Grice belongs to this domain, an activity close to that of the film journal. His journal is a notebook of forms and colors from his virtual editing table. In *Chronos Fragmented* (1995), Malcolm Le Grice attempts to work in new way with the process of organizing images according to the potential interactions of selected sounds/images in a variety of modalities and rules defined by the filmmaker. This approach gives the filmmaker free rein permitting him to overcome the obstacles which previously prevented him from bringing them to the screen. The process diverges in this way from classical linear or even expanded production techniques which film has developed so far. Le Grice's filmstrip is not that dissimilar to *Shimmer* (1995) by Nelson Henricks in which he presents an investigation into the ghosts of his childhood. Nelson Henricks makes the invisible concrete whereas Malcolm Le Grice gives precedence to the process of editing over the subject which makes it visible.

And so there are numerous films which, recording action such as those of Erik Wesselo, are closely connected to the performance art of the 1970s. These films offer self-filming, self-portraiture, and extracts from film journals. The actions they film are rigorously commonplace; anything spectacular is deliberately avoided. Celebrating one's birthday, stuffing oneself with food, knitting (Hélèna Villovitch,) bathing (Anja Czioska), sex with inflatable dolls (Frédéric Charpentier), are among these actions. All of the economics of daily life and intimacy are used in keeping with the particular limits imposed by the limits of the Super 8 cartridge, in other words, three minutes of continuous shooting in which the beginning of an action can be seen but its end can only be imagined off-screen. In all cases it is the notion of play which motivates the performance and the filming, an attitude shared by Steve Reinke with his series *100 Videos* (1995-1997). Each episode is shot with the objective of amusing himself and to provoke a reaction. The temporal constraints are particular to Super 8 and do not apply similarly to Video 8 where the nature of the project alone determines its constraints. The brief duration of the cassette does not mean these are cinematographic haiku:

in addition to series, episodes, there are also actions which differ from one reel to the next. The use of a single shot, whether fixed or not, is a common practice of these artists whatever medium they employ. These different kinds of sequences sweep away any separations without however eliminating their respective characteristics at the moment they are filmed. Things become more complicated at the moment of the projection or distribution of these works. Whenever the work is intended for an exhibition, video is the preferred medium while for projection in a cinema, film is the preferred choice of many.

This commitment to daily life is nothing new in film; it has in fact been one of the characteristics of British film since the beginning of the 1980s. It is the emergence of the creator (filming-filmed) within the frame that is new. The objective is no longer to analyze but to show as simply as possibly in order to undermine the conventions of mainstream audio-visual production which, in general, is highly sophisticated. To take back ownership of images by preferring an unsuccessful, poor quality, badly defined image. It is obvious that cheap Fisher-Price and High 8 cameras have had a preponderant influence in the development of this aesthetic.[7] A cinema of resistance. And in this context it is easy to understand the interest that filmmakers and video-makers have shown for the minor forms of cinema, above all for home movies.

I am thinking of *Passagen* (1996) by Lisl Ponger and also *Happy End* by Peter Tscherkassky (these two films use movies of vacations and New Year's Eve celebrations) as well as Matthias Müller who from one film to another incorporates images from his past as he has done again briefly in *Pensao Globo* (1997). Lisl Ponger's film has the particularity of presenting a genuine touristic atlas of rich European families. A white person's view of a world in which colonialism and exoticism are the way to understand other peoples. The private world becomes public. This appropriation of films which are cinematographic only in name seems to me fundamental in the sense that it allows a reconsideration of the interest of such images and their banal idea of beauty and composition. This use of beauty has often been minimalized because they are perceived as being without value.

This supposed absence of value, this display of kitsch beauty recalls, for example, the photographic work of Jack Pierson. A light breeze is blowing, unpretentious images take over and manage to do it whatever their medium. And in parallel to these home movies the iconography of pornography asserts itself in its capacity to portray sexual desire at a time when moralism is seen as a protective and redemptive value.

The widespread use of home movies and pornographic films in experimental cinema is consistent with the purest tradition of what can be defined as subversive film. It consists of a use of which film prioritizes expressiveness without at all minimizing formal questions of other ways of seeing, whether it consists of working with the innate materiality of the filmstrip or imagining it in relation to other media. Today the history of film is bound up with television, at least in terms of how it is seen. Filmmakers find themselves in a new situation where the choice of the distribution medium has become secondary. What motivates them and enthralls me is to witness the coexistence of cinematographic forms which have previously been completely incompatible but which I cannot imagine being without. Digitalization seems to be the ideal way to a cinema as it has for so long been thought about, written about, and promised. It seems to again be possible to dismantle images. These cinematographic practices, labelled experimental, still seem to me to be the place where art can be found.

New York, February 1998

A MINOR CINEMA, A CINEMA OF CUSTOMS, A CINEMA OF MOODS

Cinema, in all of its aspects, is going through a crisis caused mainly by its conversion to the new technology of communication and norms of television. But, at the same time, experimental cinema, which has always been in opposition to economic and industrial standards, appears to be finding new life thanks to young creators. This form of contemporary cinema, despite its enormous diversity, is characterized by the affirmation of subjectivity, identity, history. A minor cinema, a cinema of customs, a cinema of moods, whose specificity is found in its abandonment of genres and the elaboration of ways of thinking, it grows out of diverse experiences drawing in equal measure from social and political history and small family chronicles. It is a cinema which, reconnecting with the earliest days of film, offers multiple ways to see. Still, it is not possible to define it strictly as narrative or documentary cinema. A perversion of genres and categories has encouraged the development of hybrid genres, between autobiography and diary, investigation and political militancy. In this way some filmmakers outline key elements and traverse territory that amplifies and transforms our perception of the world. They give direction to contemporary cinema. I will speak about some of them who express their personal concerns in an unprecedented way: Su

Friedrich, Matthias Müller, Jürgen Reble, Cécile Fontaine and Jakobois.

Su Friedrich articulates her work around two poles: on the one hand, arguments in support of feminism, on the other, the tradition of American avant-garde film. Friedrich asserts herself as a woman, a lesbian, and a filmmaker.[1] But to reduce Su Friedrich's films to these poles is to run the risk of missing the multiplicity of combinations that they reveal through her experiments with subjectivity and its discoveries. Her work demolishes the boundaries between categories and genres, creating hybrid objects. They explore intersections between practices previously considered mutually exclusive: the film journal in the tradition of Mekas with *The Ties That Bind* (1984) but also the formalism of an alphabetical arrangement of fragments of a story in *Sink or Swim* (1980). Drawing on events in her own life, her films take on different aspects: more narrative with *Damned If You Don't* (1987), more militant with *Scar Tissue* (1980) and *First Comes Love* (1991) or more autobiographical with *Gently Down the Stream* (1981) and *Rules of the Road* (1993). Nevertheless, whatever the type of film, she has always been concerned with elements of fiction.

Starting with *Gently Down the Stream*, Su Friedrich arranges an accumulation of stories - here a series of fourteen dreams - scratched directly onto the film emulsion. Words accompany but do not relate directly to photographic sequences. In this film a relationship is established between the text and the flow of the images, between the traumatic nature of certain dreams and the waves in which women dive and swim. These waves are the agent of lesbian desire. The word-by-word presentation of dreams is juxtaposed with the continuity of the photographic sequences, threatening the interpretation of the dream by these images. The dream's narrative plunges the viewer into a peculiar mood. It warns us to be apprehensive about psychological troubles which the filmmaker's dreams reflect even if we cannot understand them. Su Friedrich here finds a way to confront independent fields of reality in a cinematic space. This disconnect between text and image is a dominant trait in her films. The text, written or spoken, does not refer directly to or explain the images; it is often beyond or below them and yet a relationship between them develops whether deliberate or not.

With *The Ties That Bind* (1984) and *Sink or Swim* (1990), the filmmaker explores parental relationships. While in the first she evokes the memory of her mother, in the second she questions the relations between a father and one of his daughters. The two films differ as much by their intentions as by their approach but share the richness and diversity of the material they employ. In *The Ties That Bind*, the images echo the mother's point of view, while in *Sink or Swim* the off-screen narration is the daughter's and that of Su herself, encouraging a certain detachment in the recounting of autobiographical stories. The narrator's voice dominates the visual content as well as the rhythm, the choice, and the treatment of the shots. In fact, the meaning permeates and is woven into the disparate visual elements, ranging from words scratched onto the film or refilmed from the screen, to found footage (recycled images) of the film journals of the filmmaker and her parents, travel films, and including more conventionally staged scenes of the filmmaker and her mother. These two films make use of personal questions but do so in a way that allows the experiences of the mother, the daughter and the father to be shared by all in a number of different ways. In fact, the questions asked of the mother, scratched word-by-word onto the film in *The Ties That Bind*, make the filmmaker's presence felt and, in a way, pose questions directly to the viewer. In *Sink or Swim*, it is the organization of the story in a backward alphabetical order, from the letter Z (Zygote) to the letter A (Atalante, Athena, Aphrodite) that divides the stories into voices in the third person.[2] The private word is at the center of Su Friedrich's films. *Damned If You Don't* (1987) continues the investigations of *Gently Down the Stream* confronting questions of Catholicism and lesbian sexuality. But, unlike all of her other films, this one uses the conventions of narrative cinema more directly in order to subvert them by intertwining several levels of story-telling. It does so by incorporating the Michael Powell film, *Black Narcissus* (1947) while calling into question its ideology, attitudes towards sexuality, etc.

Su Friedrich's work has a way of subverting genres equaled only by her skill at combining previously distinct formal strategies. The process of separation into chapters in *Sink or Swim* is accomplished through the alphabetical organization of stories. It is reminiscent of Frampton's *Zorn's Lemma* (1970), whereas the use of off-screen narration recalls his *Nostalgia* (1971). And in addition, in both films the author is not the subject of the work's concerns.

Bringing together issues associated with the documentary and a subjectivity characteristic of personal cinema, introducing filmic effects in order to question the perception of time and space in the recounting of an experience, in other words, enlisting the processes of structural cinema to evoke an emotionally charged experience, these are the salient characteristics of Su Friedrich's cinema. In *Damned If You Don't*, she explores the realm of sexuality and its portrayal dominated by the viewpoint of men. This feminine re-appropriation of the female image is accompanied by an affirmation of cinema as visual pleasure.

In the same way, Matthias Müller confronts the intimate and the social, the personal and the clichés that haunt us. The two filmmakers are both concerned with paternal relationships. In Müller's case, the understanding of absence involves the appropriation of images of the father and those of what the father does to his son. Thus, in *Final Cut* (1986), Müller reworks family images in order to find connections and meanings. Absence is dealt with by means of image appropriation. This reuse leads to cuts during editing which permit the artist to no longer be the victim of images but, on the contrary to control them from inside. This type of re-appropriation is symptomatic of the difference between Friedrich and Müller. For one, exposure through questioning drives the film, while for the other it is the reuse of the images of loved ones, mixed in with personal or found sequences, which lead to the development of new meanings. The image appropriation yields revelations not only through the juxtaposition of sequences, but also in their chemical treatment during processing, through refilming and editing. The sequences are reworked in a way that makes them lose the cold and neutral character typical of the video image.

Continental Breakfast (1985) and *The Flamethrowers* (1988) are films made collectively to allow a multiplicity of points of view. *Aus Der Ferne - The Memo Book* (1988), *Home Stories* (1990) and *Sleepy Haven* (1992) all draw from recycled images from diverse sources. All these films investigate: Germany in the case of *Home Stories*, the family in *Final Cut*; cinema in *Home Stories*, which works through compilation and reinterpretation; AIDS and anxiety about death for *Aus Der Ferne*; the representation of male homosexuality in the case of *Aus Der Ferne* and *Sleepy Haven*. The cinema of Matthias Müller is a cinema of confrontation. The sequences shot for the film as well as those borrowed from other sources collide in many different ways. An interpretative approach classifies and associates them along other lines of convergence, other desires. In *Sleepy Haven*, the blue coloration of the image contrasts with the heat of desire, a last homage to Kenneth Anger's *Eaux d'artifice* (1953).

The image is overloaded: the accumulation of waste, chemical development stains deliberately left by the filmmaker, refilming and various tints, confer on each of his films a dream-like mood. The superimpositions, the intense base notes of the soundtrack as the slow but hypnotic rhythms. Thus in *Aus Der Ferne*, dark sepia predominates, the sequences melt into one another like the backwash of surf. One sequence succeeds another by bursts or by slow progression, permitting us to isolate the body, the room, the chandelier, the garden. The sequences asphyxiate each other: a strange vision of mourning and anxiety. A wave of images about death, about absence (a friend dead from AIDS), submerges us. We are sent back into the filmmaker's eye, in close-up, which gathers fragments of the visual experience and melts the vision and progression into a magma of sensations.[3] A similar experience is to be found in *Sleepy Haven* where the filmmaker organizes multiple sequences from film journals and adventure films based on a way of looking at several male bodies. There is always the presence of the body which asserts itself through the relations it maintains with its environment, whether that be desire, sickness, death, nature, or the city.

A certain practical skill characterizes contemporary experimental film. For a number of years, certain filmmakers have been developing their films themselves, rediscovering in this way the methods of the first cameramen who developed and projected the films they had shot. Shooting film again becomes an act of magic, an alchemical process. In this vein can be found one of the members of the former Schmelzdahin collective, Jürgen Reble, who works both in his studio and in public. He creates performances in which the image of a film reveals itself, passing from negative to positive and then being tinted, before being progressively chemically destroyed or burned.

Film is an ephemeral art. The lifespan of prints is relatively short compared to the presumed eternity of other works of art. Nevertheless film is rarely seen that way; few filmmakers seem to take into account the fragility of their medium.[4] It is this fragility and the evolution over time which is at the heart of the work of Jürgen Reble. If at the beginning, it was for him above all a question of identifying the reactions of the physical medium to time and decomposition, this interest changed when he discovered that film emulsions reacted differently depending on the environment in which they had been stored or left in. The discovery of this evolution of the material medium opened possibilities for him which the use of chemical products only served to amplify. In the beginning, his work focused on films which had been discarded and buried in the ground, like *Stadt im Flammen* (1984), or submerged in water for several months, such as *Aus Den Algen* (1986). Once recovered, the films seem to have been devoured by bacteria, and strangely similar to decomposing nitrate film. The colors had turned. The emulsion had peeled away in places or entirely, causing the image to disappear and only the transparent base to be visible. Analysis of this aging process and the transformation it caused were essential for this group of filmmakers, who began to study the possibility of controlling this random process. During the time that Jürgen Reble was part of this group, he worked on found footage and, little by little, began to introduce sequences from his film journals. His introduction of this element brought about the break-up of the film collective. Starting in 1989, with *Rumpelstilzchen* (1989), Jürgen Reble's found footage of animals was accompanied by sequences from his personal and family films. The multiplicity of chromatic variations emerges in *Passion* (1990). Whatever the nature of the sequences (collected by the filmmaker), they all underwent (re)processing. Nothing was preserved. It was this aspect that his live performances revealed in a radical way, rendering every projection a visualization of a unique process, the ultimate perception of an image. The image is sacrificed to a process that simultaneously both reveals and destroys it. To make visible the nature of film, like showing the transformation (the sacrifice) of nature by man, is the task that Reble assigns himself. To do this, in *Das Goltene Tor* (1992) he juxtaposes scientific documentation with images of everyday life. He handles his material in a highly pictorial way, thus removing all realism in favor of an internalized vision. Reble is in this sense not so far from Stan Brakhage who sees in cinema an art of vision; film incorporates every modality of light devoid of all realism, realism being a purely human invention.

This primacy of luminous energy over realism, inaugurated by Len Lye, taken up by Stan Brakhage and Jürgen Reble, among others, can be found in a different way in the work of Cécile Fontaine. She too is interested in reprocessing and manipulating images. As if, faced with the accumulation of so many images, nothing remained for filmmakers to do besides recycle them in order to create other meanings, other interpretations. This would explain the incredible proliferation of found footage films in recent years.[5] Cécile Fontaine shares with Jürgen Reble a fascination with the materiality of the film medium and with the visual qualities of its emulsion. Although she works primarily from advertising films, television shows and news footage, she also uses home movies which allow her to include emotional feelings which she could not otherwise have shared. It is less the specific details of these sequences that count than their capacity to create a general impression that can be shared by everyone.

Films, for Cécile Fontaine, are to be cut up, manipulated in every sense in order to create other images, relations, and mirages. Whatever the material the filmmaker uses, she proceeds through an in-depth study of the film material itself and what comes to life when it is projected. In fact she plays as much with the subject matter of the films she uses as she does with their physical materiality. She deploys a subtle strategy to ridicule social behavior and the way it is recorded on film. Every film genre is fair game: she subverts advertising films (*Overeating*, 1984; *Cruises*, 1989), educational films (*Golf Entretien*, 1984 and *2 Made for TV Films*, 1986, made from the outtakes of the previous one), home movies, or news reports (Japon Series, 1991, conceived from a Buto dance film). This work examines the cinematographic image from several angles. First, from the point of view of its production methods. In fact, Cécile Fontaine rarely shoots film herself. She relies on already shot film which she dismantles, scratches, tints, then reassembles using a technique she shares with poster designers. She works with the filmstrip itself, lacerating it, submitting it to the worst "abuse" in order to give it a pictorial appearance whose gestures and lyricism will be highlighted during projection. The film's emulsion allows her to subsequently deploy ghosts of representation through a medium which is no longer but a shadow of itself and displays only a worrying strangeness. Representation on the brink of disappearance which resembles that deployed by Jürgen Reble. These ghosts and specks of image dust, these perforations of misplaced soundtracks, these out-of-frame images are what the filmmaker plays with, creating visual puzzles in which humor is never less powerful than its visual impact.

In Cécile Fontaine's work, a banal dailiness gives rise to the most caustic criticism. But the filmmaker never abandons her sense of humor which achieves its highest expression in her treatment of the soundtracks and home movies made by her father; as if it was necessary to not let her father have the last word in films in which his daughters and others had been excluded. The revenge of the filmmaker who, without seeming to, and without using the excuse of technology, changes the world.

To change the world through film is a project shared by Jakobois.[6] The evolution of his perception of the world is what underlies his cinematographic practice. This perception involves the collection of images which constitute his film journals and film catalogues, as he has explained himself. The films of Jakobois are often based on a number of recurrent themes: games in *Jeux et joueurs* (1987-1988), desire in *Passage du désir* (1988-1993), but also places: *Déjà ? Vu* (1980), Passage du Thermomètre (1982), *Les Ponts d'Asnières* (1987). They can be the journal of a year, as in *Un an d'une vie* (1987-1988), *Passage des petits métiers* (1989-1990), etc. Jakobois articulates intimacy and abstraction in a number of his films; this articulation opens paths that are similar but still very distinctive from those of the filmmakers already mentioned. The play of forms, responses when confronted with the unexpected, are what interest the filmmaker and it is particularly evident in certain sequences of *Passage du Thermomètre*, *Pluie de roses* (1984) and *Passage des petits métiers* just how important the mastery of Super 8 is to his way of transforming reality.

Skill in the organization of events has led him to favor thematic films. The filmmaker is drawn to the celebration of daily activities. This celebration is sometimes imbued with nostalgia and seems to capture a world that is gone forever. Film thus becomes the instrument which preserves as much as displays. Celebration of the body - an impulse he shares with Müller and Friedrich. Expression of insatiable desire in searching for one self and others, in which, from one film to another, the pleasure derives from the urgency of its recording. Jakobois shares with Hiroyuki Oki[7] the ability to render the essentiality of this quest for self, by playing with framing and rhythm. The latter, in *Yuei Kinshi* (1990) and *Tarch Trip* (1992-1993) throws himself into a frenetic quest where the torments and desires of the body, the doubts which inhabit it, are revealed by slow and tense shots. Film is what permits the display of this search by roaming off the beaten track. A cinema between places and people. A cinema which favors sudden bursts of distance while at the same time bringing things together.

Art Press spécial Cinéma, hors série n°14, Paris, 1993.

ALWAYS FAIR WEATHER

For some time now the experimental cinema scene in France has been experiencing a period of change. There is a feeling of enthusiasm with a greater number of film theaters interested in screening this type of cinema. It should be noted that traditional cinema is experiencing a period of crisis with numerous cinemas closing in Paris and the provinces. So many of these picture palaces have become Palaces of Consumption, catering for other dreams. So many filmmakers find no place to come to rest save the endless nocturnal realms, illuminated by the cathode fire flies. In the wake of this obvious deterioration of the French film industry, whether at its production or distribution levels or its direction toward the lowest common denominator, "made-for-TV movies," experimental, documentary or independent cinema, is now enjoying a resurgence of interest which is simultaneously positive, stimulating and disquieting for the filmmakers, because there is always in situations like these, a return to the established figures, that is to say, the beneficiaries of the situation are those whose history has already been designated. This is one of the dangers or weaknesses of the revival. This resurgence of interest is too fresh for the benefits to be felt by the younger generation of filmmakers, or at least those who have appeared since the early 1980s.

Experimental cinema in France, although institutionally recognized, is not subsidized in the same ways as in other countries. There are few or no subsidies for production, unless the project can be considered to fall within the field of the visual arts. Likewise there are no subsidies for distribution outside France, as is the case in Great Britain with the Arts Council of Great Britain or in Germany with the Goethe Institut, Canada etc. Subsidies do exist however for distribution: Light Cone for example, a film cooperative (900 titles in its catalogue), founded in 1982 by Miles McKane and myself, or the Paris Film Coop/Cinédoc (with 250 films), founded in 1974. In addition to funding these distribution groups, programming centers receive grants, such as Scratch Projection or the Archives of Experimental Film in Avignon, allowing them to organize weekly screenings or invest in special events. Various projects can be undertaken: festivals or specialized thematic programs, for example an event which juxtaposes the relation of film, video and electronic arts received funding for a second time. Similar support is given to the edition of books or catalogues on experimental film, whether these are edited by a large institution or by the courageous initiatives of independent editors such as Paris Expérimental. A restoration program of experimental films has recently been launched by Light Cone, with the agreement of the Centre National du Cinéma and the Film Archives at Bois d'Arcy. This ambitious program allows the restoration of works from the 1970s in Super-8 or 16mm, for example, with their eventual return to a distribution circuit, as well as historical works, say from the 1920s, which previously had only been available to archivists.

In line with what is occurring in the other arts of the western world in experimental cinema, there is no dominant aesthetic, rather many cinematographic perspectives and styles. The time of the avantgarde as a dominant category with its decrees of modernity is over. Nowadays, the aesthetic is defined by a fragmented constellation of practices which highlights the varied research and whose fruits are the different means of working and production. This is how a multiplicity of different practices which were formally mutually exclusive and ignorant of each other, now exists side by side. With this coexistence, friction no longer exists and that encourages the emergence of new filmmakers who, free from the historical and aesthetic quarrels that dogged the French scene until the beginning of the 1980s can now establish a new topography for French experimental cinema. In the next few paragraphs I shall try to illustrate these principal tendencies.

Lately there has been a return to the concerns of the "nouvelle vague:" small production units, disnarratiion and a focusing on the identity of a character often played by the filmmaker themselves. The pathway to an existential quest passes through narration, as was revealed in works of the American and French filmmakers of the late 1950s. A quest that can be seen again in the film of Nicole Blachon, *Les Bienheureuses* (1991), a lyrical evocation of Lesbian desire. Parallel to this practice, which no longer regards narration as a taboo, there is the development of a more personal cinema, transcending formalism, germinating through more liberal forms, a lyricism normally found only in "diary" films. A genre still relevant which is exposed through a diversity of techniques, an attachment to a place, district or city, the subjective eye of the filmmaker etches this into a global overview, whether by the raising of political, sexual or social issues. It is for this we can appreciate the importance of the work of the group MétroBarbèsRochechou Art initiated in the late 1970s, which was to establish a comprehensive map of the places they haunted and the exceptional people surrounding them in Paris. A similar attitude, albeit indirectly, can be found with the group Molokino which expresses itself as much by the places as by the sum of its participants. Jakobois (from MétroBarbèsRochechou Art) continues, in a personal way, to produce diaries and cine-poems, sketching maps of his everyday desires and pleasures. In a similar vein, Melih replies, in his own way, to some of the characteristics of the group (Molokino) by overlaying his super-8 images with sound poems. Within this type of filmmaking all social strata are present, explaining the use of "found" imagery, the excluded become visible, the off-screen voices are seen, we are faced with humanity in all its splendor and all its misery, allowing us to perceive some of these films as documents of a history that is beginning to dissolve having left no trace of specific representation.

In a film economy that has seen the closing of its essential laboratories over the last few years, its services and film stocks disappear to the advantage of video or new technologies, the influx of new film-makers can be characterized by their desire to control, to a greater extent than in the past, the different stages of film production which has been a reality in other countries and is now becoming a necessity here. Alternative labs are beginning to appear favoring a new approach to the materiality of film and at the same time questioning the conditions of production, consumption and distribution of the moving image. This could explain the use of found footage, be it pornographic with Frédéric Charpentier and Melih, televisual with Béatrice Slazak, Maurice Lemaître or miscellaneous with Cécile Fontaine, who has become the mastermind of a "cinema povera." A greater part of her work falls within the domain of "recycling" and the editing of different emulsion layers which make up color film. It is a minor cinema in the sense that she does not use any special technology such as cameras, optical printers etc. It uses the very materiality of the medium itself, an aesthetic and a playfulness are rendered through this radical transformation of the medium's materiality, while incorporating or being aware of film history. Fontaine takes an active position in the defense of graphic cinema as being a vital force, as does Françoise Thomas, by scratching, re-photographing and coloration, the practice of the group Metamkine is a further affirmation of this. They have developed techniques of refilming which reinforce their performance activities, which are a combination of film and music as performance. Their sound work is the sonic equivalent of the chemical breakdown or attack during the development of a film. For the last four years they have made the scene more dynamic by creating a projection room, laboratory and exhibition space all under the same roof. Here we can find the premise of an activity which escapes both the institutional and the academic, favoring the vital element of marginality which is essential both for and within experimental cinema. A presence which underlines the emergence over the last several years, in the domain of film as well as that of the visual arts, of a parallel art economy. Artists assuming themselves - outside the galleries and museums - the exhibition, the studio spaces, and the production of their work. In the domain of cinema, this means taking charge of the fabrication, the printing and the processing of films and prints in order to avoid laboratories as much as possible.

This does nothing to inhibit the 'chiseling' of Lettrist cinema, to continue their activities by way of discourses, or film-actions with Maurice Lemaître remaining as the emblematic figure and, through his activity and the revived interest for the films of the 1950s and 1960s from the younger generation, Lettrism finds itself in the spotlight. This can only serve to strengthen the links that exist between the visual arts and cinema, distancing experimental film a little further from Hollywood and therefore from an industry close to televisual concerns. The influence of experimental cinema can be felt in current advertising or independent production as a repercussion of its being, rather than an overt desire on the part of its filmmakers to make inroads into this sector. It is not the avant-garde which goes to Hollywood, but Hollywood which is desperately seeking surrogate images, free from the codes of narrative archetypes. The tradition of independence in experimental cinema can therefore serve as a model for future filmmaking. In this vein, the film journal *Omelette* (1993) by René Lange is not so far from classical cinema in that it tells a story; here however, it is his story and his confrontation with his family about it. A whole study of the social power of what is said and what is left unsaid is recorded in this film journal.

In this extremely turbulent field which is contemporary French cinema, certain individuals such as Jean-Michel Bouhours, Rose Lowder, Maria Klonaris and Katerina Thomadaki continue to work or to rework their connection with film production after having devoted their time and energy to the defense of cinema. All these filmmakers in their most recent films have gone beyond a previous practice and have stepped into a new territory of filmmaking. In *Quiproquo* (1992) Rose Lowder confronts two different types of landscape, one industrial, the other "natural," without abandoning the questioning of spatial perception through cinematographic means. We find many filmmakers from a previous generation who have been known to question their practices now opening up new areas and thus exploring a new voice. After having worked for a long period with diary film, Vivian Ostrovsky with *M.M. in Motion* (1992) now confronts the relations that may be offered between dance and cinema. This relationship is not that simple given that the means of expression in each discipline differ so greatly. Her latest film is in two distinct parts, each from different cinematographic perspectives.

The first section is experimental and is the result of the filmmaker's response to six productions of a choreographer. This is an impressionist approach as opposed to the second section which is a documentary approach focusing on one single production. The convergence of these two approaches within the same film produces a strange hybrid, held together by a state of hiatus close to that of a raised foot ready to step forward. This confrontation and state of hiatus lead us to another filmmaker, Martine Rousset, who for many years has elaborated an oeuvre showing the relationship between literature and cinema. This results in a temporal expansion and luminous flashes, permitting the possibility of speech, heard only at the moment when color dissolves. It is within this period of tension between saying and seeing that the filmmaker elaborates a work which leads cinema towards literature, by-passing the anecdote or narration, profiting from pure visual events, evoking those moments of Debussy where music becomes speech and speech becomes song. This voice is very often feminine with its inherent silences including a certain violence, which can only be compared to flashes of light and color, fading to black. This violence is also present in the work of Leonor Sherrer but is used here on the body and its treatment. Corresponding to the physical violence is an optical treatment that plays with disappearance and the disruption of sight - its exhaustion into white.

It should be noted that France lacks a militant experimental cinema as can be found in Anglo-Saxon countries. There are however numerous women making films but within this group the primary motivation is no longer feminist. The same can be said for the gay filmmakers who seem to have lost their militant tendency, as if they were no longer victims of a blatant exclusion which has been accentuated by the return to power of a strong right-wing. There is however a certain awakening of consciousness, certain issues arise to focus the attention or create a project. The confrontation of individual filmmakers with the illness of AIDS has shown the diversity of responses to this issue. I will take two films by way of example, *Broken Blossoms* (1992) by Miles McKane and one of my own, *Sid A Ids* (1992), The former gives a highly charged emotional response of a visual artist towards the ephemeral and fragile aspect of the human condition while the latter is more an attack against the French state, of its blatant policy of exclusion. One underlines mediation while the other attacks with "agitprop."

Broken Blossoms (1992) by Miles McKane is the response of a visual artist who employs an emotionally-charged symbolic evocation faced with AIDS. It is a response which grows out of the engagement of an artist. There is a similar attitude among many gay and women filmmakers, a similar commitment where her or his difference is stated without the necessity for a dogmatic discourse. This type of approach, which seems to refute an idea of community, is something specifically characteristic of films "made in France." Cinema is no longer an instrument of political activism and was rarely linked in the past to any kind of militancy. This leads to the conclusion that despite the current "crossbreeding" of practices there remains a division among the producers of moving images which will be difficult to overcome. Is this a reflection of the political crisis affecting France or is it a reflection of the sacrosanct Cartesian division which deems everything must remain separate?

If methods do overlap, they have not yet reached a point where opposition becomes an associate of militancy and cinema, as was the case of the gay activist Lionel Soukaz in the 1970s. Filmic genre is no longer restrictive, implying a renewal of approach, at present in its early stages which makes it difficult to form a hypothesis about its development. Let us hope that the institutionalization of experimental cinema, as a highly valued cultural activity, will not lead to aridity in contemporary production for the benefit of those who are ready to freeze the pages of history at the point of time when they themselves were twenty years old.

Revue de l'Institut Français de Bilbao, n°1, October 1994, in Catalan and French,

1st English version: *Innovation 93*, Manchester 1993.

MARTINE ROUSSET: A CINEMA OF SEPARATION

The encounter with another, one other to be exact, is the central concern of the cinematographic work of Martine Rousset: the appropriation of the specific mental universe of a person, of an author…but it is not a question of an adaptation in the sense proposed by traditional cinema, but much more an interpretation based on a body or a chosen text. Almost synesthesistic work which limits itself to the production of luminous and sonorous energy. The body and its gestures, the text and its style are perceived according to their breathing, according to their life as a dancing body, like a text screaming its misery, its solitude…

A synesthesia of absence.

An interpretation, almost a transcription, which would only respect the production and the emission of meaning before it was pushed back down into the psychological (novelistic?) subject.

An absent meaning.

Transcription of a universe and not of a character. That Carolyn Carlson dances is important in that she is the object of a cinematographic encounter and also in that her dance is in itself an invitation to …This encounter brings up three filmic propositions, three different ways of understanding Carolyn Carlson's dancing. Whether she is recognizable or not Carolyn Carlson is not the concern of the films, but what is the concern are the gesture and the rhythms that accompany and shape them. The film's task is not to give us an object or objects from which we can make the classic transfers of identity...

The film is simply there; almost beyond there.

If in Martine Rousset's first films the bodies are present as is the case with *Le réverbère* (1977) and in the *Carolyn* series, then they are always transformed, their specificities often erased. They become archetypes. The subject in the background fades away. The bodies are kept at a distance from the stage which is made visible, then heard. Excluded by coloration, by repetition (see *Le réverbère*), they seem to disappear or efface themselves by being refilmed (*Carolyn II*, 1980, *Carolyn III*, 1981) or by the multiplication of representations of the same body over time (*Carolyn I*, 1977) or in space (*Carolyn II*), composed of three simultaneous images.

An absent body, nevertheless present by certain of its gestures. A memory of a person even while details tend to fade away in our memory, mixing things up, covering up the tracks; thus the little girl and the woman in *Le réverbère* could be the same person at two different ages but nothing confirms it; ambiguity reigns and encourages a multiplicity of interpretations. This haziness is accentuated in *Le réverbère* by the repetition of scenes as well as the scratching-out of faces. The body becomes (is) its gesture. The gestures are selected and allow for polysemy. Gestures frozen in what they are about to become (see the *Carolyn* series). A multiplicity of meanings, the crossroads of different interpretations of a suspended gesture. This suspension, as in the work of Klossowski, a source, a foundation for fictions, but for Martine Rousset the fiction arises more easily by means of voices. In the confrontation of two shots as in *Carolyn III* where the dancer's gestures make her, by turns, woman or child, in harmony with the way she is treated visually. The suspension is created cinematographically in different ways: by freeze frames or by using photographs. The use of still photography is the most obvious technique, the easiest to identify for what it is, but not the most adequate to the degree that time is frozen rather than simply held back momentarily. For this Martine Rousset has a preference for the refilming of sequences and the resultant whiting-out which tends to make the recognizability of the figures disappear. This refilming is accompanied by the use of a blue filter which transforms and cools down the light a bit.

Refilming is also a way to turn things inside-out and, in an analogous way, it encourages the encounter and the appropriation of otherness by its differentiated and distanced exposure. The body, the person, can only be heard through the voice. Not by their voices, but a voice, some voices...

With *Laure*, the work of Martine Rousset takes on another dimension in which the literary asserts itself an original source of film. The field of literature, opened up, takes on a cinematographic body. By proposing other ways of accessing literary experience and the imperative necessity of writing, Rousset will fashion a cinematographic work that, at first sight, is rigorous and paradoxical. In fact, if cinema in a general way has made abundant use of literature, it is often done so only by being novelistic. But it is not the story in itself that interests Rousset but the evocative power of fictions, that a text reveals in the course of a sentence.

The three latest films of Rousset question the relation which sound has with the image. What is at stake here is the existence of an image whose purpose is to make seeing abstract. A cinematographic image which seems made only to prioritize listening. An image which puts itself in parentheses. An absent image which flees towards listening.

With *Laure* the process which Rousset has implemented develops in a singular way. Based on Laure's writing and principally on the story of a young girl, this text is declaimed - but not enacted - by two voices which echo the two images which constitute the film. One is confronted with a large luminous bluish and white image which contrasts with a small image in dark tones. One is of the daytime, the other of night-time. Everything separates them. They are the mirrors of two voices, one robust (an image of rebellion), the other fragile (the image of oblivion, of death). These two voices read the text about a childhood. The images are there to prepare us to experience violence, the urgency of the text is expressed by two voices. The nocturnal image shows us a street at night in the rain, an intersection, a possible analogy for discomfort, of the heaviness caused by the past: the child-hood memory of the young girl trapped in the straitjacket of a self-satisfied and upright bourgeois woman; this image is one of looking back at the past, on the way to oblivion, turning back on the self, on the way to death. The other image, in revolt, offers a panoramic views of the skylights and picture rails of the Museum of Modern Art. Hallucinatory relationships occur between sound and image; homogenous relations of completeness, while we hear: "Suspended between ceiling and floor," the image offers us a view of a roof through a window; paradoxical relations which only reinforce what is declaimed: "...or even only human," while we see that what is human has been banished from the two screens, momentarily emphasized by the eruption of a museum picture rail which comes into view offering for our contemplation only the dimming of light and the invasion of darkness; a bridge to the other voice, the other image. The large bluish image shows us an exhibition space, a place of looking: a museum with or without paintings, the space is lit up inside the frame but also outside it by the voice as well as the other image that offers only an exterior view at night, filmed from an interior. From one to the other, exteriority and interiority are shown. A situation which reinforces the text, the voices but also the image when suddenly the countryside appears in the exhibition space, the suspension which is the museum. A disconnect emphasized by the voice which speaks of the countryside. The poplars in winter echo the description of summer in the country by Laure. This intrusion of the outside into the interior (museum, text, etc.,) make possible the next film *Dehors* (1985) in which the countryside is the essential object of contemplation, of meditation, and also the basis for the play on sound which permits the viewers to formulate their own stories and relationships. Amid the greenery there are glimpses of a plane which can be heard. A veritable laboratory of literature is visible by its edges.

The countryside ending in the museum with the appearance in this space of vine shoots, traces of an installation by Mario Merz, a fragile encounter, evoking a textual residue.

Echoes of a future outside: how to make it visible. The meeting place: the museum, the film; the voices, the screens. The whole strategy of the films aims at creating the stretching of the time of "exposure" of the image so that we can enter into the time of text. The text and its voice are nevertheless threatened by their interments in the slow and fascinating scansions of the image. These images, some of which can be found again in *Mansfield K.* (1988), are subtle combinations of shadows and lights. The light which, in a museum, is what permits seeing becomes here the object seen. It allows us in *Laure* and *Mansfield K.* to hear the sound composition made from texts and sounds. While in *Laure* the refilming increases the grain and blur of forms and facilitates the transition from one voice to another, the jumps from one image to another, in *Mansfield K.* the line is heavy, the definition sharp, surgical, almost brittle. It evokes the sound of a broken rib and imminent death. A death prefigured in the image by beams of sunlight dotting the surface of a river.

An analogy between what is said and what is seen: fragments of light which outline the confined spaces, echoes, visual souvenirs of memories, of need.

Martine Rousset works from little known texts, texts that have been ignored, forgotten. Exiled texts in every sense of the term. Exiled because their authors are women, thus not yet writers. Laure dies without publishing a book. Katherine Mansfield writes in English in France. Martine Rousset exiles herself; she makes a film in English even though she does not speak it. A coming to awareness.

The cinema of Martine Rousset is slow, static - despite tightly framed panning shots in *Laure*, or the shot in *Dehors* which follows a tractor at the top of the frame, slightly behind it and just as it finally passes out of sight; as if the camera was out of sync (also out of view?) with the objects that she films - meditative, which make the image a space where time can be laid out, which explains the stretching.

A study of duration where the shots chosen (leaves in black and white in *Dehors*, or a forest lane in autumn) give us the time, time to hear the rustling and falling of leaves, to perceive the sun reflected in the river (*Mansfield K.*), the sparkle of light on glass surfaces (*Laure, Mansfield K.*) becomes the imaginary basis for a future but nevertheless a text already audible through its words and sounds. This is how the image can bury us and make us speechless, thus this cinema which, behinds its minimal content, is extraordinarily efficient, extremely high-strung, intense, on the brink of being lost. In fact there is a danger of injury in the image and the sound for it is often difficult to take them into account simultaneously. Nevertheless they have been carefully conceived to go together. The separation of image and sound recalls the Cartesian separation of body and soul. More exactly, it concerns the articulation of the difference between existence and consciousness: a case in point are the sequences in *Dehors* where a voice arises between what is said and how it is represented. It is in this space and this space itself that the films of Martine Rousset explore. In this sense it has a gravity because it forces us to share the difficulty of being.

Brochure *Cinéma du Musée*, Centre Georges Pompidou, 1989

VIVIAN OSTROVSKY

The films of Vivian Ostrovsky belong to two genres that have evolved in experimental film: the film journal and the collage film. Her films are like a delicious combination of these two categories in a single dish, defying definition and genres. Still, the films seem closer to film journals to the degree that the sequences that compose them match each other like elements of collage. The links existing between the two genres establish themselves according to the way they are handled, according to the montage of images and their relation to music and sounds. By fusing these two elements, the filmmaker ends up with a peculiar object: the mosaic-journal.

THE MOSAICS ARE MADE up of fragments which, juxtaposed with each other, create motifs and turn into a specific representation. If the mosaic can be considered as a possible cinematographic construct, then a cinema can be discovered which uses sequences as building blocks which can be cut into sparkling fragments and organized according to different criteria which each film imposes according to its own content and intentions. And it is through this practice that the unique qualities of the work of Ostrovsky emerge. In fact, more than the presence of the author, it is her absence that is felt, which works to the advantage of what is shown and manipulated. Evidence of the filmmaker's hand can nevertheless be detected in the framing and the cinematographic references of certain shots. This framing can resemble that of traditional cinema: for example in *U.S.S.A.* (1985), the manager coming out of a building to meet someone at the entrance or the scene of a woman in a telephone booth recalling early Godard films. In *Movie (V.O.)* (1982), the world of the theater is evoked, recalling news events and their discrete framing: here Ruggero Raimondi saluting the crowd, there ice skaters in beams of spotlights.

But Ostrovsky will also subvert this classicism by manipulating the facts through her montage, giving them something of the appearance of the assemblages of Kurt Schwitters and the collages of Joseph Cornell's boxes. Another connection, this one more cinematic, evokes an association with Dziga Vertov and Bruce Conner, with a nod to Medvekin in her way of treating the images that she has herself shot as if they were found objects or as documents. The filmmaker, as a creator of images, effaces herself in the service of her content, whether it consist of cultural or social records or private anecdotes. These representations mixed up between themselves, without any hierarchy besides the pleasure of happy association, create a mosaic effect that undermines the feeling of a film journal. The shift into the realm of the imaginary is brought about by, among other things, the means of recoloring the film which distances it from the original perception of the screen. Thus in *Movie (V.O.)* the orange-tinted scenes of Harlem, in *U.S.S.A.*, the reddish-brown of the front of a butcher's shop and in *** (1987), the sepia tone of certain gestures and the yellow-green of the final bucolic scene. These transformations through tonalities but also, as we will see, by editing, give precedence to film as a game over film as autobiography. A shifting of the subject of major cinematographic consequence. A cinema more neutral in its form which plays more easily with its content by turning to increasingly incisive humor.

THIS DISTANCING IS FACILITATED EVEN MORE by the fact that Ostrovsky can draw from a large quantity of images that she has already collected. She gathers images which she sorts and classifies, from which she can draw as she pleases according to the needs of any given project. It is this accumulation of many hours of footage which she had at her disposal that allowed her - for *Movie (V.O.)* a 12 minute film - to use the footage in a way that recalls certain assemblages by Joseph Cornell or Kurt Schwitters.

If the footage was drawn from her collection of documents, its montage was, in this case, a selection of sequences which would provide the main visual framework. This activity is both analytical and playful at the same time. Thus the subject which generates the images matters less and their content becomes the priority - not for its initial affectivity but for its rhythm and power to evoke other representation or other emotions which will often be accentuated by the soundtrack.

IN THE MANNER of Bruce Conner but also of Russian filmmakers and in the tradition of many great filmmakers who have worked from archives of commissioned film documents, the talent of Ostrovsky manifests itself in her capacity to make places collide - Moscow, Berlin, New York in *U.S.S.A.*; a summer house and an airport in *Allers-Venues* (1984), etc., - objects and situations (the pepper mill in ***), according to approaches which will never become systematic. In this work which puts the filmmaker in the role of parade organizer, Ostrovsky skirts around any personal attachments to the images: the exclusion of what is too personal permits her to reintroduce private places, individuals as scenes like any other: a case in point is *Allers-Venues* and, in particular, the scenes of meals, a recurring leitmotiv in all her films except *Copacabana Beach* (1983).

·   ·   ·

BUT THE CONTENT does not nevertheless turn into a purely socio-ethnological document (although if the humor is ignored, *Copacabana Beach* could be seen in this way) largely because of the way that, once the editing is completed, the filmmaker works with sound. Sound here plays a preponderant role to the degree that it provides another connotation to the primal meaning of the images. Numerous examples can be cited, such as, to name only one, the procession of the Jewish community and its rabbis dancing to a soundtrack composed of Brazilian samba drumming.

UNEXPECTED ENCOUNTERS between sound and image, often effectuated in a humorous vein, reproduce this collision effect which is one of the most frequently used techniques of Ostrovsky (an indication of changes in her personal life?). The power of these collisions derives from the association of disparate elements to provoke a critique of each one of them considered separately.

IN *MOVIE (V.O.)*, a scene in a men's room summons up a "camp" feeling by accompanying it with a Troubadour melody, "Tu mia:" the sound reinforces the eminence of the place by means of a cliché. In *Copacabana Beach*, while images in fast motion show a far-off group of women doing exercises on the beach, a popular music hall hit by Carmen Miranda can be heard. Ostrovsky plays with the sound as she plays with the images: in both cases there is research, gathering, archiving, classification followed by a contrasting which effects the nature of the game on several levels, in several voices. Plays on words and images which, from film to film, become increasingly complex, multiplying the meanings. Thus a very beautiful sequence of good-byes in the Avignon train station, in grainy black and white accentuated by the lighting and the enlargement of the image, while the voice of Elvis Presley is heard on the soundtrack, "What now, my love?" The departure of a loved one occurs before our eyes, while the choice of black and white evokes all the farewell scenes of our cinematic memory. By these means, the film becomes powerfully evocative of filmic memories where lie the differences between what has been seen on the screen and what has been actually experienced.

To FILM IMPLIES the recovery of memories of films, of Hollywood films, for example, in the cases of a Russian scene at the beginning of *U.S.S.A.*, of Jonas Mekas's films in certain sequences of *Allers-Venues*, *Movie (V.O.)* and *U.S.S.A.*, or of Kubelka's *Unsere Afrikareise* (1961-1966) as regards the complex relations between sound and image (although in Ostrovsky's case the humor is more striking).

OSTROVSKY PLAYS with the codes of representation and with the clichés as they are used in classical cinema. She plays the codes off against each other, as in the scene in *U.S.S.A.* when the funeral of Andropov recorded off a television screen and reframed is shown, on the soundtrack can be heard an orchestra rehearsal in which the conductor complains, as the parade of dignitaries and the army are seen, that things are "Stiff, a bit too stiff..." An amused commentary on the political world. In the same way, in *Allers-Venues*, while people bathe in a swimming pool and a man sips his drink, the voice of Boris
Karloff on the soundtrack introduces another way to read the images and transports the viewer from a vacation home movie to a police thriller.

WITH VIVIAN OSTROVSKY, experimental film rediscovers the humor which it so often lacks. Playing with images and sounds, she succeeds at avoiding much of the artifice of film (whether experimental or not) and does so without ever appearing to. Without any apparent effort,

she upends and tries to transform our cinematographic expectations
- I was about to say culinary expectations, thinking again of this
connection, previously developed by Kubelka, between cooking and
film: a question of measuring ingredients and know-how. An art of
accompaniment.

- Brochure of the *Cinéma du Musée*, Centre Georges Pompidou, 1988

ROSE LOWDER: THE LITTLE FEELING

The upsurge in conceptual and minimal art in the 1960s led certain artists to extol a new approach that was to modify both the concept of a work of art and that of the artists themselves. Their work featured a process which was almost phenomenological in the relations it established between the physical work, its space, and the spectator, through simple processes which were nevertheless complex in the way they were developed and their consequences, and they made use of seriality as well as repetition. The artist advocated a new sensibility which could be described as "detached," to the degree that subjectivity did not necessarily mean an affirmation of individuality but more its elimination in favor of the work itself in the process it displayed and everything that could result from it. The artist became almost a parenthesis, preferring to pursue studies about, with, and of the work of art - a quasi-scientific approach.

Rose Lowder belongs to this tendency of artistic thought. It is through it that she occupies a specific place in the field of experimental cinema in France. But the roots of her work do not lie solely in the contribution of minimalism. Her process ranges from the simple (a single proposition is illustrated in a film such as *Roulement, rouerie, aubage* (1978), to the complex (already in *Rue des Teinturiers*,

1979, and even more in her later films such as *Scènes de la vie française*, 1985-1986). But her path has not been so schematic or restrictive as this phrase might suggest in so far as in all her films, whatever the complexity/simplicity they employ, Lowder examines the differential intervals that cinematography displays, in other words the difference existing between the perception of the reality of a phenomenon seen by the naked eye and the view of it through a cinematographic device. The object that the filmmaker analyzes - that she practically auscultates - is not reality in itself but its perception by the tool which is cinema. This investigation is not a documentary one. It is actually not a question of knowing whether or not film is a reflection of reality, or if it transforms and manipulates it or not. This analysis - shared by many other experimental filmmakers who nevertheless do not draw the same conclusions from it - involves concentrating on the components implemented by the cinematographic device, in other words the frames, their continuous or discontinuous succession, focus and depth of field, temporality, the movement and associations of all these elements on a strip of film... The process of Lowder involves searching in directions which, even while taking into account the accomplishments of filmmakers since the 1960s, lead her to prefer returning to techniques from which cinema was originally born, by re-examining the ambiguous status of the cinematographic image and its relation to perception. Thus *Parcelle* (1979) plays with visual effects close to those developed for the praxinoscope. This return to the instruments of pre-cinema allows her to distance herself from classical, or to be more precise, dominant, cinema that is more concerned with narration than the status of the image and its making. In another way, *Scènes de la vie française : la Ciotat* (1981) works in continuity with shots that serve as a reference point in the history of cinema (the Lumières' *Arrival of a Train at La Ciotat*, 1895), but mixes representations of the same scene at two distinct moments. The two moments woven together create jumps of continuity in the otherwise peaceful progression of images. *La Ciotat* could be seen as the encounter of the inventivity of Meliès with the framing of the Lumière brothers.

Roulement, rouerie, aubage (1978), *Couleurs mécaniques* (1979), *Certaines observations* (1979) and *Rapprochements* (1979) share, for their part, an axis of continuity while *Parcelle, Rue des Teinturiers* (1979), *Champ provençal* (1979), *Retour d'un repère* (all versions, 1979) and *Les Tournesols* (1982) align along an axis of frame-by-frame exploration. In both of the axes with which Rose Lowder's work is concerned a similarity can be discerned in spite of the disparities between what appears on the screen.

In the totality of her work, no editing is done outside the camera. Every reel of film retained is shown exactly as it was shot. Each reel shot is analyzed according to several criteria: whether the pre-conceived idea with which a reel was shot functions or not, and then how the reels differ between themselves in relation to the approach and what those differences are. Then, to re-examine what has been cinematographically created on the reels, which entails taking into account their temporal development, requiring an analysis of the way they progress through rather than just the nature of each single frame. And finally these reels, whether used or not, must be examined to determine if they close or open one or more areas to explore further, and if the latter is the case, what new axes or new films do they suggest?

The reels are at the same time the basis for what is analyzed and also (in themselves) the objects of analysis: both the object analyzing and the object analyzed. Each film is sustained by the problems of perception that it poses, uncovers or tries to resolve. For a reel to become a film, it is still necessary for the filmmaker to explore and master conceptually a certain number of perceptual problems that film raises. This conceptual mastery and the interest in clarifying these questions determine whether the reel becomes either a film (*Les Tournesols, Parcelle*), a part of a film (the three reels of *Champ provençal* and the twelve of *Rue des Teinturiers*).

All of these aspects lend a scientific character to the process. It can be noted not just in the precision of the points examined in each film - the variations of depth of field and their manifestation in the film as an object which reveals the difference between the way film perceives reality differently from the eye (*Champ provençal*), a study accompanied by a questioning of perspective, the serialization of single frames encourage an almost simultaneous perception of otherwise separate events in real-life perception (*Rue des Teinturiers*), the simultaneous presence of two distinct moments taking place in the same scene (in the series *Scènes de la vie française*) - but also in the notational system which is created before, during, and above all after each film. In fact, the film can be perceived differently depending on whether it is projected or examined on a light table. The latter, highly meticulous way, permits the filmmaker to find the points at which a given reel addresses a different problem from the preceding ones: a case in point is *Rue des Teinturiers* which announces a more restrictive approach to the study of the domain and anticipates *Retour d'un repère*. These graphic studies are the record of effects created in and by the film and take into account the criteria by which they were made. The partitions allow her to isolate certain components for further work among the many that she judges pertinent.

Beyond the scientific precision that Lowder brings to her cinematographic actions, certain components can be noticed which make her work unique, recognizable among all others even when it is not purely a question of style. First of all the choice of scenes brilliantly displays a stunning rejection of any compositional academicism. The choice of framing. A balcony is visually transformed through her vision into the echo of a jungle, a tree branch resembles a caress, a field of peach trees or sunflowers. But these masks will always be thwarted by the process Lowder employs. Often one is confronted by a point of view precisely chosen for the way it is set back, its capacity to undermine the effects of classical perspective; thus the vista of a peach tree in different seasons in *Champ provençal*, the close-up of a tree branch overlooking a lake in *Retour d'un repère*, the telephoto shot flattening its subject, apparently a water wheel, in *Roulement, rouerie, aubage*, close-ups of colors in rotation, actually a merry-go-round in *Couleurs mécaniques*, perfectly inconsequential, almost documentary scenes, in *Scènes de la vie française*, principally *Paris* and *La Ciotat*.

Most of the time, in the case of the frame-by-frame axis, a depth is perceptible which is not at first a characteristic of any given frame but which together create a sense of serialization. This disposition differs radically from that proposed by American structural cinema in the sense that the latter treats the frame as the smallest cinematographic unit. Whereas Lowder's cinematographic work calls into question precisely this supremacy of the frame and rejects it as a delusion. By the play of variation between one frame and another in the same scene, she shows that by placing these intervals within the frames it can be shown that the frames are not the fundamental unit of cinema, but that it lies much more in the disposition of the component parts and their relations between each other within the composition which shapes the frame.

The axis of continuity for its part reveals how the perception of a phenomenon is made evident through cinema, whether it is by framing as in *Couleurs mécaniques* and *Rapprochements* - the latter calling depth perception into question with the same tree branch used in *Retour d'un repère* but by means of an uncontrolled element: wind (with this film and its incorporation of chance as a process that generates filmic events, Lowder reiterates certain Modernist approaches already employed by such artists as Marcel Duchamp, Chris Welsby or Jan Dibbets, which raise the idea of assisted chance) or whether it is by coloration which call into question the idea of a truth, a fidelity, a conformity to the cinematographic representation of reality, thus the different approaches to the coloration of a field of sunflowers in *Les Tournesols colorés* or in *La Ciotat*. Color is an integral part of the process which Lowder develops in her films as an element that can be controlled during the printing of the film in order to alter the scene represented. The colors, those of childhood, are in in fact warm, often saturated in the eyes of those who have grown up in the northern hemisphere. This saturation is contemptuous of pedantic theories contending that color must be dim and fade away, which is not reflected by the clarity and highly defined contrast of colors created in the southern hemisphere.

Colors, objects, and their treatment go beyond the scientific character that the filmmaker often ascribes to them when she speaks. It is impossible to ignore a strong sensuality in the scenes and in her choices of them. Lowder prefers scenes of nature, natural landscapes, even when she films certain scenes in the city. Their cinematographic transformation is such that they no longer seem to emanate from an urban setting but from natural landscapes. In this sense, Rose Lowder perpetuates an Impressionist tradition: working from nature versus working in the studio; in the manner of Cézanne, working on site is the *sine qua non* for capturing the "little feeling" and representing it.

Brochure *Cinéma du Musée*, Paris, Centre Georges Pompidou, 1987

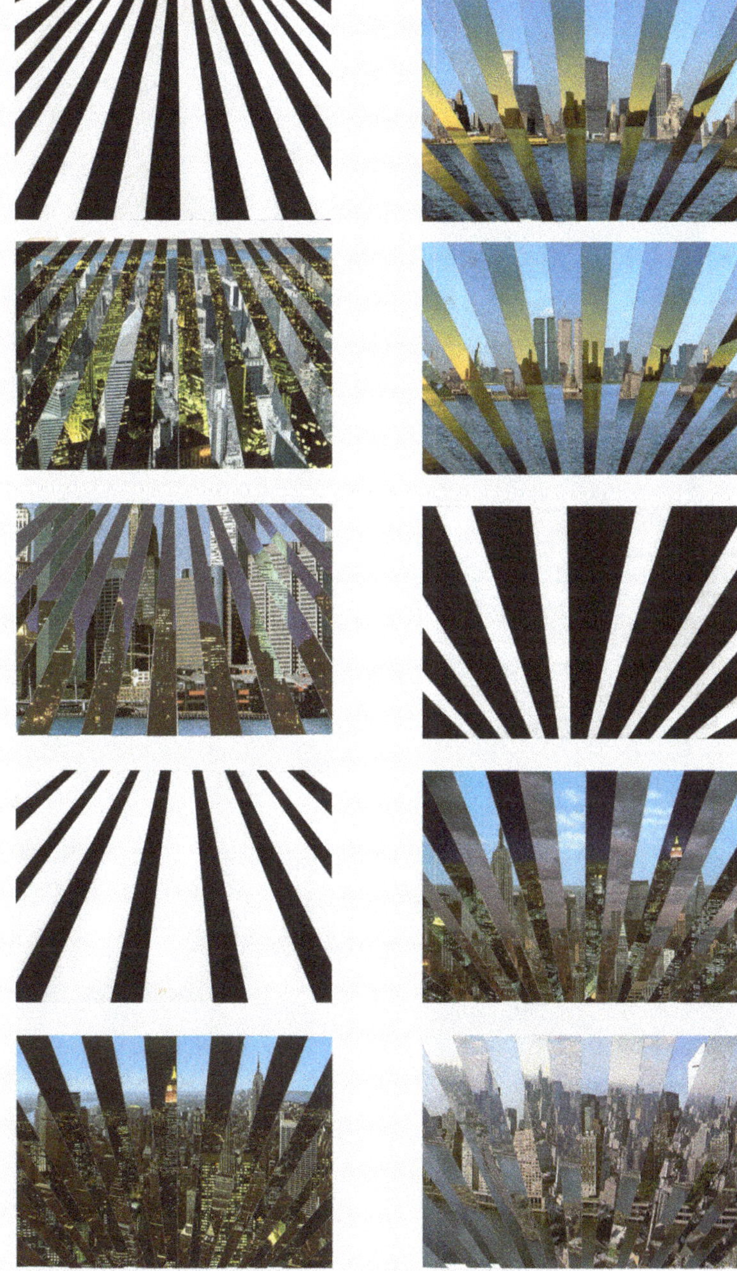

2

UNDERGROUND CINEMA

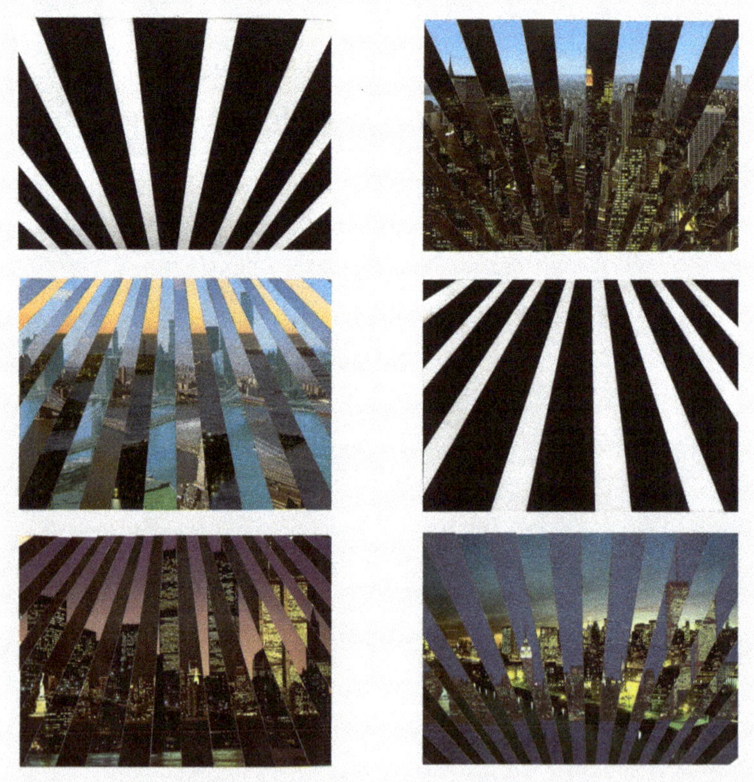

REMINISCENCES...
ON TWO JONAS MEKAS AND ANDY WARHOL PROGRAMS

To mention the names Mekas and Warhol is to evoke indirectly all of the 1960s in America. They can be found together on numerous occasions. Mekas was the cameraman for *Empire* (the eight hour film on the Empire State Building, 1965) and defended Warhol's films in his column published in the *Village Voice*; Warhol projected his films at Mekas's Cinematheque. A twenty-five year old friendship united them, a friendship recorded in Mekas's films.

BOTH BECAME major figures of the *underground* for almost opposite reasons. Warhol shook up th
e high art world with methods and techniques that were considered minor - illustration, advertising, etc. - while Mekas became an apostle of experimental cinema.

ALL OF WARHOL'S art is haunted by cinema, whether by its subjects (Marilyn Monroe, Elvis Presley, Elizabeth Taylor) or its media: silkscreens, different photographic techniques, multiples and series.[1]

As soon as Mekas had settled in the United States, film, along with poetry, became his principal interest.

JONAS MEKAS ARRIVED at the end of 1949, after having spent almost five years in displaced person camps. Starting in 1951, he attended Hans Richter's classes[2] and in 1955, with his brother Adolfas founded the magazine *Film Culture* which over the years would become the bible of independent and experimental film. Starting in 1958, he began writing his "Movie Journal" column for the *Village Voice,* continuing until 1976.

HIS INTEREST in cinema was expressed as much by his writing as by the different film projects he undertook by himself or with his brother. From 1950 on, he shot the New York Lithuanian exile community and peace demonstrations in black-and-white with the intention of making documentaries. Then, progressively, after having made *Guns of the Trees*[3] (1961) he devoted himself to the New American Cinema through articles and screenings in different places such as Spoleto in 1962. During the same period, he founded the New York Filmmakers Cooperative which influenced the organization and distribution of experimental cinema in a number of countries.[4] This activity as a promoter of experimental film left him little time for personal work. He developed a particular form of filmmaking which dispensed with the scenario as the first step in the production of a film. In this way he could film in the time he had available: "If I can film a minute, I film a minute. If I can film ten seconds, I film ten seconds. I desperately grab whatever I can."[5] Jonas Mekas created a particular style, moving away from traditional film and extolling home movies made from fragments of events, flashes of objects. He brings out the poetry of everyday life and makes its fleeting impressions resemble those of Action Painting. This personal cinema had been developed by Marie Menken and Stan Brakhage who had succeeded in creating a form of filmmaking completely free of all literary influences "where the filmic syntax achieves a spontaneous fluidity and where the images are truly like words that appear and disappear and repeat themselves as they create clusters and blotches of visual meanings, impressions.[6] The understanding of images as words translates visually into a spontaneity and fluidity of camera work which no longer seeks to faithfully reproduce reality. The dynamic of filming, its movements, rhythms and syncopations allow for the capturing of the truth of a moment and to extract its poetry. The same process can be found in Mekas's work, doubtlessly influenced by the freedom of tone and expression in the films of Marie Menken.[7] The out-of-focus shots, the jerky rhythms, the over- and under-exposures are not eliminated in the editing but serve to accentuate the presence of the subject filmed. When Marie Menken films Warhol in *Andy Warhol* (1965), she transforms the artist into a wild machine churning out silkscreens of flowers or Jackie Kennedy. Her manner of constantly returning to a theme is reminiscent of the canvases or Brillo boxes made by Warhol and Gerard Malanga. She seems to be more interested in the process itself than the result. On the other hand, Mekas, in *Scenes from the Life of Andy Warhol* (1990), concentrates on the Warhol retrospective at the Whitney Museum or the artist's working sessions with Polaroid photography. Mekas's observation uncovers less known facets of Warhol's life. They seem to be images snatched from a certain form of reality. But if this isolating of images does not create a feeling of distance, it enables, on the contrary, an addition, later, by means of the soundtrack or intertitles, supplemental information which marks the passage of time. Everything filmed is put aside for several years before being worked on. It creates a confrontation with time, with memories or with the screen of memory. It bears witness to Mekas's vision of New York, invaded by nature: the snowy winter scenes are like distant memories of his youth in Lithuania. In this way, his evocation of Warhol permits him to resume his lament: that of an eternal wanderer who loses his friends as he had already lost his country. In *Reminiscences of a Journey to Lithuania* and *Paradise Not Yet Lost* (1977-1979), he returns to the long-lost roads of his childhood.[8] *Lost, Lost, Lost* (1976) explores the problem of the loss of identity caused by immigration. As opposed to these disappearances, these losses, the rebirth and return of the seasons are essential elements which permit the perpetuation of a memory and protect from forgetting. The apparent fluidity of the shots is accomplished in spite of the inclusion of blocks of single frames capturing bursts of motion, actions, textures, and light: spinning bodies in *Notes on the Circus* (1988) or in *Cup/Saucer/Two Dancers/Radio* (1965-1983). Bursts that, through interwoven shots, create a mosaic of sensations and specifically cinematographic visions and which evoke the dazzle of the circus. Mekas frequently juxtaposes masterfully highly disjunctive sequences with more drawn out sequences such as in *Award Presentation to Andy Warhol* (1964),[9] or in *Cassis* (1966): a meditation on the port of Cassis, the residence of Jerome Hill, a major benefactor of Mekas and most of his initiatives.[10]

IN HIS WRITINGS, Jonas Mekas has always recognized the important filmmaker, those destined to mark the history of experimental film and make it important. Among these, Jack Smith and Andy Warhol hold a prominent place. The influence of Jack Smith, in film as much as in theater or performance, was enormous: he could use any character who happened to be present when he was shooting.[11] His baroque and provocative work pays homage to the stars of Mexican musical comedies and his films use derision and mockery with rare elegance. The incisive aspect of their derision, his taste for the artifice of social codes and stereotypes would be re-used by Ronald Tavel in some of Warhol's first sound films. Jack Smith was his favorite director[12] even though his films did not formally have much to do with those of Smith, his deliberately static camera and action reduced to a minimum.[13] Nevertheless, the transvestism, the homosexuality and the androgyny are themes that both filmmakers explore, themes in phase with the sexual liberation movements that were appearing in the wake of the movements demanding civil rights for black Americans.

. . .

JACK SMITH WAS, along with Jean Genet, an instigator of scandal. His film *Flaming Creatures* (1963), attacked as obscene, provoked a highly public outcry and was condemned by a New York court in 1964: an echo of the similar censorship of Kenneth Anger's *Scorpio Rising* (1963) in California. It was in relation to *Flaming Creatures* that Mekas spoke of Baudelairean cinema. He would always defend this film and recognize it as one of the greatest films of the American *underground*.

IF, for many American artists, there was no doubt about Jack Smith's importance, Smith was largely overshadowed by the aura of celebrity surrounding the Warhol enterprise, as much during the Warhol Factory years as after. This is reflected in the multitude of films made around this 20th century legend. Some of them, such as the films of Willard Maas, Ron Nameth, or Marie Menken were made in the 1960s and were part of the period - Marie Menken in fact appeared in some Warhol films - others, such as Pascal Auger's, use them as a point of reference and reflect Warhol's power of fascination. If Warhol's films are about absence, putting viewers in a position in which they cannot see what they are looking for - *Blow Job* (1964) is the archetypical example - then this program works well since it employs the strategy frequently used by Warhol: be conspicuous by your absence. There remains a series of films which, like ghost images, allow us to perceive the appropriation of someone else's image as borrowed from Warhol.

ANDY WARHOL
FROM THE SILVER SCREEN TO THE CATHODE
RAY TUBE

Both the name and the oeuvre of "Warhol" are inextricably linked to film; the artist's constant, quasi-obsessive pursuit in this medium yielded a surfeit of cinematic material, the scope of which still remains elusive. Indeed the known films represent only the tangible "tip of the iceberg."

THE BODY of Warhol's material oeuvre is haunted by the cinema; it is apparent in all aspects of his artistic production. The movies generated works where Warhol cited and recycled such symbols as Hollywood stars and their entourage. The influence of film seems, nevertheless, to have been automatic - as opposed to meditated. In fact, the intervals between one "photogram" and the next are more or less measured according to the films and their respective structures. Continuous shooting of a stationary subject minimized these intervals, whereas camera movement and the use of strobe lights maximized them. But the cinema is also a prolific source of clichés. From 1963 to 1968, the Factory saw itself as a site for "happenings", a place where one could place images before even considering how to formalize them. The latter process was nevertheless far from passive, for it conditioned the characteristics and processing of the frames, the poses etc...

WARHOL BEGAN MAKING films in 1963, the year he shot *Sleep*. Filming became his chief activity from 1963 through 1968, when he shot film after film in the inexorable rhythm he had already developed while making his silkscreens of Campbell's Soup Cans or Marilyns, and would pursue with photo booth images and Polaroids. The constant production and accumulation of work minimized the impact of slight variations or differences from frame to frame.

WARHOL'S FILMS and videos provoked a great deal of written theory that frequently offers only a fragmented vision of his work. For in such analyses, the works were regarded and rationalized conceptually, without addressing their screen impact. This is paradoxical, given that Warhol's early films are known to function according to an elastic timeline, akin to contemplation.

THE RESULT MIMICS the effect of certain drugs, which dilate time. Out of time, cognitively absent, one experiences a detachment from the reality of the self.

BEGINNING IN 1982, at the behest of John G. Hanhardt, Warhol allowed the Whitney Museum to establish a film archive, presenting the artist's movies and videos as they were successively restored. For the last few years, Callie Angell has been responsible for protecting, cataloguing and restoring these films - so that they may once again be distributed. Gradual access to these films call for a true reassessment of Warhol's cinematic career. Until recently, most of these films had never been seen, beyond the underground network of the 1960s, and the major retrospective exhibits staged in the 1980s. The few films exhibited afforded only a partial vision. Indeed, far more than the videos, those films kept largely out of circulation for the last twenty years became tantamount to myth. However, their disappearance from public venues was a strategy orchestrated for the purpose of promoting Warhol's production. The rarity of screenings enhanced the importance and reputation of the films; the routine ploy of the publicity and public relations. The project of establishing an index has revealed the abundance and richness of Warhol's cinematic oeuvre, not to mention some hundred or so films that were never before distributed.

WARHOL'S first films focused on simple, domestic acts, often of a homo-erotic nature: a blow job session, a haircut, a kiss. While taking up the theme of eroticism, the later films recontextualized it, staging comedies where young men in sexual situations are prey to both the camera's and the spectator's eye. Warhol's voyeurism deeply affected his painting as well as his film; it was after all intrinsic to continual coverage, and a constant in his film work, which lead him to "collecting". As if the accumulation of images and sounds (in fact he recorded a phenomenal number of both audio and video cassettes) can ensure that none of the action is lost, nor any of the event that unfolds before camera and microphone, regardless of how much real time is manipulated.

THE MOST STRIKING examples of this process are found not only in both his film and photographic portraits (according to the ongoing inventory, some 500 Screen Tests exist, not including the video portraits beginning at 70), but also in the "performance" films where a given action is recorded in its entirety, its duration determined by the amount of film attributed to it: two 45 minute reels for a portrait of Henry Geldzahler smoking a cigar; nine 30 meter reels for *Blow Job*

(1964); two 33 minute reels for *Beauty N° 2* (1965), and *Paul Swan* (1965), and 24 audio cassettes of Ondine, whose transcription became the book, *A Novel* (1968).

IF WARHOL'S initial interest in the cinema was shared by the cultural milieu, by its fascination with stars and divas of every ilk, he did not limit himself to it, but decided to create stars in his own right - whether by championing the more active personalities of the American underground movement since the late 1950s, including producers, actors, performers and writers such as Jack Smith, Taylor Mead, Mario Montez, Ronald Tavel-or by "producing" new stars, such as Online, Candy Darling, Joe Dallesandro, Edie Sedgwick, Viva, Ingrid Superstar... The films seem to belong to the first Factory, sealed in silver paper, while video emerged from a new Factory, more reminiscent of a well-run business than a meeting place for the marginal denizens of the demi-monde of drugs and prostitution, transvestism and homosexuality, all mingling with the art world, the media, the mass interpreters of golden youth. The "cinema" Factory is where one went to play one's game hoping it would last as long as possible. The film documents what occurred in this space confined to the camera's field of view, and sometimes what was outside that field. Space where seduction and provocation were the essential behavioral elements. Promiscuous transactions and sexual provocations predominated; one may recall Mario Montez and his banana in Mario Banana, or better yet various episodes of *Chelsea Girls* (1966). These movies inspired a certain attitude, or reflected it, whether it was part of the script or not. As always, Warhol's interest was in the portrait of the person in the act; for example, Robert Indiana eating his mushroom in *Eat* (1963), Paul Swan recreating representations of the past in his namesake film. Participants were not asked to play a role per se, to be other than themselves, and this directive holds true as well for the "sexploitation" films such as: *My Hustler* (1965), *I, A Man* (1967), *Chelsea Girls* or *The Loves of Ondine* (1968).

. . .

When a video camera was loaned to Warhol in 1965, he had produced a series of Factory Diaries that had evolved out of the action performances of the first factory. Beginning in the 1970s, video seemed to have both sealed and symbolized the end of the Underground era, newly eclipsed by the bourgeoisie and the Jet Set, despite the efforts of the series *Vivian's Girls* (1973) which shows transvestites and models living together. The challenges and the resulting portraits were no longer the same. If the video portraits can be linked to *Screen Tests* (1964-66), and to the painted portraits (commissioned), a major part of the video work was, at least in theory, destined for television viewing. The "Talk Show" project was derived in large part from *Interview*, the magazine Warhol launched in 1969, and which championed his camp humor and sometimes cruel sense of wit adopted as ammunition by gays.

There has been insufficient emphasis on the provocative aspect of some of Warhol's films. In his oblique homage to the Dadaist and the Surrealists, notably Marcel Duchamp, Warhol explored the perverse practicability of certain domestic objects and/or their images (urinals, bottle holders, Coca Cola bottles, soup cans, an electric chair, a building). Provocation is as intentional in the duration of *Sleep* (1964) and of *Empire* (1964) as it is in the subjects which belong to Pop iconography and their treatment by select interpreters -.in this case via one artist's "film."

A performance of fellatio in *Blow Job* (1964), kisses in *Kiss* (1963), multiple couplings in *Couch* (1964), a crotch shot in *Taylor Mead's Ass* (1964), sadomasochistic encounters in *Horse* (1965) or *Vinyl* (1965)... While low budget films dominate the first period, narration is not altogether absent, as evidenced as early as 1963 with *Tarzan and Jane Regained...Sort Of*. The premise of *My Hustler*, which documents a rehearsal by the Velvet Underground and Nico, is not beyond allowing erratic camera movement and even intermittent use of zooms. The strobe cuts in *Bufferin* (1966) provoke the actors as much as the spectators by briefly interrupting image and sound, thereby chopping up the narrative. This represents a new kind of camera montage, which breaks the continuity of the action and thus calls on other techniques Warhol used to deliberately upset the film's essential structure, as he did in *Kitchen* (1965) or *Lonesome Cowboys* (1968) etc. The narrative films do not compromise Warhol's interest in multiple screenings, which telescoped the unfolding of a story line, such as in *Lupe* (1966) and *Chelsea Girls*.

WARHOL EXPLORED all aspects of cinematography, ultimately focusing on a certain direction while maintaining full autonomy in terms of choice of genre. This spectrum invariably inspired myriad interpretations of his work. This held true for Warhol's entire oeuvre, which made the mass distribution of his name and products, and their imitations his chief preoccupation. These interpretations proved a boon to distribution, as did advertising a business which became, in its own right, Warhol's oeuvre.

THIS EVENTUALLY BRINGS us to question the way in which we perceive Warhol's films and videos, and to go beyond the formal, reductionist interpretation which takes material elements into consideration over actual content. But one cannot ignore the matter or quality of the frames, the velvet elasticity and sparkle of silent films thanks to the use of 16 images per second which induces in the viewer a state of inertia akin to hypnosis or meditation...

IN RELATIVELY FEW years of cinematic production, Warhol went from making films for the pleasure of making them, to the making films for "the movies" - an evolution which altered the way in which he worked, his status and even his role as an artist. Moving from back-room bootlegs to mass-produced products, Warhol went for the brand name. The craftsmanship of the Factory was ultimately lost, left back somewhere in the dust.

WARHOL FILM & Television, Paris, American Center, 1994.

HOMAGE TO PAUL SHARITS

I met Paul Sharits in 1980 at the Hyères Festival which had that year organized a major presentation of his latest films, which had never been shown in France. There followed a friendship which was strengthened over time by numerous meetings here and there, on the occasion of different screenings of our respective films. His sudden death was an intense aesthetic shock that was shared, I believe, with many young filmmakers of my generation. Knowledge of this fundamental work undeniably opened, as much for film in general as for the filmmakers themselves, whole areas of possibilities which were, to say the least, radical; whether one thinks of his Fluxus episode or his installations which, starting in 1971, confirmed the status of film as an artistic practice and challenged it by a questioning of (among other things) the fixed duration of film presentation based on criteria foreign to the film itself. In addition, Paul Sharits proved himself an uncommonly gifted "colorist." He allowed color to be perceived according to previously unexplored harmonics and rhythms. Through his *flicker* films he created temporal color harmonies which, in the manner of the monochromes of Yves Klein, opened unexplored spaces and volumes close to the spirit of all-over painting.

The violence of images, the opposition between pure color and the photographic image, making use of looped sound, the uses of scratches and burns, everything conspired to make his films amazing for the admirer that I was at the time. His films made us experience other temporalities. A specifically cinematographic space opened up whose impact was never diminished with a deeper familiarity with the work but was, on the contrary, reinforced.

Paul Sharits removed film from the hinges of classical representation, progressively discarding any traces of narrative that his early films such as *Ray Gun Virus* (1966), *Piece Mandala/End War* (1966), *T,O,U,C,H,I,N,G* (1968), *Razor Blades* (1965-1968), *N:O:T:H:I:N:G* (1968) might contain. This removal of narrative elements in no way precluded the presence of autobiographic, obsessional, or emotional elements; they haunt his films and reappear in the filmmaker's prolific writing both public and private. Nevertheless, for some years (at the same time his return to painting occurred) some discursive elements, fragments of stories, could be glimpsed in a more prominent way in his last works such as *Rapture* (1987), *Figment* (1977-1986) which blended both his first films (*Wintercourse*, 1962, which was lost then found again in 1985) and fragments of Super 8 film journals, of which his trip to Romania seems to be a prefiguration in *Brancusi's Sculpture Ensemble at Tirgu Jiu* (1977-1984).

The film work of Paul Sharits is at once extraordinarily formal and analytic, but also incredibly personal and objective.

Sharits's entire life was characterized by profound, often violent, disruptions, which touched him in horrendous ways both physically and psychologically and which can found in both his films and paintings. This violence is expressed as much by the way in which he approaches the medium and its extrinsic fragility as by the way he explores the very limits of film. This calling into question of limits is carried out according to processes inherent to the mechanics of cinematography and by the "locational pieces," to use one of his own terms. Despite the apparent diversity of the processes he used, Sharits remains true to the questioning and attitudes which, depending on the period, were in the foreground or background of his work. Based on whatever frame of reference dominated at the time, different aspects of his work attracted commentary, sometimes forgetting the continuity of his artistic activity. Thus his progressive abandonment of narrative elements in favor of a questioning of the nature of the medium through analytical films often calls on models which share their strategies of organization with repetitive music. By determining a limited number of components (a series of notes, a few frames of pure color) he concentrated on the gradual augmentation of certain precise visual effects by modifying little by little one of the elements of the initial series or, in other instances, dividing the film according to distinct parts which, each in its turn, exploits and develops an idea though different modalities. It is also by this manner that the exhibition of *Frozen Film Frames* can be understood; they are another way to show the film and permit an overall spatial under-standing of it all at once: the image of the complete score of the film - combining the parts that have already been projected with what is to come. This type of exhibition permits the deferral of time, the suspension of its passing. A suspension similar to that which leads to the understanding of what occurs in the act of projecting a film such as *N:O:T:H:I:N:G*. The moment of capture recorded simultaneously with the moment of release, the setting aside of continuity; a perception which freezes time in order to fully appreciate it and its object. This exhibition leads almost automatically to a conception of film as a concrete visual art work, removing it from a temporal event with a fixed duration. Simultaneously, film inhabits space and plays out over time, it explores the timelessness of endless projection. In the manner of a painting, a work fixed in place, the installation makes of film an art which escapes the contingencies of moving through time and must submit or respond to the demands, even if minimal, of a fixed, established form. The work can be approached at any moment for an indeterminate length of time. Sharits's installations use ribbons of film which are laid out and extended from one screen to another as in *3rd Degree* (1982), in which the smallest image is incrusted into a second larger one which is in its turn incrusted into a third. *Sound Strip/Film Strip* (1971), with its short loops of scratched frames develops an infinite number of variations which make the piece completely perceptible at first glance but always different at every moment. The analysis of the medium includes the study of the film ribbon according to the way it was recorded and the different ways it can be reconstituted when projected. Sharits often plays with the ambiguity between the recording of the ribbon composed of single frames of pure color and its projection, in which the frames produce their own intense flickering effects. He questions the para-doxical movements that are generated by the passage of the ribbon through the projector depending on whether or not they have been refilmed alone and depending on whether they go by forwards or backwards. The illusion of spinning which results during projection is itself questioned even if it means modifying the projection condi-tions by using multiple screens or, more simply, either hiding or showing the frame lines as in *Analytical Studies II: Un-Framed Lines* (1971-1976) or the sprocket holes as in *Synchronousoundtracks* (1975) or *3rd Degree* as well as the optical soundtrack as in *Episodic Generation* (1979).

The films feature material dysfunction which results in the ensemble functioning perfectly. It is precisely because bits of film are scratched, broken, burnt, or missing that everything works. It is in its fragility that the violence is most perceptible, a fragility not unlike human vulnerability and of which the films *T,O,U,C,H,I,N,G*, *Epileptic Seizure Comparison*, and *3rd Degree* are among the most eloquent expressions. Human beings find themselves in extreme situations on the brink of crisis, just before everything is upended. Painters in recent years have exploited these states doubtlessly in relation to their own personal histories, echoes of a violence ever-present in their bodies.

Thanks to Miles McKane

L'Armateur, n° 8, October-November 1993.

GREGORY J. MARKOPOULOS

THE SONG OF THE POET

t

The cinematographic work of Gregory J. Markopoulos is as singular as it is exemplary. Its specificity has marked cinema as a whole. In 1947, with *Du sang, de la volupté et de la mort*, Markopoulos opened a new era in the cinematographic treatment of narrative forms. If he has remained a little-known figure, it is because of the difficulty of seeing his work over the last twenty years. Markopoulos settled in Europe in the late 1960s in order to devote himself entirely to his work. He only showed his films on rare occasions, always attempting to guarantee the quality of the projection and of the attendant documents. His oeuvre is that of a solitary precursor creating new cinematographic forms which have left a lasting imprint on the art of cinema.

Each film by Markopoulos transforms our gaze and our manner of understanding the world. The visual quality of his work is remarkable. It appears in the compositions within the frame, the linkage of sequences, the rhythm of colors, the symbolism of objects, the interpretation of characters, and the consummate perfection of the editing, as well as in the relations between image and sound. To see a

Markopoulos film is to experience a mixture of admiration and fascination for his implacable skill and elegant mastery of the medium - confirming that cinema is a genuine art, capable of influencing all the others.

The door swings open, the threshold is crossed, and like the protagonist of Psyche we leave the everyday world behind, to step into one of the most brilliant manifestations of the song of art. The filmmaker is interested in wanderings and quests for the self, when they are accompanied by an affirmation of the beautiful and thus of the good (as in Platonic equation). This is the way we should approach the first masterpiece, the trilogy *Du sang, de la volupté et de la mort*, which proposes an errant path through the mental landscape of a few characters over the length of three films. The fate of the individual is inscribed as a fulfillment taking place within similar worlds, despite the disparities between the characters. Access to this plenitude is not easy; and sexuality changes nothing here, since these young people cannot fulfill themselves completely outside the discovery and acceptance of love. This delicate affirmation maintains that love is a destiny, particularly when it is forbidden. In *Psyche* (1948) — the first film of the trilogy — one sees various viewpoints on an encounter in which the heroine experiences great difficulty in giving voice to her sensuality. The fear of such expressivity reappears in her fainting spell at the touch of the young man. The framings bear the mark of this same distancing, in the chromatic opposition between foreground and backgrounds.

The subtleties of the editing and the gradual weaving of the narrative through the use of short sequences always seems to anticipate or defer what we actually see, leading us into another temporality, closer to that of certain dreams in their capacity to suspend or collapse time. The admirable sequences of wandering journeys through Los Angeles in pursuit of an ungraspable image offer an exemplary prefiguration of *The Dead Ones* (1949). In this latter film, the various scenes of pursuit and escape confirm the artist's desire for Paul. The quest for the other is simultaneously accompanied by an identification of the self, which is inseparable from the affirmation of homosexuality - even if the recognition of this reality provokes the errancy of a soul with respect to its place in the world, and therefore its place in society. The theme of homosexual love is a constant in the oeuvre of Markopoulos. It is approached in different ways in the fictions and the portraits. Already in *Du sang, de la volupté et de la mort* a deep sensibility is unveiled, a love of beauty is affirmed: we see it in the shots of the young man turning into a tree, in a scene near a lake in Lysis (at the center of the trilogy). In the last of the three films, *Charmides* (1949), sequences of a bare-chested young man gazing intensely at a river, with adolescents throwing stones in the distance, evoke an aesthetic sometimes close to that of the photographer Herbert List; but here the work is in color. The encounter of the two adolescents is announced by a juxtaposition of shots showing us the bare chest of the one, followed by a detail of the other's torso and breast, then by a shot of the river, before returning to the first boy moving off into a park. The protagonist of *Charmides* leaves a university campus, then walks across a park and finds himself in an industrial wasteland, caught in a tangle of metal bars and raw concrete: the embodiment of a desire whose reality is unveiled by means of superimpositions of the young man wandering through the sunset at the close of the film.

The trilogy already displays a great mastery of unconventional narration, related more closely to myth; the narrative is stripped of all psychology, in favor of fragments of an initiatory tale bordering on ritual, death, and transfiguration.[1] The film inscribes the passage from an undifferentiated state toward the discovery of the self. Even the sleeping Eros - close to hypnosis - of *Eros, O Basileus* (1967) evokes initiatory rites celebrating the power of life and desire.

In *Psyche*, Markopoulos demonstrates an extraordinary virtuosity in recapitulative editing, selecting a few frames from each of the sequences that structure the work. In *Swain* (1950) we rediscover this same kind of recapitulation, preceding a series of superimpositions which complete the film. This use of very short shots will be employed again later on, and becomes preponderant in *The Illiac Passion* (1967) and *Gammelion* (1967), both of which exploit a similar distribution of single frames and shape the narrative on the basis of those clues alone. This filmic treatment gains its autonomy with respect to the mythological content of *The Illiac Passion*, while *Gammelion* more radically exploits the separation of individual frames, leading us to the sublime view of a "chateau" and its surrounding park.

With *The Illiac Passion* there is no longer any need to fall back on a psychological alibi in order to establish character; the symbolism of an object or a color suffices. The character's mark or mythological inscription can be glimpsed by these signs, which make the film into a creation of intuitive thinking. Its deployment is visually organized according to a particular rhythm: either by the rate of the single frames (varying from one to twenty four), by the layering of superimpositions (from one to four), or by the use of dissolves. Effected inside the camera, the superimpositions work on the vision of the characters, manifesting an interiority that is suddenly rendered public. We dream with *Twice a Man* (1963),[2] in which the narrative of forbidden love is elaborated by the serialization of distinct times. Time is underlined disjunctively by the soundtrack, which breaks the fluidity of memory by syncopation. Delays of meaning manifest the unconscious of all the characters at once, as though the production of myth took place outside the characters who embody it. This same split returns with the representation of the maternal figure: at once old for the son and always young for herself, she is a timeless image. The confrontation of these two "image-temps" is linked in the unfolding of the film, but not in the chronology of the story. The times meet, denouncing the accuracy of representation. This is how Markopoulos envisages the reactualization of myth. Myth eludes the logic of narrative, it founds its chronology through a condensation which is not that of the dream, since it is intertwined with an aesthetic aim as precise as it is refined.

It would take pages to describe the extraordinary acuity with which Markopoulos works on memory, knowledge, and the anticipation of events which have already happened. In his "portrait films" (*Galaxie*, 1966, *The Olympian*, 1969) he composes times as others do motifs, by means of superimpositions, just as he composes space in his "landscape films" (*Ming Green*, 1966, Bliss, 1967, and *Sorrows*, 1969). In *Twice a Man* and *The Illiac Passion*, he mingles sequences encouraging a diffuse perception of events, freed of any discursive logic. He accomplishes this through abrupt transitions and explosions of single frames (veritable pyrotechnics) - sudden eruptions of sequences that upset the linear development to the benefit of a suspended time. One can also consider the use of the color. The use of colored filters and the play of exposures, swinging from saturated to faded hues (*Swain*), are essential. In *Psyche*, we pass from a "normal exposure" to a shot that has been shifted to blue, punctuated by a few red frames. The rhythmic use of color reinforces the meaning; the myth is tinted, literally and metaphorically, with the addition of a unique symbolics that is neither secondary nor anecdotal. One recalls the opening of *Gammelion*, where the use of the flicker lends pulsation to matter, light, and color, propelling us into another world. This same wealth of invention is also found in the interruption, of detail shots which breaks the continuity of an action, cutting into a character's course or a camera movement, as in *Twice a Man*. This form points to significations which we must activate. It is as though we were placed before hieroglyphics, or a musical score, and had to propose a reading without any key to the code except that of the aesthetic and plastic substance. It is in this sense that the photographic quality of Markopoulos's films should be understood. The composition within the frame is of first importance. It responds to precise criteria, whereby the lighting facilitates a blurring of details or a sudden appearance of traits, an emergence of shadow zones. All this favors the production of an aesthetic ensemble that puts the very constituents of cinema at risk. In the same way, the use of the dissolve in the trilogy announces the fade-overs between superimposed sequences in *Galaxie*, then the kaleidoscopically interlocking superimpositions of the later films, *The Olympian* (superimpositions made within the camera), *Index - Hans Richter,* 1969), (overlap made while shooting as well as in the printing, mixing the fadings), and *Saint Acteon,* 1971 (no superimpositions. It is the rhythm of the very short shots that creates the illusion); it also strangely prefigures the land-scape films such as *Gammelion*, *Bliss*, and *Sorrows*. The precision of the superimpositions in *Eros, O Basileus* and The Illiac Passion or *Bliss* refers us to the idea of annunciation and thus reveals the sacred nature of Markopoulos's art, while the delicate superimpositions in *Sorrows* inflect the tonality of the motif (Wagner's home and gardens in Triebschen).

The sound of the films partakes in these same strategies. It is not muted, obscured; quite to the contrary, it encourages confrontations. The outbursting sound of the rain and the storm in *Twice a Man*, the birdsong in *The Illiac Passion* and in *Himself as Herself*, the song of crickets in *Eros, o' Basileus*, the sound of horse's hooves in *Gammelion*, all reinscribe myth into a natural dimension. Human adventures cannot be torn away from the cycles of nature, its fatum. The force of the overture in *Twice a Man*, which lets the sound of the rain be heard from the dark screen for almost two minutes, is unforgettable. Else-where, when off-screen voices proffer texts they decompose the sentences into a disjointed sequence of accentuated words, some of which are run together with the preceding or following ones, upset-ting the linearity of demonstrative prose. Here we are in the field of poetry and of the rhythmic apprehension of the word. Like images, words become material to be shaped artistically: for example, the handful of sentences in *Gammelion*. The voices in *Twice a Man* and *The Illiac Passion* do not explain what is happening, but produce effects of meaning which are supplementary to the images and sequences. The return of the same word against different shots induces an indetermination of references. But one cannot speak of a discrepant sound montage. Because relations exist between the images and sounds, we must activate the potentials they enclose: it is a matter of an idea shared out between sound and sight. The use of music follows criteria no less precise than those for the composition within the frame. The music is not there to signify the image. By its articulation with the image it allows a better communion of the shared and divided idea.

Markopoulos works on images and sounds in such a way as to

transport us beyond, in a state near hypnosis, where we reach the domain of "film as film." Here lies the meaning of the resonating gong that punctuates all the portraits of *Galaxie*, marking a tension that grows more intense as the film unfolds.

Markopoulos' oeuvre inscribes and promotes the idea of an art that elevates, that takes off from its ground. Thus it rejoins the idea defended by Nietzsche: "He who takes away is an artist, he who adds is a slanderer."[3] Like any major body of work, these films speak of another world that only a select few can share. Let us wager that this first retrospective can open a space of communion between a unique oeuvre and its viewers.

Gregory J. Markopoulos 1928-1982 Retrospective 1940-1971, American Center, Paris, October 1995

KENNETH ANGER

American experimental filmmaker of the first generation, a magician for himself, a filmmaker for others; he uses film as a means of casting a spell.

His film production follows the path that can be found in *Scorpio Rising* (1963), *Fireworks* (1947) and others: a series of disasters (loss, theft, fire, censorship) and their repercussions.

His work is the stuff of legend, which explains Kenneth Anger's fascination with Hollywood as a factory of fake myths which he catches in the act of falsification. The ruse of Kenneth Anger is to take old myths and give them a new outward appearance (either in the image itself or in the way they are sequenced in relation to each other), simultaneously repudiating and exploiting illusory Hollywood myths - see, in this regard, *Scorpio Rising* in which can be seen on a television *The Road to Jerusalem* (1952), Hitler, Marlon Brando in *The Wild One* (1954), while the bikers get ready, get dressed, and set things up for a future orgy. A filmmaker of scandal, violence, sexuality, for whom each of these terms is an occasion for casting spells and rituals.

In *Fireworks*, homosexuality is perceived as a form of fleeting violence with night as its backdrop. The dreaming teenager, who dreams of being kidnapped by sailors; in an atmosphere of sado-masochism. In Anger's films a formal style sticks to the subject filmed, like the skintight t-shirts of his teenage subjects. Form itself is an erotic symbol.

One sees without seeing, glimpsing masks, fancy dress, and jewelry that the camera seems to show us in the blink of an eye, without dwelling on them, and we, the viewers, seem to desperately scrutinize the screen to get another glimpse of our heart's desire. This could be characterized as sliding cinema? There is much wakeful-ness, waking up in Anger's work. When one wakes up, the eye blinks; this blinking, this oscillation, is the collapse of vision and sometimes of reason - in *K.K.K.* or *Kustom Kar Kommandos* (1965) a teenager in a tight t-shirt lovingly polishes, with extreme delicacy, a superb 1930s car with a pink powder puff. The relations between the man and the machine are carried out with gentleness, in a soft way, as if under a gauze veneer, with tender gestures, the light touch brings a shiver of desire. The machine with its chrome, its brass, its mirrored surfaces, its interlacing of angles and straight lines, its very coldness, is eroti-cized by contact with the sliding caress of the "masculine'" powder puff. The eroticism is at its height, the camera follows the trajectory of the powder puff. The car is no substitute for something missing, it is not there by default. It is rather the coupling of machine/desire which is at work. The different positions reverberate visually. When Anger scrutinizes, he does not do it in the manner of Warhol (*Sleep*, 1963), *Blow Job*, 1963, *Empire*, 1964...), he is not a "neutral" witness, he is the right witness for this rare, privileged moment that he has prepared and staged.

Scorpio Rising is, in Anger's words, a film about the "myth of the young American biker as a totem, a terrifying toy, "Thanatos in chrome and black leather." The dressing up of the rockers before their nocturnal orgy and the polishing of their machine; an integral part of the party (and not just what permits them to attend). The film focusses dialectically on the mythology using very short cuts (just a few frames) - such as the scene of the biker in ecstasy while shots of disaster appear on a television screen. The dressing-up of the rockers before their all-male party which takes place according to a pre-determined ritual. Each sequence collides with the beginning of the next, all the while offering within itself a series of collisions on the same theme. Above and beyond this, songs impact the images, with provocations, bursts of laughter and other sounds. A veritable assault is mounted by the soundtrack which sometimes overwhelms the eroticism (by disconnection) of the image, increasing the over-charging until the ultimate charge.

One passes from old myth to another, newer one: the gay biker. All in an *Allegro assai*, with which one cannot be too satisfied with the presentation because one is waiting for its return.

The camera proposes, in flight, a mythology from light to dark. The strength of the film comes from the harmony of its form with the images, going by ever faster, paradoxically more detailed, more perceived, more syncopated, as if an image, by what it shows, avoids a certain ambiguity of gaze at the moment that desire appears.

Le Gai Pied, n° 2, May 1979

KEN JACOBS

Ken Jacobs is one of the most important figures of American experimental film. For thirty-five years Jacobs has questioned the nature of images in motion through a multiplicity of approaches. His work, in whatever genre it is executed (film journal, analytical film, personal film, picaresque, performance, 3D), has always been interested in film as a process of recording and restitution (at the moment of projection) of an event including a more or less open narrative. The story is never absent from Ken Jacob's films, even if in certain films he blasts apart classical representation and its modes of narration. Film replays in the present a time that is past, another life. Cinema is like a business producing ghosts and chimera whose visual performances constitute a magnificent outcome. A work based on the ephemeral and the fragility of cinematographic illusion unveiled by Ken Jacobs's devices.

Since his first films, which celebrated in *Orchard Street* (1956) and *Little Stabs at Happiness* (1959-1963), a now-vanished way of life (New York bohemian life in the 1950s), to the latest performances of electric shadows, Ken Jacobs has often occupied an awkward position in experimental film. He has always favored and even insisted on a cinema free of any professional constraints, a cinema close to home movies, such as those of his wife Flo in *Urban Peasants* (1975), resembling those of Jack Smith and Ron Rice. Several of his early films were in fact made with Jack Smith (sometimes despite disagreements with him). This work is a sumptuous manifestation of personal cinema. These films open up spaces of freedom as much in the tone as in the character of the events filmed. The filmmaker moves with great mastery from composed, prepared scenes to improvised, assisted ready-mades of great lyricism as in *Little Stabs at Happiness* or *Star Spangled to Death* (1958-1960).

Jacobs puts previously separated styles together, the frequent use of found footage permitting him to address the question of story-telling in *Doctor's Dream* (1978), that of the authenticity of the subject filmed in *Perfect Film* (1986) through the use of outtakes from news footage of the assassination of Malcolm X. With *Tom, Tom, the Piper's Son* (1969-1971), the themes and variations transform the codes of story-telling using a recycled primitive film. This recycling of film is just as deftly applied to his performance pieces: *XCXHXEXRXRXIXEXSX* uses a 1920 French pornographic film, *Making Light of History: The Philippines Adventure* (1983), newsreel footage. In his 3D films, Jacobs refers to the history of cinema, the Lumières in *Opening the Nineteenth Century: 1896* (1990), to which is added relief, while with *Keaton's Cops* (1991), the masking of a major part of the screen does not prevent the understanding and the recapitulation of an eminently classic chase sequence.

His new performance piece, *Bitemporal the Sea* (1994) is an extraordinary Rorschach test in relief which makes use of the viewers' imagination and their ability to create visual phenomena from a view of a few waves filmed by Phil Solomon. With this performance piece whose actual creation took place this winter at the American Center, we enter the virtual realm. In fact, each viewer can amplify or obliterate the illusion of depth and volume by putting gelatin filters in front of their eyes. Free to manipulate the projection and its effects, the viewer becomes the agent without whom the mirage cannot flourish nor the miracle occur.

Sound and music occupy as preponderant a place in his performance pieces as in his films. The music is never redundant, it incorporates silence just as the films use the absence of image. The disappearance of sound as much as that of the image in the dark of the screen allow the fragility of the event to be affirmed. Sometimes the sound suddenly disappears and does so in an even more marked way in the performances. It no longer supports the image, does not recycle it, but did it ever? It encourages the distancing and a return to the images; it facilitates the transitions, the suspensions, the wavering and the return of concentration, essential agents in the elaboration of a cinema which conjures up ghosts.

Jacobs works by appropriating sounds, music, noises as well as found, then reappropriated images. The work of recycling applies as well to his own films, which are never totally completed, always in the process of becoming something else. The soundtrack of *Blonde Cobra* (1959-1963) uses a radio to pierce the layers of black silence, interspersed between the sequences, in order to contrast the present moment of vision with scenes that took place at other times and places. The eruption of parasites into the ghosts of a story still to be told for viewers in the present. The characters of the picaresque films are themselves called into question by shots which interrupt the advancement of the action in *Star Spangled to Death* and *The Sky Socialist* (1965). The interruptions in *Star Spangled to Death* by means of documentaries (like the report on the politician defending his record in his re-election campaign), advertising, facilitating the understanding of an epoch by dynamically juxtaposing cinematographic elements normally kept apart.

His work is on the periphery, always on the margins. In *Tom, Tom...*, the re-reading of history, its abstraction, leads us to see details in the image to which we would not have paid attention, the same is true for *Perfect Film* where nothing that had been found was modified. By this appropriation and this identification, Jacobs pushes us to exercise critical judgement. This attitude is reinforced by the fact that the filmmaker in all of his work has always juxtaposed personal images with anonymous sequences, demonstrating, if it were necessary, that film is a question of how to look at things and the adoption of a particular point of view.

Always, Ken Jacobs proposes to shift how we see things in order to become conscious of everything that a filmed image can contain. Poetry is never far off and bursts through in many of his films. The subtle variations of the depth of field in *Airshaft* (1967) reveal a window sill with a flower pot and a sunbathing cat. The modification and transformation which the passage of a gust of air evokes. An image takes shape by the quivering of the depth of field. The representation is haunted by a multitude of imperceptible events which the filmmaker's insistence, as much as that of the viewers, bring out. Ghost images become incarnate for those who take the time to see.

Revue et Corrigée, n°24, June-July 1995.

English and German versions:

42 Internationale Kurzfilmtage Oberhausen, 1996.

1st version in *Rétrospective Ken Jacobs : le cinéma comme image fantôme*,

Paris, American Center, 1994.

3
____

RECYCLING

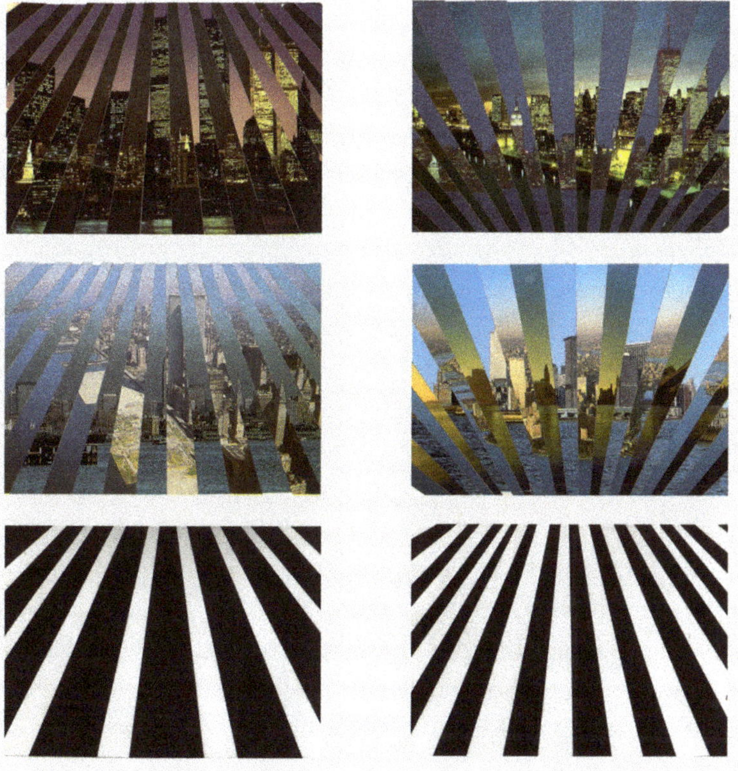

THE HARDER THEY FALL

Parallel to a cinema which requires making images for narratives, militant or formal documentaries, there exist other practices which focus on using images created in another way. It is a cinema of sampling and of salvaging which does not require shooting new film. It is a cinema which springs from strips of film already shot to make of it something new.

The salvaged film starts from the premise that editing is a second moment of creation. As soon as editing begins, cutting bins and closets fill with shots that are left behind; librarians, archivists, and zealous creators scoop up this abandoned content. Collecting it and storing it gives birth to a different kind of cinema of which the compilation and found footage films are brilliant expressions.

At first glance, the use of this kind of film would appear to be economic; no shooting is needed because the material already exists in the form of scraps and outtakes. These films are collages in the literal sense as they are film segments glued together end-to-end, or parts of an existing film which have been rearranged by piecing them together differently. The collage can be understood as a way to bring out new meanings. The links between sequences can be logical, analogical, or absurd in character. And, very often, social criticism grows out of the found footage through the juxtaposition of seemingly unrelated shots. Within a collage film can lurk ideas of disjunction and reconstruction.

The filmmakers considered here work with this disjunction and its manifestations. The notion of found footage evokes the idea of a found object and calls up the notion of "ready-made" so dear to Marcel Duchamp, but nevertheless with an obvious tendency to turn it into a deliberately fabricated object. While found footage may indeed have been found (not always by accident), it remains above all selected and re-presented film. Altering its original intention, which can include anything from sampling to a form of appropriation which could be called "pruning," actions which involve both manipulation and transformation and which demonstrate, by their very process, a critical interpretation. Changing the context of footage is often a way of subverting its meaning (not yet conceptualized) in which the use of *found footage* serves only as a reiteration. This process frequently makes use of quotation and parody, referring back to its source as a point of reference. Found footage necessarily accentuates editing as an eminently playful process completely independent of the intentions of the original film. The filmmakers' footprints, their skill at manipulating external images is revealed by their ability to master the relationships between the shots and sequences that they make use of. All filmmakers use the material according to their own needs and purposes.

Thus, in the case of Adrian Brunel, the utilization of found footage reveals a corrosive humor and demonstrates that it is not the source material itself (stock shots) which matter but the way they are used. This filmmaker, who has a special place in British cinema, that of a talented eccentric, became a master of the art of contriving narrative continuity by the use of intertitles and a dialogue between filmed sequences.[1] In a wickedly clever way, he plays with intertitles in several found footage films. At the end of the 1910s, it was common for editors and producers to draw from a well-indexed catalogue of existing sequences in order to add "color" to their story. In this way, shots already used in one film could be recycled in another so as to create particular effects. Think of the number of scenes of war, costume balls, ships at sea that you have already seen in movie theaters. If you look carefully, you will notice that these atmospheric shots have all been grafted onto other films by means of lap dissolves and superimpositions.[2] Found footage is borrowed and sorted out to fit into another context. Adrian Brunel specialized in these borrowings and parodies. In working this way, he departed from the established idea that stock shots were just a way to compensate for missing images; he was to use them for what they were, creating stories that were full of nonsense which in general gave them a heightened realism and meaning.[3] He created a new genre of crazy comedy which parodied big-budget productions and, in their black humor, prefigured certain works of the Kuchar brothers. Thus, as he acknowledged, he "made a film almost completely out of scraps of travelogs (such as 'Knowledge of the World' in the tradition of the earliest films)." The result was *Crossing the Great Sagrada* (1924), in which he used intertitles which he then sub-titled and shots taken from different films - the first third of the film was made up of staged shots. This process of double sub-titling favored plays on words and created a simultaneity of cinematographic events in a spirit which recalled the playful calligraphics of the Dadaists, and later exploited more systematically by the Surrealists in the *Exquisite Corpses*.

Thus *Crossing the Great Sagrada, Pathetic Gazette, So This Is Jolly Good* and *A Typical Budget* (1925) are skillful pastiches. Adrian Brunel assigns a particular role to the sequences he shoots, one that is generally reserved for advertisements and intertitles, facilitating dramatic continuity. In so doing, he displaces the arrangement of shots by changing their status. This displacement echoes what is at work in the use of found footage: the isolation and extraction of a shot and its emergence through insertion into a new context.

In *Crossing the Great Sagrada*, the intertitles are attached to sequences that have nothing to do with what they portray. In one version of the film, a title card proclaims "Mass jubilation in New York," while the image shown is one of the Royal Guard in London; this sequence is followed by another which stipulates "Only a few savages dancing." The previous intertitle could be an ironic reference either to the Royal Guard or the mass jubilation. The intertitle creates an imprecision, an ambiguity, playing with the visual or textual content. This approach is central to *Crossing the Great Sagrada*, so much so that the intertitles themselves are subjected to subtitles which call into question and parody their informational nature. The film offers a fictional voyage to unexpected places and plays with the gap separating the voyage from its cinematographic representation. The gaps are made all the more visible by the fact that the intertitles do not describe what is seen but follow their own logic which does not correspond to that of the viewers' dumbstruck gaze. The whole film plays on this kind of disconnect between verbal description and seeing, between expectation and delay or result.

Adrian Brunel uses stock shots in a casual way and his film is not drawn from a single source of images. He combines different approaches and, in this sense, seems closer to contemporary film-makers such as Viénet, Schub or even Bruce Conner. In fact if, like Esfir Schub, Brunel depends mainly on libraries for his films, his approach is not only based on newsreels or film archives; he also draws on comedies from Britain and other countries. Without any specific political intent, he creates a purely cinematographic spec-tacle from whatever means are at his disposal.[4]

In this sense, his work is distinct from the early films of Esfir Schub or *Three Songs of Lenin* (1934) by Dziga Vertov. Esfir Schub's name is inseparable from compilation films:[5] she inaugurated the genre, in 1927, with *The Fall of the Romanov Dynasty* and *The Great Road*, then, in 1928, with *The Russia of Nicolas II and Leo Tolstoy*. For these three films, she drew on a mass of documents of sequences to which she gave a new dimension; in juxtaposing two worlds alien to each other, she brings out the ironic and the absurd, and gives these documents an emotional force which they had not seemed to have previously had. In *The Fall of the Romanov Dynasty*, she contrasts scenes of the aristocracy with others of farmers, and through the collision of these two previously separated worlds points out the inevitable fall of the dynasty. Her editing is nevertheless not as dynamic as that advocated by Vertov in his *Kino-Pravda* (1922-1925) or in his documentary symphonies. Schub sacrifices nothing to either the associations nor to the formalism for which Vertov and Ruttmann - with *Melody of the World* (1929) - would be so often reproached. Schub's use of archival footage and newsreels respects the actions and gestures represented; she believes in the truth of the cinematographic document and preserves its integrity whereas Vertov galvanizes his vision of the world by means of a formidable machine for seeing and creating associations. The projects differ as much in the editing as in the goals they assign to film. Nevertheless, in *Three Songs of Lenin*, correspondences can be seen. For once, Vertov calls upon other images (and sounds) than those recorded by his team; he searches for raw material in order to create his ode to Lenin. Suddenly, iconography and representation predominate, while before only dynamism counted. In this film, the formal approach dissolves in reconstitution and memory. An approach of mourning or advocacy which confers on the documents a status closer to the one seen in the work of Esfir Schub or Bruce Conner - one of the founders of found footage films - in *Report* (1963-1967) or *Valse triste* (1979).

Political vision allows the organization of raw material according to an efficient dialectic, even if it can sometimes seem schematic or reductive (see the oppositions in Schub's early films). In these compilation films, criticism emerges from the document by isolating it out of its original context and by its juxtaposition with other elements. The criticism makes it possible to not have the nostalgic view inherent to compilation films due to the nature of the documents and their emotional impact. Schub, as much as Vertov, makes use of intertitles which encourage distancing from representation. Nevertheless, in Schub's work, there is not to be found the irony which is in *The Fall of the Romanov Dynasty* - an irony which recalls that of Brunel when he subverted the meaning of a shot with the use of a title. But here the poetic dimension is effaced in favor of a political message, the criticism is transmitted through the commentary and in this way denatures the activity depicted. The same text, "by the sweat of his brow...," applied to two distinct scenes - a scene of a ball on a boat during a cruise and a scene of farmers slaving away like convicts - renews our apprehension about the documents by their mutual interrogation. Could it be the juxtaposition which creates the distance and the criticism, as if by a sensory effect? Does this critical distance from the work in a compilation film come from the very act of extracting it and its recycling as is the case with collage, photomontage, and found footage films?

And yet, not all found footage films are films of criticism. Or do they become so independently of the filmmaker's aims? The employment of found footage encourages, by the introduction of new relationships, the emergence of incongruity and, consequently, facilitates the impression of strangeness and inadequacy of the images in relation to each other, thus leading to a questioning of their relationship itself and of the images associated with it. So the found footage film questions the organization of sequences, as close as possible to the image itself, as in *Sur les bords de la caméra* (1932) by Henri Storck where newsreel sequences on the relation of the individual to the crowd are put together in a comic fashion. He returns to pacifistic criticism in *Histoire du soldat inconnu* (1932). The film investigates men's fascination with war through the alternation of official images (from Eclair newsreels) of statesmen, sequences of the wounded, cadavers and skeletons. Its pacifism is evidence in the use of shots of the signing of the Kellogg-Briand pact (which, in 1928, condemned war), anti-war demonstrators, and the collapse of a smokestack, evoking the coming annihilation of the world, as Cocteau had already done in *Le Sang d'un poète* (1930). Here Henri Storck departs from the Surrealism which dominated his first works to play, as a patient editor, with images of the representation of power, thus questioning the authoritarian nature of this representation. Despite the differences with Schub's first film, Henri Storck's films and the late works of Germaine Dulac, all work from newsreel footage, in other words with official, practically authorized, images. This should have made their distribution easier but the selection and rearrangement of these same images often made them problematic - for example the fate of *Histoire du soldat inconnu* which was censored for several years in France. In addition, in *Le Cinéma au service de l'Histoire* (1935), Germaine Dulac edited a series of Gaumont newsreel documentaries which she had patiently collected in order to confer a meaning to these anonymous reels, a precise stamp, in the continuity of her action to reveal "the true universal human and social character of cinema."[6] The use of found footage seemed to institute an opening up of other domains, putting to work images which were not created by the filmmaker. The filmmaker manipulates, arranges them, sometimes making them look ridiculous, favoring a neutrality in the way they are assembled; the filmmakers erase themselves from their content; they disappear before the evocative power of the images they use. Yet manipulations are numerous. The erasure is in appearance only. They make their mark on the film, if only through references or quotes. In fact, through the appropriation and the use of a more or less well-known document, the chosen sequence or extract becomes a sign to be played with, upon which the work is organized. It is in this sense that the extracts of films in Kenneth Anger's *Scorpio Rising* (1963) must be understood; the sequences from *The Wild One* (1953) emphasize the fascination that Scorpio feels from incidents of violence, while those from *The King of Kings* (1927) place Christ and Brando in the same category, that of "leaders." Thus, the anonymous extracts or identifiable films using clichés without invoking the same referential space; nevertheless, they all execute a change of attribution and function. The same goes for the extracts of musical comedies used by Matthias Müller in *Aus Der Ferne* (1989) or *Sleepy Haven* (1993), and the extracts from films of Murnau, which evoke a time when the image considered itself innocent. In addition, the extract or the entirety of a film can become the basis for an analysis which investigates the effects of narration such as *Tom, Tom, the Piper's Son* (1969-1971) by Ken Jacobs, or can study the decomposition of movement such as *Surfacing on the Thames* (1970) by David Rimmer. Thus do films explore the ability to analyze seeing by splitting up the initial image. The accumulation of quotes allows the development of a study of the image of women in *Schmeerguntz* (1966) by Gunvor

Nelson or to subvert the voyeurism in the consumption of pornographic films as in *Sodom* by Luther Price. The film can also limit itself to the quotation, as in *Trade Tattoo* (1937) by Len Lye or *Une œuvre* (1968) and Un navet (1976) by Maurice Lemaître.

Sometimes the quote is only the wink of an eye, sometimes it is the central motif of the film from which ways of organizing fiction can be studied: for example *Rose Hobart* (1936-1939) by Joseph Cornell, *The Doctor's Dream* (1978) or *Keaton's Cops* (1991) by Ken Jacobs, *Pièce touchée* (1989) by Martin Arnold, *The Great Blondino* (1967) by Robert Nelson. David Rimmer has several times explored the details of the reproduction of movement by playing with reiterations and differences in *The Dance* (1970), or chromatic variations on loops in *Variations on a Cellophane Wrapper* (1970). With *The Secret Garden* (1988), Phil Solomon plays with the national myth that *The Wizard of Oz* (1939) has become; in *Home Stories* (1991), Matthias Müller questions the codes and clichés in the representation of movie stars. The quotation is drawn from journalism with the footage of the Kennedy assassination in *Report* by Bruce Conner or from the documentary in *Perfect Film* (1986) by Ken Jacobs and from the movie trailer in *The Politics of Perception* (1973) by Kirk Tougas.

Images can have meanings that many would prefer to be unique. It is not the least of the accomplishments of René Viénet to have subverted this uniqueness in the earliest films which he distorts just by the means of subtitles: *La Dialectique peut-elle casser des briques ?* (1972). This film hijacks a karate film by inserting subtitles which tell a story of power and how it is represented. A subtle game which plays with cinematographic genres, recording and, should it be necessary, demonstrating that often the image only acquires meaning from its caption, the sub-title, the story, and its author's signature. By hijacking a minor genre, the karate film or the pornographic film (*Les Filles de Kamare*, 1974), Viénet comes back to his original objective in 1967: "Film which is the newest medium of expressions and doubtless the most useful of our era has trampled on almost three quarters of a century (...) Let us appropriate above all the most fully-realized examples, the most modern, those which have eluded artistic ideology even more than American B movies: the newsreels, the coming attraction announcements and above all advertising films."[7] It is what Guy Debord had already achieved by using advertising films and newsreels in *Sur le passage de quelques personnes à travers une assez courte unité de temps* (1960). The incorporation of these external elements facilitates the analysis of society that will be developed even more radically in *La Critique de la séparation* (1961) and above all *La Societé du spectacle* (1973) which juxtaposes the reading of texts from the work of the same name with images from many different sources and, by so doing, creates a formidable machine for denouncing a certain use of cinema as a "phagocytosis" of society. Whether it be by Debord or Viénet, one characteristic of this diversion asserts itself: one which consists of playing with graphic elements and intertitles which interrupt the flow of realistic images by calling up the catch-words and slogans found in movie trailers and commercials, a refer-ence-reverence to what Lemaître accomplished with his first film. But quite often in the case of Viénet, the intertitles are superimposed on the hijacked image and are accompanied by a soundtrack with narra-tion which reinforces and underlines the hijacking by its commen-tary on the source material, as he does in *Chinois encore un effort pour être révolutionnaires* (1978) where, on the appearance of Mrs. Mao, several intertitles, accompanied by a French song saying "I am not who I say I am...," comment on the three intertitles placed between the different images: "In the role of Mrs. Mao," "the famous actress Lan Ping," "otherwise known as chiang ching." Here the letters block the representation interposing another diversion to the appropriation of Chinese newsreel footage. These actions of diversion pervert with great humor the seriousness of many compilation films but without ever becoming just entertainment since the subtitles provide captions to the image.

The history of film offers many examples of borrowings which provide the impetus for a new film. Again Ken Jacobs has a special place both for his performances (*XCXHXEXRXRXIXEXS*,1980), or his 3D films (*Opening the Nineteeth Century: 1896,* 1990), but also Al Razutis, Jean-Claude Bustros, or Maurice Lemaître, who opens *Le*

Film est déjà commence ? (1951) with a sequence from *The Birth of a Nation* (1915) and who uses multiple quotes and borrowings from all cinematographic genres. All filmmakers expresses their reverence according to their own aesthetic.

The quote is particularly powerful when it is used only on the soundtrack. Thus, in *The Song of Rio Jim* (1978), Lemaître creates, using a piece of found music, a Western which distinguishes itself from others by the fact that the sound narration does not correspond to a single image: in fact, the screen is completely black. The sound is the deviation and challenges cinematographic genres by its very presence on the screen. This challenge differs from the one proposed by Al Razutis in the series of *Visual Essays: Origins of Film* (1973-1984) in that it confronts the filmmaker's project with the very actions or political conditions that have led to the work's creation. In this way Lumière, Méliès, Eisenstein are challenged. Confronted with each of them, Al Razutis proposes a critical contextualization. He connects the potentialities of their actions with an analysis of cinematographic technique. In this way in *Storming the Winter Palace* (1984) the shot, the focus, the sequence, the editing and their ideological importance are all challenged.

There has been a tradition of incorporating shots in order to emphasize a point or affirm an observation on society; the Vietnam War has been a major issue for Americans: it has been reflected in, among others, *Quixote* (1964-1965) by Bruce Baillie and *23rd Psalm Branch* (1966-1978) by Stan Brakhage. Political, social, ethnic, or existential causes often motivate the use of found footage, leading to the appropriation of problematic representations. Thus Craig Baldwin creates marvelous stories of anticipation by a paranoid reading of film documents of every kind in *Tribulation 99: Alien Anomalies Under America* (1990) which seems to apply to film what the Situationists did when they subverted comic books: a critical view by exaggerating in the process of subverting its meaning.

There exists a contrast between the anonymity of found images and the sequences used by filmmakers in the 1960s and 1970s, which analyze the medium, and by the makers of compilation films, such as

Germaine Dulac, Esfir Schub and Henri Storck; in documentaries, this practice also exists as can be seen in the introduction to *Le fond de l'air est rouge* (1977) by Chris Marker which, working from stock images, builds an argument and proposes an interpretation. The question seems to have moved from being one of the signified to one of the signifier. A shift in inquiry of which the Al Razutis is a prime example, and which restates the two approaches and thereby allows them to open new paths of inquiry. Still, the positions are not so entrenched, we tend to get caught up in the net of an only partly defined argument. *Passage à l'acte* (1993) and *Pièce touchée* (1989) by Martin Arnold are exemplary works. By using an optical printer, the filmmaker disrupts the continuous play of a scene from a classic film by pausing it, running it backwards, and starting it again - as if inflicting it with Parkinson's disease. By running it in reverse, turning it into its mirror image, he brings out a polysemy of meaning from a scene which originally depicted a banal domestic event (a husband returning home to his wife or a family breakfast in the case of the more recent film).

Many filmmakers occasionally use found footage at the heart of their filmic proposition. In this case, the sequence can expand to extreme dimensions. The film delineates possibilities contained in the original document; see for example *Tom, Tom, the Piper's Son* by Ken Jacobs which examines the way in which primitive films told their stories; *Eureka* by Ernie Gehr which focusses on a San Francisco cable car and investigates how an image is remembered; *Berlin Horse* (1970) by Malcolm Le Grice which studies loops and how their differences emerge through repetition, as does *Seashore* (1971) or *Watching for the Queen* (1973) both by David Rimmer. The focus on and attempt to analyze loops allow certain filmmakers to understand how film communicates its information and to rearrange or re-establish it through subtle manipulation - the film loops of Wolf Vostell are among the most striking examples. Working from a series of very short shot and sometimes still images running in a loop, as in *TV Décoll/age for Millions* (1967), he investigates the nature of images that we gorge ourselves on, such as those of fighter planes preparing to take off in *Starfighter* (1967), or Americans bombarding Vietnamese with napalm in *Vietnam* (1967-1971)...The repetition of these brief sequences, instead of the images extracted from televised documents that seem banal, endows them with a power that they would have lost amid the multitude of war images broadcast every day.

Artavazd Peleshian made a number of found footage films. *Au début* (1967) commemorates the 50th anniversary of the October 1917 revolution by mixing films by Eisenstein and Vertov with newsreel footage from various sources. He explodes the representation of the revolution by trying to breathe life into it with an irresistible blast of fresh air. He works with short sequences which he manipulates in several ways: looping and thus repetition of the sequence, re-photography which heightens contrasts, in order to make the subject abstract and reduce it to just the power of its lines, the movement of mass. Peleshian edits and structures his films by employing a circular form, an ellipse which permits by the return of shots to transform and make resonate the blocks of images of which they are the vectors. He is not as interested in the single frame as Vertov is in *Man with a Movie Camera* (1929) or in sequencing as in *Three Songs of Lenin*, nor does he reuse a montage of attractions.[8] His concern is with a montage that makes the shots resonate, within each block of images and from block to block.[9] Peleshian is interested in the disjunction of shots and not in the interval which links them. He shatters any single meaning to benefit the resonance which tints it, he colors but does not freeze.

Numerous found footage films employ a secondary process bobbing on the surface of the tide of images: the addition of different texts on the intertitles. Words, phrases, and more explicitly, the application of not always readable graphic elements have been used by Guy Debord, Isidore Isou, Maurice Lemaître, Cécile Fontaine and Frédérique Devaux...This graphic element scrambles the "diversion:" a figurative kidnapping, a supplement to the diversion which modifies what would have been the initial perception of sequences. An example of this tactic can already be found in the Len Lye film, *Trade Tattoo,* in which the advertising message determines the logic behind

the order of the chanting of words and phrases in the film. The words
or phrases are painted directly on the film strip between the documentary sequences skillfully reworked by means of colorizations,
solarizations... Sometimes, they are stenciled onto the photographic
image, leading to a textual counterpoint to the tide of images. Their
positions and their movements within the frame are conjugated with
the movement depicted in the image. The melody of multiple voices
developed by Lye only reinforces the pertinence of the image. The
sequences gleaned from the archives of his peers serves to instrumen-
talize the efficacy of the institution delivering the message all over the
place.[10] This message is quite obviously far from those of Hellen
Biggar and Norman McLaren in *Hell Unltd*[11] (1936), or Len Lye in
Rainbow Dance (1936) or *Trade Tattoo which* overflow with information.

The graphics, the playing with letters would take on a greater
importance with the Lettrists who would make it their predominant
tool and label it "chiseling." Chiseling represents a direct intervention
on the film strip as a malleable medium, also accomplished through
scratching, scraping, piercing, all means of attacking the film surface
directly. Corresponding to the chiseling is the "discrepant"[12] sound,
in other words the autonomy of the soundtrack in relation to the
ribbon of images. The images are sabotaged rather than diverted.
This independence of graphic elements from sound is common to all
documents. The history of cinema and classic films are invoked in *Le
Film est déjà commencé ?*, then Méliès in *Un navet*, and in the series *Vie
de M.B.* (1986)...A large part of the Lettrist production (Maurice
Lemaître, Roland Sabatier) consists of arranging images after having
chiseled them, in order to mount an orderly attack of anecdote and
realistic reproduction, which are not often challenged in film, experimental or otherwise. The chiselings operate on the image to give it a
supplemental sense; almost a non-sense, at least if it is not possible to
examine the film-strip itself, in order to decipher the phrases laid
onto it as in *Le Film est déjà commencé ?*, *Une histoire d'amour* (1978)...
This supplement of graphic elements, of letters resembles a blurring,
a loss of the photographic quality of the image. The image is attacked
by the chiseling in a way that makes its lisibility dissolve into the raw

material of the film-strip; the dissipation of its details melts into the underlying whiteness of its celluloid base - as a homage to the artists who worked on lacerating billboards who can be seen in *Scratch Pad* (1960) by Hy Hirsh and also in *Ça* (1965-1966) by Jean Clareboudt.

There is in the origins of Lettrism a primacy of the gesture on film, an attack which recalls Pollock's Action Painting, where the gesture and the spontaneity of the act create its characteristics and appearance. This gesture of graphic elements on the film-strip, begun by Len Lye and Norman McLaren takes on a violent quality which links it to a new aesthetic category, reminiscent of the avant-garde manifestos of the beginning of the 20th century. In contrast to Len Lye, for whom graphic elements were only a way to choreograph energy with colors and forms, the Lettrists play with the relationship of photographic representation and their chiseling. Thus, in *Le Soulèvement de la jeunesse, Mai 68*, Lemaître uses news footage of student protests and military sequences, alternating the original soundtrack of the news footage with the reading of a text by Isidore Isou on the past and the future of the political economy. Here the spectacular dimension of the images is sometimes offset by the monotone of the voice reading the text, in this way creating a dichotomy between what is commented on, its announcement, and the images. In addition, the sound spills over onto the images on soldiers on patrol. Despite the laughter it provokes, this juxtaposition seems to reinforce the pertinence of Isou's declaration. It is here, above all, that the sound is discrepant, while in *Un navet* the sound intervenes to emphasize the diversion begun by the different graphic elements. *Un navet* intertwines a large number of films. Can several films be a "navet" (bad film)? By disqualifying parts of images, or by commenting on them with drawings, Lemaître creates image games and puzzles. The covering of all or part of an image makes it possible to draw attention to certain zones of the screen which has a still more striking effect when the images are from a pornographic film. In this way, voyeurism is simultaneously featured and denounced. The denunciation is particularly cheerful here. The intervention breaking up all continuity or linearity provokes an outburst of polysemy, drowning the spectator in the provocation of pure gestures which fly in the face of common sense. It is an art of harassment (doubtless a homage to Erik Satie) which, by repetition ends up by being seductive. *Un navet* is characteristic of the numerous strategies that Lemaître resorts to in his use of found footage, strategies he shares with the incontestable master of the genre: Bruce Conner. There are numerous differences between Lemaître and Conner; among them, I will cite two. The first is that Bruce Conner uses only black and white films from the 1940s and 1950s whereas Lemaître is less limited in his choice. In addition, Lemaître deals with the physical substance of film, while Conner, by his use of fade-ins and fade-outs, black leader or flicker effects reminds viewers that they are allowed in the presence of a film.[13] The second difference has to do with the use of the soundtrack by these two filmmakers. The accompaniment does not have the same value nor the same function; the necessity for sound does not relate to the same political or aesthetic choices. In fact for Bruce Conner the soundtrack is not discrepant, it tints the film with a nostalgia that mourns the loss of the American dream. Maurice Lemaître, like Bruce Conner, has a weakness for coming attraction movie trailers, and projectionists' leader. There are troubling similarities in the use of projectionists' leader in *A Movie* (1958), *Cosmic Ray* (1961), *Ten Second Film* (1965) and *Le Film est déjà commencé ?* For Conner, the leader allows him to isolate sequences and show them in contrast with the fluidity of classic narrative form. Each filmmaker in his own way questions the traditional way of projecting film, removing from projection precisely what would be the center of attention. But for Lemaître this questioning goes further in the sense that for him it includes the entire event of showing a film.[14] Lemaître systematizes what Isidore Isou had introduced in regard to the manipulation, the transformation, the construction of a visual reality by the use of signs, in order to reveal the impossibility of the faithful reproduction of images. In this work initiated by Isou and Lemaître, then pursued by a host of other artists, it is evident that there still existed numerous possibilities for recycling to explore. To name just one, the idea of making a film with just scraps of film. One of the characteristics of the films of the 1980s and 1990s is the mastery of every stage of the filmmaking process, including the development and the printing of filmed or refilmed shots. This does not just mean questioning the order of the elements - sequences, shots - but also the texture, the surface and the thickness of the film-strip. Attention to the raw material and the surface of the image. The filmmakers of the 1980s play with the basic material of which film is made, multiplying the processes of intervention and innovation: manual development, the stripping away of emulsion and its reattachment to other media, the use of different format and the employment of other base materials...

Whether working with anonymous images as do Yervant Gianikian and Angela Ricci Lucchi in most of their films, or Paolo Gioli in *L'Operatore perforato* (1979), or with television series as does Frédérique Devaux in *Imagogie* (1981), or educational films as do Caroline Avery in *Midweekend* (1985-1986) and *Big Brother* (1983) and Cécile Fontaine in *Golf Entretien* (1984) and *Overeating* (1984), the possibilities for the visual treatment of the basic physical material of film are infinite. Different filmmakers perceive found footage in different ways, but certain convergences of attitudes and ways of intervening are perceptible in relation to how the original material can be transformed by extreme manipulation. The Schmelzdahin group and Jürgen Reble, as well as Metamkine, are the most excessive; taking possession of their films, they copy, then chemically attack them, transforming their visual qualities, giving them a new meaning as much as editing them would - see *Stadt in Flammen* (1984), and *Aus den Algen* (1986). The use of primitive films does not have the same result when it is done by Gianikian and Ricci Lucchi, who explore the nature of representation of a world condemned to disappear, as is the case with *Dal Polo al'Equatore* (1986), as it does when done by Paolo Gioli who, in *L'Operatore perforato*, which investigates the base material through the particular characteristics of the 9.5 mm format (which uses a central sprocket hole between frames) and in which can be seen a cameraman overwhelmed by a projected film and transformed into the cameraman of his own private visions.[15]

These old films depicting a lost world (in its reality as much as in its representation) nevertheless reflect the full power of newborn cinematography by its capacity to record unknown scenes and landscapes; thus *Lyrisch Nitrant* (1990) by Peter Delpeut paints the portrait of an epoch at the height of Romanticism through the depiction of desolate landscapes and bodies given over to hysterical passion - an epoch which saw in cinema the ideal medium for the depiction of vertiginous transports of passion...the fragile medium is transformed and decomposes. This transformation and this ephemeral character are the source for the cinematographic alchemy of Jürgen Reble. The sudden burst of primitive films makes it still more possible to write the history of film through these types of representations by confronting them either just by their technique, as in *The Death Train* (1993) by Bill Morrison which evokes the movement of images through railways, or by evoking the collapse of the contemporary landscape, creating only mock situations as in the series *Peggy and Fred in Hell* (1984-1994) by Leslie Thornton which juxtaposes sequences of children shot by the filmmaker with images from the period intended to be educational as well as bucolic. The world fabricated by children is a world of borrowings and appropriation. Their mental landscape is made up of found images and sounds arranged by their subjective modalities.[16] Here history becomes the object of quotation and refers back to the compilation film using just a few sequences. It is in this sense that *Displaced Person* (1981) by Daniel Eisenberg and *In Memory* (1994) by Abraham Ravett can be understood. Both films investigate Nazism but by different strategies, in one case by trying to understand the irrational while in the other case by the tragic consequences of this irrationality for the Jews.

This appropriation takes on different forms in the 1980s and involves dealing with films by deforming them, by tinting them or attacking them chemically. The attack is all the more interesting when it is carried out on images that the filmmakers themselves have not shot. Thus the Schmelzdahin group, then Jürgen Reble or Matthias Müller in Germany, Phil Solomon, Caroline Avery, Nina Fonoroff in the U.S., Sabine Hiebler and Gerhard Ertl in Austria,

Cécile Fontaine, Metamkine and, to a certain degree, Michel Amarger in France, working with these manipulations to different degrees. Some similar effects can be found in the films of Frédéric Charpentier who re-photographs sequences from pornographic films until complete deterioration in *The Dog Star Man Has a Too Big Flaming Cock for the Sheba Queen* (1991). In *Imagogie*, Frédérique Devaux applies parts of photographic strips onto the 16mm film-strip to create a dichotomy between the film's projection and its appearance to the naked eye on the editing table; in the same manner as *Retour à la raison* (1924) by Man Ray with the nude female body or *Filmfinish* (1986) by Paolo Gioli with deformed photos of athletes in action, this film contrasts two ways to understand the film-strip. Between the flow of images and the graphic manipulation of the source material, are grafted the photographic interventions which apply the principles of collage to the strip, and in so doing produce conflagrations of scale, objects and spaces.

The eruption of the photographic strip glued onto the exposed or unexposed film-strip shifts the notion of editing towards the idea of a visual composition in space applied to time. Thus, the relationship between multiple Super 8 images glued onto 16mm interacts with a large image rendered unreadable during projection. A play on the memory of forms. Rendering visible something that has disappeared; a filmic memory is thus worked out. These images can only exist by the manipulation of older images; they are at the heart of the practice of Cécile Fontaine and Caroline Avery, who from one film to another create new ways to see what could in certain respects recall certain films by Stan Brakhage and in particular his "stained glass" films: *Mothlight* (1963) and *The Dante Quartet* (1987).

The films of Caroline Avery are conceived according to the nature of the base material she had found. The filmmaker colors and scratches on parts of the image of *Midweekend* (1985) and applies fragments of images in *Big Brother* (1983). These two films shatter the representation of human behavior by the addition of paint on the base material, evoking Brakhage by their colors and Len Lye by the motion of the painted areas. *The Living Rock* (1989) elaborates these manipulations of images still more radically by alternating shots of pure color with painted ones. The sequences which result are refilmed in order to make the contrast between photographic and painted textures greater than it would have been had the photographic black and white simply been juxtaposed with the painted color. In her films Caroline Avery edits in a very tight way in order to create a visual shock, a montage of opposites which reinforces the painting - for example the car accident in *Midweekend*. For her part, Cécile Fontaine literally scrapes different layers of emulsion from color film and then redistributes them onto the same film-strip out of synch by a few frames or, as in *Japon Series* (1991), plays with the separation of colors, or pastes them on other emulsions and other film stocks, as can be seen in *Almaba* (1988) or *Cruises* (1988-89).[17] Each time the detachment does not reflect the re-attachment so in this sense they cannot really be called *ready-mades* because the manipulations depend on the success of the original scraping-off. In this case, the dysfunction is an integral part of the cinematography and reinforces the understanding of film as a form of alchemy in the way it is conceived by Jürgen Reble.[18] With *Overeating*, it is evident that luck was on the filmmaker's side because the effects created by the soaking of the film do not necessarily end up visually recalling the act of gluing it all together. In this film a man stuffs himself and the film seems to get twisted, crumpled, and torn like the chicken that he is devouring. The repetition of the same loop strengthens the disgracefulness of the feast shown in the film. There are continuous allusions, mockery, irreverence, toying with the images and symbols which allow the filmmaker to play with the contents in ways that recall those of Schmelzdahin in *Der General* (1987): Nosferatu who raises his eyes is terrified by the vision of a duck... Cécile Fontaine works with what can be called the margins, the scraps of cinema; in other words scrapes, scratches, soakings, peelings, and so transforms film into a totally visual activity fabricated out of nothing, thereby allying with the practice begun by the Dadaists with their collages, the canvases of Schwitters and even more with the *Cut with the Kitchen Knife Dada through the Beer-Belly of the Weimar Republic* of Hannah Höch. An act of salvage or how to make an art work without seeming to touch it. Which recalls *Curried 7302* (1977), *Deep Friend 7360* (1973) and the "raw films" by Tony Conrad which ask how it is still possible to make films in your kitchen.

Cécile Fontaine transforms her raw material by detaching it from its base. On this, depending on the quality of the film, how old it is, how it has aged and been stored, she obtains a certain type of texture: mosaic or stained glass, etc. This detachment of the emulsion calls attention to the physical gesture that accomplished it and re-introduces into cinematographic practice an element of chance specific to the medium itself. Scraping it off reveals new forms and new relationships between the found objects (filmed) which interject, at the core of the photographic representation, the material nature of the medium, the recording of the gesture and its displaced inscription.

The detachment creates two elements, the base and the emulsion, the base on which a phantom-like trace of the image remains: its shadow; and all or part of the emulsion. *Cruises* can be considered as, up to now, one of the filmmaker's most beautiful films. At its source is an American commercial for a cruise in the Gulf of Mexico, the film journal of a German soldier in the region of Colmar[19] during World War II and a ludicrous comedy. The incongruous encounter of these three elements will create magnificent conflagrations and collisions of meaning. Fontaine connects the films in two distinct ways. Thus scenes of meal, dancing, relaxing follow one upon another, moving from black and white to saturated color. But the relationships engage with each other within each sequence, inside the image itself. In fact, several sequences display an incrustation of color film at the center of a black and white image, as in the scene of passengers on the deck of a boat; two moments collide within the same image. It should be noted that the images are in motion. As are the scenes where several people are swimming. The incrustation is not meticulous, it is more of a patching together that shows the materiality of the torn ends, recalling the zip paintings of Barnett Newman, or stripes in certain Paul Sharits films. Here the constituent elements become the filmmaker's objects of predilection and she plays wondrously with all the gaps and bumps that she includes in her work. Work that has numerous similarities to Schmelzdahin to the degree that they make use of all the accidents which are normally discarded. They are fond of attacking the film with various chemical products which dissolve the emulsion and melt it into a magma of flamboyant color.

The materiality of film is not challenged in order to analyze how or why, but to examine its expressive possibilities with which the filmmakers play. It is a far cry from certain structural films which use found footage for analytical purposes as do Birgit and Wilhelm Hein, Sharits and Le Grice. For them, the initial representation does not seem, at first sight, to be the most important object of their consideration.

Alongside the use of found footage which gives priority to the materiality of the image, a new use can be observed which allows the filmmaker to focus on autobiography: the film journal. These films are drawn entirely from extracts and a few sequences. Gustav Deutsch, in *Adria 1954-1968* (1990), explores the use of home movies, primarily vacation footage. This particular use encourages the transition from film journal to a form of essay and allows the film to be pulled back into subjectivity and the personal history of the filmmaker, as is the case with Cécile Fontaine in *Histoires parallèles* (1990). This pulling back in often occurs when an identity as a member of a minority is affirmed or demanded. The affirmation of a difference of race, sexual preference, etc., which involves the taking over and deflecting of images creating by and for the white male majority. The affirmation of a subjectivity, of a history that is made by taking charge of the deflection of images and redirecting them to other purposes. Thus can be seen in all films made by minorities another distribution of the images that concern them. This use of home movies and erotic films by Abigail Child in the series *Is This What You Were Born For?* (1981-88) clearly places the film as a protest and a commitment to the establishment of a history controlled by minorities themselves and not imposed on them and making them submissive. *Ecce Homo* (1989) by Jerry Tartaglia plays with images of gay sexuality with a full knowledge that any representation of gay sexuality today will be considered as pornography. In a classic manner of diversion, the use of found footage becomes for ethnic and sexual minorities one of the most efficient ways to overturn the established values through their reappropriation and thus to create and circulate new images. *Covert Action* (1984) by Abigail Child questions the representation of women in home movies. In parallel to this generalized reappropriation of images by minorities is the making of film journals which consist, either totally or partially, of found footage. Among these, I can see two types. The first are those which use souvenirs of a past era to bring out a personal history as is the case with *Decodings* (1988) by Michael Wallin. Working from sequences from the 1940s and 1950s - thus contemporaneous with those used by Bruce Connor - Michael Wallin succeeds at evoking the difficulties that adolescents experience at affirming a homosexual identity. But this film, with its slow rhythms, offers a nostalgic look back at a past in which elements can be discovered which would explain a personal history. *The Smell of Burning Ants* (1994) by Jay Rosenblatt can also be understood in this way with its analysis of the "creation of the male." There also exist other ways of using found footage which involve forging new connections between previously separated categories of films. Using home movies or anonymous film journals in order to convoke and promote the emergence of memories and situate the activity and power of subjective memory from a personal or social source seems to be one of the characteristics of contemporary film and video. One could cite *Fast Trip, Long Drop* (1993) by Gregg Bordowitz in which found footage allows the filmmaker to orient himself in history when faced with sickness and imminent death. Or one could cite *Passion* (1990) by Jürgen Reble which, by means of a film journal over a year, reveals his fascination with wildlife and scientific films and thus evokes the existence of a world parallel to our own in which the cycles of life and death are respected. In the same vein, in *Sink or Swim* (1990), Su Friedrich, through the use of a backward alphabet, recounts in the voice of a young girl, stories of her childhood: amid commercials and television series that embody the father figure of an American family, several sequences use images filmed by her grandparents and incidentally reveal the figure who haunts both the filmmaker and her father: childhood images of her father and her aunt swimming in a lake. The insertion of personal documents encourage an understanding of the film as a powerful memory which the filmmaker constantly updates - thus Noll Brinckmann in *Der Fater* (1986), with films shot by her father in China, or Malcolm Le Grice with *Little Dog for Roger* (1967). In fact the footage is no longer collective but belongs to an individual domain and allows family history to become a universal experience by emancipating it and placing it in the public arena. Thus Nina Fonoroff in *The Accursed Mazurka* (1994) mixes up layers of images and numerous extracts from Hollywood films to evoke a psychological breakdown. The images as well as the soundtrack of her film create a depersonalization through the accumulation of images and contribute to the establishment of a form of labyrinth which evokes and attempts to reconstitute obsessional processes. Work which involves both memory and at the same time the process which allows filmmakers to reveal the breakdowns in their own story as part of history.

The multiplicity of images no longer belong outside the domain personal or historical, they operate through this fragmentation and circulation that authorizes the use of found footage and permits the simultaneous affirmation of different compositions of time, proposing a genuine social deconstruction, and in so doing, the use of found footage mirrors the history of 20th century art.

Found Footage, Paris, Galerie nationale du Jeu de Paume, 1995.

JOSEPH CORNELL: MONSIEUR PHOT

Film played a preponderant role in the artistic training and career of Joseph Cornell. Film is both what permits us to explore unknown lands and a formidable tool of montage, of collage, which encourages a multiplicity of linguistic associations: plays on words and images. Cornell made films but also collected silent films with which he put together both public and private programs.

THE CINEMA ENCOURAGES a wandering of the spirit as much as recording physical travel; a whole eroticism of nostalgia, of loss can be found in the relations Cornell maintained with cinema. Film works with nostalgia in several ways. There is the fascination with movie stars expressed in the articles and scenarios published by Cornell: *Monsieur Phot (Seen Through the Stereoscope)*, in 1933, and *Theater of Hans Christian Andersen*, written the same year and only published in 1945. This nostalgia can also be found in certain of his boxes, as in the *Penny Arcade Portrait of Lauren Bacall* (1945-1946) and, of course, in his films which, most often, recycle images from different sources. It is in this sense that one can understand the replacement of the original soundtrack with Brazilian music in *Rose*

Hobart (1936) and its projection at silent film speed. The slowing down places the film in the realm of the marvelous. Its mauve color (in fact, the film is tinted) reinforces this atmosphere of strangeness and reflects the unreal experience of a dream.

READING *Monsieur Phot* reveals the implementation of this unreality, this realm of the fantastic which uproots conventions and narrative links through the use of formal and thematic associations. In the manner of the Surrealists, Joseph Cornell employs montage, whether in his boxes or his films. These associations allow him to establish connections, a sliding from one form to another: a pheasant pops out of the laundry basket of a street urchin, in *Monsieur Phot*, or a lunar eclipse follows a sunset over water, in *Rose Hobart*. This form of condensation occurs more often in his collages and boxes than in his films themselves, as Cornell employs an iconography that is largely pre-cinematographic. A collage of fragments of engravings, of letters, that can surround the reproduction of a photograph. The use of engravings reinforces a detachment from reality and makes possible the rediscovery of the particular enchantment evoked by black and white dictionary illustrations. Skidding into the beyond, a return to a childhood playground. A use of engravings and photography by a collector who, with a box, a label, one scene or another, created a world both romantic and distant in which eroticism is not yet encrypted.

WITH THIS SCENARIO, Cornell pays homage to the Surrealists and their love for incongruous situations (for example the sequence of the servant or the one with the pianist, two scenes evoking Germaine Dulac as well as Luis Buñuel), but perhaps even more late 19th century French musical and literary culture, which can be found as well in the fantasies of Georges Méliès, to which Cornell alludes when the photographer must wait for a carriage to go by before taking his picture (to cite just one example). Renaldo Hahn, Claude

Debussy are evoked as much for the evocative power of their melodies as for their atmospheres - a street scene in the snow. But Cornell counters the Surrealists' provocations and violence with a search for a lost paradise: an age of innocence. This nostalgia is again visible in the five images that accompany the scenario which function as clues and catalyzers for the imaginary journey that *Monsieur Phot* represents. The photos, the engravings, allow the spirit to move off onto other shores, which cinematographic representation, being too realistic, can only suggest.

Anthologie du cinéma invisible, Paris, Jean-Michel Place/Arte Editions, 1995.

CÉCILE FONTAINE: FILM UNBOUND

Films can be made in all different ways. There is not a single (dominant) practice which would dictate and impose the correct way to make a film; it would be impossible to limit cinema to just fiction or a trailer of coming attractions, etc. Cécile Fontaine imagines film as above all a raw material that she can manipulate in its very physicality, a receptacle for previously recorded images to be manipulated after having extracted them from their original context in order to replace them organized in another way. For her, film is an open field where she can spread out through a richness of textures, graphic elements and collage, the qualities of light and its arrangement according to the transparencies offered by the different reflective surfaces available to filmmakers.

Her works are characterized by the primacy she gives to disassembling and re-editing, and to her choice of images - even if most have not been shot by her since she uses found footage - which tend to be scenes of daily domestic life. Nevertheless this process does not exclude all the Super 8 films which she creates with or without a camera. It is often in her short films that she highlights the possibilities of calibrating light by undefined forms: *Le Calvaire* (1984), *Light* (1986), *Abstract film en couleur* (1991).

Fontaine belongs to the school of filmmaking that favors direct contact with the film material itself: in other words films that do not necessarily need to contain photographic images to exist, films that make cinema into a tactile as much as a visual art and extol skill at the material processes of a filmmaking. A concrete cinema whose visual effects are often abstract. The paradox of Fontaine comes from how these oppositions manifest themselves in each film. Her mastery of her tools is what permits her to connect to both the tradition begun in the 1930s by Len Lye, followed by Stan Brakhage at the end of the 1950s and one that a new generation rediscovered on the eve of the 1980s, when they began developing and processing their films themselves.

The film work of Fontaine makes use of found footage, in other words, film sequences that she has not shot herself. Unlike many filmmakers working with found footage who just excerpt short sequences or a few images from a single film, she recycles the entirety of the films she uses (whether she has just found them or they have been given to her is of little importance). The use of the totality of the found object involves a certain number of manipulations and treatments that are particular to her work. By preserving the integrity of the object - the found film - there is an affirmation about the nature of editing, designating it as a catalyst for variations. Editing is not taken to mean a way of joining together different elements but a way of transforming identical ones into different ones (difference and repetition). A shift which establishes, by an economy of means, boundaries which the filmmaker will rarely overstep. It is always a question of controlling the elements directly even while the result of the chemical and graphic manipulations, while known in advance, are never certain or even stable. These manipulations, whether consisting of detaching and re-fixing the emulsion on other base material, or scraping and cutting up parts of the emulsion, are always subject to a skidding out of control that radically transforms the sequence and can even result in its total disappearance. This tension, this risk, is to be found in all the processes she develops, that she creates. In fact, when she detaches the film emulsion, Fontaine brings about a transfer; the deterioration of the base material results in a loss of part of the initial information contained in the content but is compensated for by a gain in what comes to life. The alternation of one of the layers of the color film is accompanied by the appearance of multiple layers and results in a kind of multiple screen vision over which the filmmaker exercises an admirable mastery by combining the relationships between colors according to which burst forth - an effect recalling both the work of the sculptor Duchamp-Villon and that of Len Lye in *Rainbow Dance* (1936); one thinks of the golfers in purple, green and yellow in *Golf-Entretien* (1984) and its close relation, the first part of *Two Made for TV Films* (1986), or the dancers whose movements interlock with each other in a choreography of color as in *Japon series* (1991). In these three films, the editing plays with the discrepancies between the three layers of emulsion in the same scene. This chromatic montage nevertheless relates to other criteria which assert the specificity of purely filmic elements: the optical soundtrack, the frame line between single frames, the three layers making up the color emulsion, "the cadence disrupted by stretching the initial image and thereby changing the format." But the films do not stop at just these manipulations, they operate on the base material through a variety of techniques that the filmmaker began to discover in 1983 with *A Color Movie* (1983). This film uses a variety of strategies which will characterize Fontaine's work, while grounding them in a vein of experimental film that emphasizes the physical attributes of the medium whether through development or processing: printing, deformation of emulsion colors, or refilming. But unlike many other filmmakers, Fontaine uses none of these sophisticated techniques, she is more direct. She tears, scrapes, punches holes, scratches or burns the emulsion, re-glues it, repositions it, without regard for the original continuity of the filmed sequence. *A Color Movie* is, in this respect, a veritable encyclopedia of cinematographic deconstruction. This film, which she considers her first, allowed the filmmaker to imagine a cinema from the point of view of graphic and pictorial element, not so much in the final result as in the working methods applied to the base material. Film is no longer seen as only a surface to be exposed to light but as one to be drawn on. The shifting which disrupts "photo-graphic" realism, and makes it "kino-graphic." The only limit to these additions are the dimensions of the film gate in the projector which can no longer handle a filmstrip that has been thickened in this way. In the manner of Brakhage's *Mothlight* (1963), Fontaine renews this approach by gluing different pieces of colored paper and plastic to the film base in *L'Atelier* (1984) as much as in *A Color Movie*. She applies the same techniques to the entire film-strip, subjecting the different layers of removed emulsion to similar treatments which become increasingly complex from one film to the next. These first experiments were fundamental to Fontaine's approach to the nature of film: "a transparent object infiltrated by the light of the projector to create motifs and colors to be seen above all as moving visual objects without any specific reference to the real world except for the physical reality of the film itself."

This consideration of film as a producer of moving colored motifs often results in making the chromatic compositions that she creates resemble stained glass. The comparison with stained glass is reinforced by the fact that, although most of the 16mm films she uses portray trivial scenes of daily life, their cumulative effect gives them a ritualistic character. Examples include the local dignitaries and police forces on parade in official visits to French overseas territories in *Histoires parallèles* (1990); a sardonic reference to the filmmaker's childhood. She literally scrubs them down by dipping the strips of the film in soapy liquid to give them a unique speckled quality. She also juxtaposes the official shots with sequences that seem to come from the Suez Crisis, echoing the potential conflicts portrayed in the subject with those visible on the screen caused by the diversity of textures and processes. There is irony and humor in Fontaine's work, a pleasure in the jokes that emerge from the underlying images through her editing, whether it is from the sequencing which emphasizes analogous forms: gas tanks of German motorcycles in black and white and swimmers in color in *Cruises* (1989) or the matching of the subject with the processing of the emulsion in *Overeating* (1985). In this film, the jaw of a person eating chicken seems itself to be under the spell of a strange form of chewing. Its representation is folded, torn up in every direction, the filmstrip is ground up by the sharp bites of a ravenous hunger. This work is exemplary for several reasons: there is a perfect balance between the way it is treated and its content, after having been soaked in different liquids, the emulsion of the film has been stretched and become detached from its base; the second, the use of loops allows the process and its consequences to be displayed several times; and the third, the filmmaker applies the same treatment to the soundtrack as to the image. The result is a discrepant montage that has destroyed the original synchrony between sound and image. Certain films follow the original soundtrack to generate the continuity of another film. Here, in the case of *Cruises*, there is a use of three types of found footage, but the commercial for a cruise from Norway to the Caribbean serves as a common thread on the soundtrack for the succession of other sequences which compose the film: a film journal of a German officer during the war (Agfa, dated 1941) and comedies from the 1920s. The initial cruise, the vector for a new cruise out of time, creates moments which juxtapose territorial conquest and tourism. It is in this sense that the relation between the sequences of the German soldiers visiting and relaxing in bucolic settings and the scenes of colored beaches in the 1980s can be imagined. This film, one of the filmmaker's most accomplished, makes the ghost image one of the most characteristic of her cinematographic palette. When the filmmaker detaches the colored emulsion from a given length of film, she obtains two elements: one is the film base, often pale yellow, the ghost of images to come; the other made up of two layers of emulsion is both more fragile and, at the same time, more defined. In *Cruises*, in *Home Movie* (1986), as well as in *Sans Titre Mai* (1988), the ghosts come to inhabit a more distinct present, and infiltrate themselves as parasites into the serene progression of images. The ghost image becomes the basis of a battle which brings together several distinct times, places, and stories. In *Stories* (1989), a dog's life is mixed up with a Western (from a random 1960s television series) and shots of a family meal; the filmmaker's family to be exact. Time is compacted, the images overlap and sometimes, as in *Cruises* and *Sunday* (1993) create peculiar patchworks and mosaics: a 1920s dancing couple in black and white mix with dancers on a cruise ship in the 1970s, German children playing with a ball that transforms itself into a yellow tennis racket, etc. One could go on and on citing the examples which highlight Fontaine's incredible precision and mastery of her tools; especially since certain of the effects she employs coincide with the work that others were developing during the same period (1983-84), in the same city (Boston), through the use of an optical printer (Caroline Avery and Phil Solomon). Fontaine and Avery go so far as to share the same banal scenes of daily life in all its aspects, whether they are the scenes of communions in *Home Movie*, or of housework in *The Living Rock* (1989), or the different processions in *Home Movie*, *Histoires Parallèles*, *Cruises*, or *Sunday*.

Although the use of found footage is highly important to the filmmaker, it nevertheless becomes a constraint in the sense that she looks above all for films which deal with daily life and are not spectacular in any way. Her work is not an advocate of spectacle, she is interested in small, unimportant events, individuals and their families. How to make films simply about what surrounds us and not get caught up in a technological mirage? She makes use of a domestic environment as much for her images as for their instrumentation in order to, so it seems, never lose sight of the individual, thus revealing an economical, quintessential cinema, with no unnecessary elements. From one film to another, the scratching on the emulsion image by image and the color shifts provoked by soaking the film in various corrosive chemicals become a leitmotif. The films are often preceded by leader which the filmmaker makes by hand and are often condensed summaries of Fontaine cinema. Plays on words scratched onto the film, sardonic commentary on the image, scratching that masks or reveals a particular aspect of the image are at play both in the short intervals of leader that introduce the films and in the leader between each film when the filmmaker assembles them onto a single reel. This accumulation of signs, of scratching, of marks on photographic images disrupt the photographic representation and once again call attention to the physical nature of the film. This is reinforced by numerous scratches, folds, tears, appearing in the photo; nothing is meticulous here, there is something raw, even brutal. The traces of scotch tape allow the peeling off of colored emulsion, as well as their re-application, marks like grain or patchwork patterns made by the successive soakings in *Histoires Parallèles* or *L'Irréversible chapitre III d'un roman 3D* (1987) are asserted as essential elements. Without them, there would be no film. Fontaine thus presents her case against the fastidiously beautiful image, so full of meaning that it has lost all interest. She works with the left-overs, the debris, the scraps. Close in this way to Schwitters and the affichistes, Fontaine presents film in all its aspects, and principally those who have been excluded. Her cinema is haunted by a critical reading of the "sacred family;" in several films she works from film journal (*Home Movie*) or from scenes filmed by her father (*Correspondances*, 1985, *Stories*), sequences that she manipulates and connects to other events which also affirm the disappearance of times past, the illusion of searching for a mythic era. Film is what permits the revelation of this social criticism out of the mythology of the every day.

Initially written for *Blimp* n°16, 1991, expanded version published in the catalogue *Desmontage: Film Video/appropriacion, reciclaj IVAM*, Museu Rainer Sofia, Artleku, 1993,

Brochure, *Cinéma du Musée*, Centre Georges Pompidou, 1994

BRUCE CONNER: AN AESTHETIC OF DIVERSION

Bruce Conner worked in different media before concentrating for several years on film. But films have nevertheless eclipsed the artist, and more precisely, the assemblagist, the collagist, the painter and the photographer. Whatever material he uses, Bruce Conner assembles incongruous objects, often scraps and trash. Found objects par excellence, but which are above all objects lost to consumption: leftovers. Popular culture clichés, objects or images functioning as signs that the artist arranges and displays in specific assemblages which will provoke one or more questions about society as a whole.

THE FILM WORK of Bruce Conner is characterized by his use of outtakes, extracts from films or newsreel footage from which he constructs his collages. His cinema is characterized by a given type of image. While the sound is drawn from contemporary composers such as Terry Riley or singers, such as Ray Charles and the Beatles, the sequences he uses are all in black and white and come from films of the 1940s or 1950s, except for *Report* (1963-67) whose sequences are from the 1950s and 1960s, during the Kennedy presidency.

. . .

His work distances itself from classic experimental film in that it draws from images that he has not shot - except for three or four short films which portray a person, such as in *Vivian* (1964) and *Breakaway* (1966), a situation (moving a painting) in *The White Rose* (1961-67) - but also because he practically creates narration on his films by manipulating the effects that are usually employed in narrative films by, for example, beginning a film with a character who seems to be the person telling the story, the catalyst for the representations and dreams for what is about to be shown. The system he uses - salvaging parts or all of films and re-editing them from disparate sequences - encourages ironic but also nostalgic critical examination. The nostalgia emerges all the more easily when the film is sepia-toned as in *Take the 5:10 to Dreamland* (1976) and *Valse Triste* (1977). Bruce Conner plays with narrative structure which he manipulates without relying on words.

Starting with *A Movie* (1958) a certain number of elements are already in play which will reappear in one film or another: use of newsreel sequences, a thematic arrangement of the selected sequences, a play of contrast and conflict in the chosen sequences according to varying rhythms. The use of repetition and Academy Leader - *Ten Second Film* (1965) is the archetypal example: it features ten sequences of projection leader, one after another - and in general everything visible to the projectionist but not to the audience, the interruption of the flow of images by black of white leader, flicker as in *Report* -, the use of pre-existing sounds or music, except for *Crossroads* (1976) and *Take the 5:10 to Dreamland* which use original compositions.

The contrasts and provocation in the sequencing or in the images are what connect the early films of Bruce Conner with his sculptures. *A Movie, Cosmic Ray* (1960-62) and *Marilyn Times Five* (1968-73) use, in part or in their entirety, images with sexual connotations, as do certain assemblages: *Black Dahlia* (1960) in which nails are driven into a woman's flesh. A definite encounter between eroticism and death emerges in this work as well as a fascination held by destruction and its portrayal. Thus *Movie* presents a whole anthology of catastrophes, death, conflict, and atomic explosions to the viewer who can only be left stunned by their accumulation. Atomic explosion becomes the subject of a film: *Crossroads*, a strange combination of the fascination and horror of the atomic explosion at Bikini Atoll shown from different angles and at different speeds, forcing us to confront the fascination/repulsion of the recordings. A fascination that the music of Terry Riley reinforces in the way it moves from falsely realistic sounds by Patrick Gleeson to a meditative melody: a repetitive stretch that forces us to contemplate the endless repetitions of the same explosion. We become the victims of an enchantment that we cannot admit to: we pass from the realism of the explosion to its abstraction caused by the stretching out of the recording speed which totally changes our way of understanding the phenomenon, its reality.

IN THE SAME WAY, starting with *Report*, the endlessly deferred repetition of an endlessly rehashed event confirms the displacement that exists between it and its recording or, more exactly, by its restitution by the imposition of a recording. The word "report" signifies both the detonation and reporting in the journalistic sense. The whole film plays with the gap between these two meanings, with the distance that separates the recounting of the event by the narrator's voice and the detonation which implies, explains Kennedy's death, and its coverage by the image that is interposed. The detonation is visually reenacted by a loop of the murder weapon held aloft in a hallway in front of the news media's cameras. The gunshot is never shown on the screen because it was not filmed, we see only the presidential couple before the assassination. The shock of the gunshot is recreated on the screen by the use of a flicker effect which constantly recalls the narrator's voice, the fatal moment: the killing, whose echo is felt through vibrant repetitions. On the screen Academy leader runs interminably in a constantly repeating countdown. The emergence and reconstitution of a life connects, in the second part of the film, with the classic work of Bruce Conner; the sometimes irreverent assemblage of news sequences showing Kennedy on different public occasions with extracts from commercials. This combination starkly illustrates the saturation of media coverage of our culture and the juxtaposition of disparate elements to which it has accustomed us.

Along with these films of criticism, another genre of film can be identified which, even while using the same editing techniques, brings out other meanings by taking a different, more nostalgic , look at the world of the 1950s and 1960s. *Take the 5:10 to Dreamland* is the exact counterpoint to *Crossroads*, made the same year; it seems to offer another vision of the world, an innocent world, an emerging world where the waters do not yet seem to have been troubled. But all the images of the film contain signs of another, darker world, ready to burst forth at the slightest pretext: lap dissolves and slower rhythms allowing other meanings to slip in and cast a veil over the gentle harmony. This film, as well as *Valse Triste*, takes a look at a past not yet afflicted by the accumulation of images of death or catastrophes, an era where the myth of America was still being created and not yet questioned. There was not yet the slightest thought of questioning the tender organization of states and people, despite the possible ravages that adolescence would leave. In fact, with Valse Triste and Take the 5:10 to Dreamland, we are still in a joyous childhood. The other side of this America, not so innocent, even in its child's play will be thoroughly explored in *Mongoloid* (1978) and *America is Waiting* (1981) in which music (by Devo in the former, David Byrne and Brian Eno in the latter) functions as the determinant element in the organization of the sequences. There is no more innocence because the time of ambiguity has begun. It is impossible to assign a single meaning to images, to people, to society. That time has passed as if it had never existed. It is by creating this ambiguity and thus by the possibility of multiple ways of reading and interpreting that the films of Bruce Connor are so relevant today. In fact, there is no longer a single truth, aesthetic, ideology, but a multitude of truths. Recycling and the use of clichéd representations as a means of questioning and diverting.

L'Armateur, n°5, January-February 1993

4

LEN LYE AND LÁSZLÓ MOHOLY-NAGY

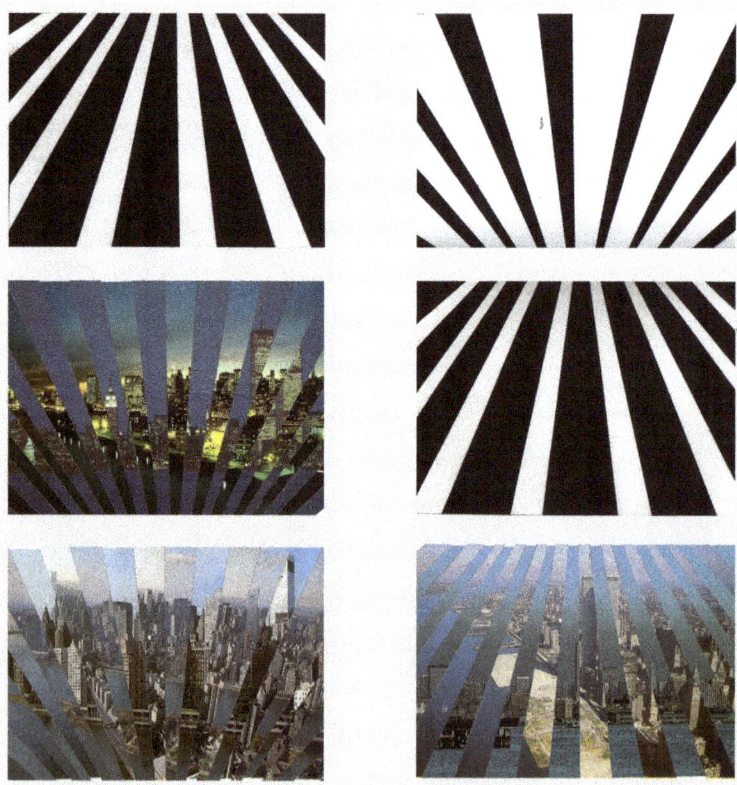

RELATIONS BETWEEN LEN LYE AND LÁSZLÓ MOHOLY-NAGY

Relations Between Len Lye and László Moholy-Nagy

Len Lye and László Moholy-Nagy shared the social and artistic experiences of the same period. As artists, both were polyvalent and worked in different media: painting sculpture, photography, and film. They published numerous texts, more theoretical, pedagogical, in a Constructivist vein in the case of Moholy-Nagy, Lye preferring at certain times a more poetic approach in his rhythms.

They were also both expatriates who had had to leave their native country, (one for political reasons: the fall of the Hungarian Republic in 1920; the other to escape the cultural isolation of New Zealand). They emigrated from one country to another before settling definitively in the 1940s in the U.S. During the 1930s, they were both in London. If they had any direct contact it was through their interactions with the musician and sound engineer that they both worked with: Jack Ellit.

The specificity of their artistic and theoretical predilections constitute two sides of the same coin played out in the context of the art of the 20th century. They embodied two attitudes in relation to art and modernity, to the age of reproduction through the techniques of the means of production and of creation. For Moholy-Nagy, it was the challenge of expressing light, while for Len Lye it was that of making motion the object of artistic creation. In both cases, this quest was pursued whatever the medium they chose.

The question of light as Moholy-Nagy understood it pushed him to develop and attempt to express it through material that effaced as much as possible the intermediaries between the light and the medium that made it visible. In painting, the use of transparencies allowed successive views of a composition to penetrate each other and overlap. The use of a medium such as plastic and metals encouraged reflections and the passage of light across surfaces and forms. It was photography, the art of the photogram (exploited by Moholy-Nagy in the same period as Man Ray) that led him most adequately to express this idea of an art of light. It was thus a question of a constructed, geometric, balanced, rational art, in the field of painting sculpture, and design: an art oriented to collective work, while his photography and films displayed the human side of Moholy-Nagy. By resorting to the anecdote, a sociological aspect develops in his films: it was work that resembled documentary in which by its angles and framing, the same subjects are to be found. The question was whether the photographs were studies for films or if the films were made to facilitate the photograph.

A constructed art, bearing social concerns, transforms the artist's position as it was advocated in the 19th century. This position could no longer be defended at a time of technical transformation not only of production equipment but also of men and, consequently, of their environment without changing the perception of technique and its purposes. In fact, he stated as much: "As production (productive creation) serves mankind and above all its development, we must struggle to adopt the tools (the means) used up to this point for the ends of production to productive ends."

Len Lye had a similar attitude to that of Moholy-Nagy but with the difference that he devoted all his work not to light but to the quest for motion. An important difference in the sense that the energy is the source of motion. Motion is the visual and aural trace of the transmission of energy. This energy manifests itself over time according to a multiplicity of forms and figures, it is rhythmic. So every artistic practice must discover its motion, which means allowing forms and gestures to express themselves, the psychic energy before meaning, before entertainment. To compose motion: this is the idea that explains the creation of direct films, the rayograms that need no camera and kinetic sculpture.

Likewise, Len Lye favors organic forms, those to be found in primitive art of South Pacific culture (he in fact learned about and recopied African and Aboriginal drawings in libraries.[1]) His artistic practice consisted of breaking free of rationalization in order to rediscover the expressive brute force of "our old brain," the one from which energy is not yet imprinted with codes (according to biology, it is the part of the brain which develops first). The quest for this expressivity is actually accompanied by an affirmation of the primacy of gesture over construction and composition. This work disrupts the subject in another way than that of the Constructivists. It erases the civilized subject in favor of the primitive alter ego, the one lodged deep inside us, the one which can express the profound rhythms of the self before the coding and rationalization of civilization. One of the most obvious manifestations of this old brain can be found in tribal art, children's art, graffiti, etc. All types of expression that can be found in the film work and sculpture of Len Lye.

Of course the positions are not as distinct as that, and closer analysis of the films and writings of the two artists reveal that exchanges and mixtures occur.

If Moholy-Nagy's writing on film favors a cinematographic avant-garde as in the book *Painting, Photography, Film* published by the Bauhaus in 1925,[2] it is impossible not to notice that Moholy-Nagy's films have nothing to do with his writings. It is as if there is an enormous gap in the thinking behind them. As if so many years had passed between the promulgation of the ideas and the making of the films that the proposals advocated by the author were no longer up-to-date. He made his first film (*Marseille Vieux Port*) in 1929 (which was the same year as Lye's first film.)

At the moment he wrote *Painting, Photography, Film* (1924), avant-garde cinema offered artists one of the richest fields for experimentation with radical ways of expanding forms through time. It was during this period that Moholy-Nagy developed the scenario *Dynamic of the Metropolis* (1921), a film project which, like many of his others, was never completed.

The design of the scenario for the film owed much to the photomontages and collages that Moholy-Nagy made starting in 1921. It was concerned with the extension of space not of time. And one more point: the scenario used images from disparate sources, reinforcing the idea of a correspondence between Constructivists' photomontage and that of the Dadaists. It extracted different elements in order to produce new arrangements by placing them into other contexts. The montage of graphic rather than cinematographic, it works with the single image on the surface not with sequences and even less with time; Moholy-Nagy did not make films from sequences drawn from here and there (while Len Lye did just that). He applied diverse techniques of pictorial collage (from Braque to Picasso) and of photomontage (Hausmann, Schwitters) elevated by the importance he attached to typography, to reinforce the key elements of the page compositions.

Even if his most theoretical writing preceded his actual filmmaking, in the 1930s (in an open letter sent to *Sight and Sound* in 1932[3]) and 1940s (in a chapter of film in *Vision in Motion*, 1947), he nevertheless always defended the idea of an avant-garde cinema as an artistic as much as an economic necessity, to insure the development of the medium itself; a similar idea was extolled by Len Lye in 1959 in the U.S.

LÁSZLÓ MOHOLY-NAGY

Today the list of films made by László Moholy-Nagy still stands at seven. The film *Tönendes ABC* (1932) has still not been found. Most of his films concern cities and architecture or human activity. There is only one exception, *Lichtspiel* (1930), in which he filmed his "Light-Space Modulator," his light-reflecting sculpture. This work certainly owes much to the light projections of Ludwick Hirschfeld-Mack and Kurt Schwerdtfeger created at the Bauhaus in the 1920s (1921-1923) in which luminous colored forms move across a wall according to a fixed scenario and which became, with Alexander László, a visualization of color and sound.

MOST OF MOHOLY-NAGY'S films were made outside the film industry and financed by himself (the first four) or through commissions (the last three). There is however one exception: the special effects sequences commissioned from Moholy-Nagy

in England in 1936 for the film *Things to Come* (William Menzies) and which were eliminated in the final editing.[1]

. . .

IN *BERLINER STILLEBEN*, *Marseille Vieux Port*, *Grosstadt Zigeuner* (1932), can be found the framing, the angles, the dynamics, the compositional lines of certain photographs that Moholy-Nagy had been making earlier or at the same time (see the photographs of gutters in Marseille, the aerial shots of the streets of Berlin and Marseille, the close-ups of gypsies' faces in *Grosstadt Zigeuner*). Another obvious characteristic of these films is the play of light, with grays and contrasts, the contrast between lighted courtyards at the end of dark entranceways (in *Berliner*), dark interiors and over-exposed exteriors, the play of shadows of workers (*Marseille*), the play of street lights accentuating shadows (*Grosstadt Zigeuner*) or erasing them (*Berliner*), etc. All this qualifying of light and the expressive possibilities that it implies reinforces the concern for social issues in his city films. For the avant-garde, city films (city symphonies) became a genre unto itself (Strand, Ruttmann, Vertov, Chomette, Ivens, Kirsanov, Vigo, etc.). But nevertheless the city films of Moholy-Nagy are different in the sense that they do not offer a day in the life of a city but rather a collection of particular notes which highlight certain prominent aspects of daily life. The films do not illustrate the day in the life of a city, their rhythm is not accelerated and syncopated, but slow. The rhythm is fluid, objects move within the frame, the speed of their movement is respected.[2] The camera does not capture multiple points of view, the rhythm is not broken up. The fragmentation is effectuated by the framing as in a photograph with the foreground cut out. The fluidity of motion inside the frame and the recurrence of several motifs evoke melodic verses and make his films almost musical compositions.

NEVERTHELESS, his work is more reminiscent of Vertov in the sense that social issues predominate through the juxtaposition of man and machine. In *Marseille Vieux Port* a sequence underlines Moholy-Nagy's adherence to the modernist tradition. In the sequence of the "pont transbordeur" (aerial ferry bridge), can be found the formal play of inhuman metallic construction in motion. The realistic framing revealing the bridge's mechanics recall *De Brug* (The Bridge) made by Joris Ivens in 1928), but at the same time the choice of the subject in the film only emphasizes the Modernism which celebrates the advent of the machine and the man-machine. The abstraction of this sequence contrasts with the realistic daily scenes of the city. The fluid operation of the bridge is a counterpoint to the squalor of Marseille. The operation of the aerial ferry bridge is not shown as it is in Joris Ivens' film where all of the mechanical details of the machine are shown. In Moholy-Nagy's film, the bridge allows Marseille to be seen in another way. In dynamic contrast to the forms and lights of the bridge are the dark, grey sequences, showing poverty and misery, the dirtiness of a large part of Marseille and its population. In this way the sharp, well-defined shots are contrasted with bodies, waste, and garbage.

THERE IS a similar sequence in his film on the architecture of the London Zoo where the demonstration of the mechanical elements which rotate the gorilla cage are a reminder of Moholy-Nagy's fascination with machines.

BY THESE CONTRASTS, Moholy-Nagy uses the documentary film as a means of social and political activism. He aligns himself with the German and Soviet avant-garde but also with social criticism as it is presented in a more narrative way by Ernö Metzner in *Überfall* (1929). Cinema, becoming a political instrument, denounces the separation between man and machine (in fact, no human activities are visible on the aerial ferry bridge). He approaches industrialization from a Marxist viewpoint and does not mix in aesthetic genres. There is no particular formal intervention on the image whereas Len Lye in *Trade Tattoo* made frenetic commercial and industrial activity correspond to color and numerous image manipulations. In this case there is no criticism just observation and a celebration of the speed of trade. With Moholy-Nagy, a distance is maintained. There is no manipulation of the images as there are in the photo collages (the juxtaposition of the general filth in the streets and port in contrast with the cold elegance of the bridge), the slow rhythm and the juxtaposition of objects empowers the criticism (it is not derision in the French tradition such as in the way Vigo viewed Nice). With Len Lye, on the contrary, the viewer is drawn into the object. The visual treatment only reinforces the dynamic to be promoted, which is also the objective of the film's "propaganda;" in one case the slow rhythm raises a consciousness of mankind's inability to adapt to its world; in the other it is a piece of advertising for parcel delivery by the British Royal Mail. *Marseille* and *Grosstadt Zigeuner* seem to participate in the tendency of 1900s filmmaking to refrain from an exploration of the potential of the filmic image in favor of the use of film as a means of awakening political consciousness.

IN THE FACE of the financial crisis and the rise of economic, political and social unrest, filmmakers seem to have retreated into more traditional forms.[3] This retreat was reinforced by the advent of sound films and the progressive disappearance of funding for independent production. This evolution parallels the return to more ordered structures in the visual arts and music. So efficiency was sought in film which, all things considered, paralleled certain theoretical preconceptions to be found both with the Constructivists and at the Bauhaus, namely "a creative work strives to establish a harmony with a new social order and to instill a balance between the human world and the technological one."[4]

IN PARALLEL TO THESE PREOCCUPATIONS, the film *Lichtspiel* (1930) appears to be the only attempt by Moholy-Nagy to create truly abstract cinema that worked with light and not pigment, to use his own terms.

· · ·

IN A STILL-FAMOUS ARTICLE *The Problems of Modern Film* (1928),[5] he identified the elements of film: vision, motion, sound. The psychological content, which he left to the Surrealists, did not interest him, he preferred to work with light itself. Thus did *Lichtspiel* operate, producing, from its "Modulator," a first approach to what would become a cinema of light and movement. Again, the paradox was the obvious gap between the written theory and the film. Indeed, the text of the article stated that film must work from projection and the reflection of light and not of pigment, that film itself must lead to motion in space. But *Lichtspiel* in no way embodies this theory. It is, on the contrary, a creative recording of the "Light-Space Modulator." All of the effects of transparence, of mirroring, of the play of surfaces absorbing and reflecting light come from the recording of the sculpture in motion, except in what relates to the high contrast negatives and superimpositions. It is not the film which produces the light effects but the machine itself: the editing, the superimpositions and the kaleidoscopic shots (which can be found also in *Ballet mécanique*, 1924, by Léger and Murphy), the variations in depth of field represent an abstract cinema based on a machine recording, but it is not a "tabula rasa" like the one used by Malevitch in painting. As Barbara Rose quite rightly remarks,[6] Moholy-Nagy works with black, white and grey in the manner of the Cubists. The film, highly sculptural, permits a glimpse of what a cinema of research could be.

GROSSTADT ZIGEUNER WAS MADE under difficult conditions and offers a slice of the life of gypsies in Berlin. As in earlier city films, Moholy-Nagy is able to evoke daily life with diverse objects or actions (rags floating in the wind...) He goes as far as sketching the feeling of exclusion by showing in short sequences the gypsies' separation from the rest of the city (for example the sale of horses in the street and also the reactions of passersby to the fortune tellers). The last sequence of dancing is spectacular: it portrays, through jerky but nevertheless slow editing, the dancers and their accentuated shadows on the ground with the details of their gestures: faces, violin players, dance steps.

IN 1933, he made a special film, *Architektur Kongress*, a film journal of the voyage of architects to the International Congress of Modern Architecture in Athens. This film again abandons all experimental intentions in favor of those of a proficient amateur filmmaker. It is not so much a classic documentary as a journal of the congress participants' trip to the Athens conference. After a studious evocation of the first days which offer views of all the great modern architects giving speeches, the film turns to relaxation and tourism, showing modernist villas and monuments of antiquity.

MOHOLY-NAGY WOULD MAKE two more films in England, *The Life of the Lobster* (1936) and *The New Architecture at London Zoo* (1936). These two films seem to go even further from the cinema of experimentation which he advocated in the direction of educational filmmaking. The film on lobsters recalls the rules of documentary followed by John Grierson in *Drifters* (1929). For Grierson, the fishermen were the main subject whereas Moholy-Nagy contrasts the fishermen with their prey: lobsters. The film features framing that recalls that used by Moholy-Nagy or Rodchenko when they photographed cities. Using contrasting diagonals and key elements (as in the sequence of the boat returning to port).

LEN LYE

Len Lye began making films in 1929 in London at the beginning of the sound film era. His first film *Tusalava* revolutionized animation imagery already dominated by cartoons at the time. The title of the film, which means "just the same" in Samoan, is illustrated by the fact that the pointed and circular forms at the beginning of the film appear again at the end. With this first film, in a still superficial way, Len Lye makes representational elements dance. The forms he uses are organic and in the spirit of motifs used by Australian Aborigines and Samoans.[1] These organic forms are in contrast to all of the experimental animation of the time: Eggeling, Richter, Fischinger and Ruttmann, who favored geometric forms, stark contrasts, and syncopated rhythms. Lye's film, while it uses the techniques of classical animation, disrupts, by the linear development of its drawing and its progressive pulsation, the animation which up to that time was dominated by notions of objective art. It should be noted that Lye was inspired by primitive forms which allowed him to access what he called his "primitive brain." He aimed to promote the affirmation of primitive forms of art, the artistic expressions closest to its energy and movement before it was polished.[2] His second film was made six years later in the film unit directed by John Grierson of the British General Post Office. This cinematographic section was a formidable production unit which nurtured the British documentary movement throughout the 1930s and 1940s. Basil Wright, Alberto Cavalcanti, Humphrey Jennings, John Grierson, and Norman McLaren were among its important members.

Colour Box (1935) was one of the first "direct" films that have survived to this day. Direct meant made without a camera. Of course the Dadaists - Man Ray with *Retour à la Raison* (1923) had made a film from his rayograms - and other filmmakers had included parts of rayograms, hand-painted frames, etc., in their films, but up to then no filmmaker had made color films without the help of a camera. Lye painted directly on the celluloid film. He rapidly became aware of all the advantages he could obtain from this discovery and how it was eminently suited to his quest for an art of motion. Indeed he did not need to reproduce and respect the configuration of objects. He sought motion. To express it as well as possible, he preferred to work quickly and employ doodles, scrawls or automatic drawing resembling the automatic writing of the Surrealists, which enabled him to avoid rationalization in favor of graphic dynamism. Lye painted arabesques along the film strip which gave his colored composition a trembling quality that recalled the transmission of energy as he perceived it.

With *Colour Box*, he made lines and fields of color dance. Several techniques were used: stretching out, combing color, scratching on the film once the painting was dry, applying stencils of forms and texts onto color backgrounds. A montage organizing these elements was then created. To this dance of color he added text and music; these films were made on commission for the G.P.O. and used as advertising.

Lye always added popular music to his films in order to reinforce their choreographic aspect. It was not a question of presenting a visualization of the music but simply to make the visual image dance. The music came afterwards, as a form of resonance. The synchronization between the music and the images gave supremacy to the image.[3] He uses popular music, blues, jazz. The selections are highly rhythmic, danceable, full of energy and reminded Lye of the energy he found in tribal dances.

After his first direct film, Lye developed new tools and diversified his approach, mixing different techniques in his film work. *Colour Box* and *Kaleidoscope* (1935) changed the course of animated film and showed that it was not necessary to respect the classical norms of cinematography to make films. *Kaleidoscope* displays marvelous oppositions to textures and colors. In this film, Lye plays with the width of the strips of color that he paints. He contrasts the delicate forms of stencils (stars, bars...) multiplying the effects of transparency, with rougher, almost flat fields of color applied directly to the filmstrip. At the beginning of the film, Lye uses the perforations as a stencil and has them run laterally across the entire surface of the screen.

These films seem to illustrate what Moholy-Nagy said about the creative use of new technology but they do it in another way: Len Lye has an intuitive approach, his actions or methods are not scientific in the way recommended by Moholy-Nagy at the Bauhaus.

Lye did not want to repeat himself: from one film to another he tried to do something different. Thus he animated objects, figurines, cars and robots in flamboyant decors in *The Birth of a Robot* (1936) for *Schell* (a highly kitsch piece of classical music accompanying a kitsch parody of an enchanted world). Then, before working with Gaspacolor, a three-color film process, one of the systems of color film production - a system that Oskar Fischinger helped to develop in Germany - he made a film with characters. It was a commissioned film in which Lye tried to dispense with the editing techniques that had been developed by D.W. Griffith: "I wanted to get away from D.W. Griffith's technique. In my opinion, all film has obeyed Griffith."[4] In *N. or N.W.* (1937), a film commissioned to describe the mishaps of a love letter caused by an erroneous postal code, Lye opts for a sequence of shots that transform a bedroom floor into a sidewalk on which the heroine walks. By this means, Lye aims to short-circuit the concrete naturalism established by the editing technique of Griffith. Unfortunately, this sequence which strayed too far from realism, was removed by the G.P.O. when the film was distributed. It was also in this film that he used a weaving together of superimposition and repetition using different angles in order to evoke the lovers' expectations and attempts at reconciliation.

With *Rainbow Dance* (1936) and *Trade Tattoo* (1937), he opened new territories to film by radically transforming the appearance of filmed sequences by manipulating the three layers of color in the Gaspacolor process. With these films, Lye perfected the technique of the optical printer which permits sequences to be colored either entirely or in isolation and to manipulate the elements of an image by recoloring each differently by using selective mattes. His system of mattes was more elaborate than the one used by Moholy-Nagy in *Marseille* where the city is animated in the center of a map. Thus in *Rainbow Dance* and *Trade Tattoo* black and white sequences become sepia-toned and serve as a background in front of which a character, object, or colored motif moves with a different color tone or thickness. It should be noted that Gasparcolor required that the same scene be filmed three times in black and white, each time with a different filter: yellow, red, blue. In this way pure bidimensional colors were obtained on predetermined forms which develop within a tri-dimensional decor (see the sequence of a tennis player in *Rainbow Dance*)[5] Certain visual effects produced by Len Lye evoke paintings by Duchamp-Villon or Man Ray, while others recall or anticipate the results of the color photographic experiments carried out by Moholy-Nagy and the New Bauhaus in the 1930s and 1940s (photographs made with the Dufay process). The color in motion passes from pictorial to cinematic to almost kinetic.

In *Rainbow Dance*, colors are used spatially while in the earlier films they dance on the surface of the film; despite several superimpositions made by stencils, there are no volume or depth effects. In *Rainbow Dance*, color plays with space, it is the motion counterpart of photographic representation. The color makes itself independent of the subjects filmed, taking away their naturalistic configurations to bring them into the cinematographic realm: a Pop use of color. There is a skillful contrast between pure acidic colors, and the pastel tones of the backgrounds or stencils. Color takes flight and shatters figuration. This characteristic will be accentuated in *Trade Tattoo*.

This film opens with 35mm film glued onto the filmstrip which sweeps from left to right across the screen, almost like an echo of the colored arabesques of *Color Box*. By this introduction, Lye indicates that *Trade Tattoo* is concerned above all with the components of film as much at the physical level : the filmstrip, perforations, as at the level of what is shown in the image: shots and sequences. In this film, Len Lye did not himself shoot the sequences that he would use but dips into the reservoir of G.P.O. images. He would take documentary images and intensively rework them; either by using them in negative or by the coloration of positives, or by the addition of stenciled geometric motifs, the texts, almost like watchwords, are much better integrated than in the earlier films. Their appearance, their frequency, their size are closely related to the rhythm of the film because of the very tight editing. This montage highlights the sequences either by the editing (jump cuts which chop up the continuity of a single action or of the narration and which he will illustrate with *Rhythm* in 1957), or by the superimpositions in associating motion inside the image with parallel movement of colored geometrical motifs and texts which sweep across and sometimes scan the image. Thus an impression of a sweeping fluidity, a perpetual oscillation is produced by the montage, emphasized by the appearance of colors and geometrical motifs which seem to chase after time, burning away the image on behalf of the rhythm of commercial remarks that the film promotes. It is in this way that he gets rid of the reference to Griffith whose techniques of montage have become the obligatory norm of all cinematographic grammar. These animated films were also a rejection of the realistic animation of Disney which was beginning to become the inevitable model for the production of all animated films. He would make a few more experimental animated films including *Musical Poster* (1940) in which politics and resistance to the Nazis constituted the main theme expressed through original graphics mixing drawings, letters, and signs. During the Second World War, he would make a large number of documentaries for the British War Office for the *March of Time* series. Among these, *Kill or Be Killed* (1942) in which Lye has an ambushed German sharp-shooter confront a British soldier, deserves mention as does the compilation film *Cameraman at War* (1943).

It was only after moving to the U.S. that he resumed making films. *Colour Cry* (1952) returned to a systematic use of rayograms in attempting to multiply the textures and transparency effects of substances that move in opposite ways. A few years later, he made two important films for different reasons. The first Rhythm was a one-minute condensation using jump cuts of a 90 minute documentary on the making of a car on the Chrysler assembly lines. It is almost a work of recycling, but the diversion is effectuated through time and not by the contrasting of scenes: shortening of sequences to create a dynamism in the montage in reference to the assembly line as much to the film. Len Lye's next-to-last film, *Free Radicals* (1958, re-edited in 1979), uses a minimum of visual components. The entire film is made up of scratches directly on film (black leader) using different tools. This film as well as *Particles in Space* (1979) still constitute one of the highest achievements of film art, in which an economy of means combines with a power and majesty of execution. Out of simple scratches he opens depths and fields of energy which up to that time only his kinetic sculpture had achieved: *Fountain* and *Rotating Harmony*, in the 1960s exploited the spinning and vibration of bands of metal, thus creating, depending on the speed of rotation, motions and flashes of light resembling those of his films.

But it was not easy. "The other day, I was experimenting with forms coming out of abstract scribbling for a film I was making. The forms were vibrant dots and lines which were spinning around, pulsating, undulating, and hitting the screen in a repetitive way. I didn't have the slightest idea what they could be, so I called them energy particles in space, but God only knows what sort of energy particles they were." Films which, by their minimalism, could recall certain later works of structural film, but which in fact stand in contrast to it by their gestures and lyricism. It is not a systematic world but one of freely affirmed energy. In these two films, Len Lye pushes the logic of direct film to its limit, drawing luminous energy of motion out of the shadows. Once again, certain connections between Len Lye and László Moholy-Nagy are visible, but as opposites. One seems to accomplish in the field of film what the other advocates theoretically. In these two films, the composition of the soundtrack is vital in the sense that it allows the image, the beat and the rhythms not to be repeated, but to be offset by something corporal. In this circumstance, in the case of *Particles in Space*, the African percussions become the support for the luminous particles. Here again the cinema of Len Lye favors motion which is always connected in one way or another to the body, to its expression through dance, to its motion.

Confronted with the incredible difficulties he encountered to make experimental films, Len Lye decided in a famous text, *Is Film Art?*,[6] to go on strike and make no more films until an institution agreed to fund him. This strike and the declarations that accompanied it recall what László Moholy-Nagy had already said in 1937. From the 1960s on, Len Lye concentrated even more on sculpture.

If many things separate László Moholy-Nagy and Len Lye, the fact nevertheless remains that the cinema of one truly seems to have accomplished visually the expectations of the other; in fact Len Lye worked on motion and light in an immediate, instinctive way and, in doing so, differed from Moholy-Nagy whose cinema favored political awareness. But Lye refused the naturalism and realism and was more interested in the expressive possibilities of film. In this sense, he could not subscribe to conventionally made cinema even though he had made many advertising films. With these two artists and their film work there seems to be in play the never-ending contrast in modern art oscillating between the objective and the subjective. The creation of one does not prevent that of another. A paradox which results in experimental art not always being on the side of the disciples of a constructed art. Nevertheless, both call for and demand an amateur cinema opposed to industry and commerce in order to encourage the flowering of film art.

Geneva, Ma Dai/Fonction : Cinéma, 1992

5

GAY CINEMA

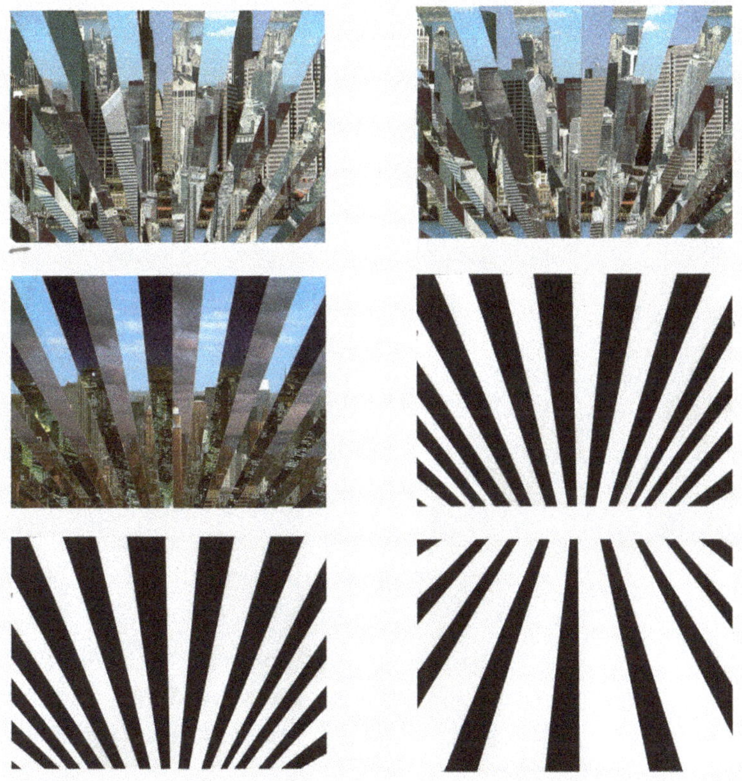

A HOMAGE TO MARIO MONTEZ

This program centered around Mario Montez is above all a homage to one of the actors who, like Taylor Mead, put his stamp on the American underground under the banner of camp. He was a (shooting) star of underground cinema, and, above all, one of the first American drag queens of the 1960s.

An essential figure in the cinema since 1963, he first appeared in Jack Smith's *Flaming Creatures* (1963) under the name of Dolores Flores and would subsequently become one of Smith's muses. He was unforgettable in the role of the mermaid bathing in a giant seashell in *Normal Love* (1964) by the same filmmaker. He could be found again in *Chumlum* (1964) by Ron Rice which was made with the costumed actors of Jack Smith's film. Mario and Jack were fervent promoters of the Mexican actress Maria Montez and her world to which Jack Smith would consecrate several essays.

Mario went on to appear in many Warhol films: *The Life of Juanita Castro* (1965), *Mario Banana* (1964), *Hedy* (1966), *More Milk Yvette* (1966) and *Harlot* (1964), *Camp* (1965). The life of Lupe Velez and above all her death seemed to have been scripted for the underground. Montez can be found in the extraordinary *Lupe* (1966) by Jose Rodriguez Soltero, of which Warhol had made another version a few months earlier with Edie Sedgwick (*Lupe*, 1965).

Montez played marvelously with ambiguity, parody, and caricature. Like all drag queens, he knew how to distill with remarkable skill the most perverse mimicry with total candor and innocence. His presence was the manifestation of a performance. It harkened back to silent film in the sense that it exaggerated, emphasized, or isolated certain traits that were characteristic of the pose or attitudes of a character. A piece of cloth, accidentally misplaced could have consequences that were, at the very least tragic. It was necessary to deploy a singular skill to taste a banana, the hungry look anticipating an unforgettable blow job.

Great art consists of equipping oneself with the bare minimum to bring to life an epoch, a character. Everything is manipulated to the benefit of a minimal presentation, close to that of a scene by Paul Swan who, by just the suggestion of a dance step, conjured up a period, an atmosphere. This is what is shown so well by the film that Warhol made about him (*Paul Swan*, 1965), and in which the choreographer attempts from a few pieces of clothing, jewelry and shoes, to summon up the spirit of his performances in the 1920s. In any case, whether it is Paul Swan, Mario Montez, or Francis Francine....it is not the fidelity to an image which counts, but the power of evocation which bursts from the taking on of each role through transvestism. In the theater of Jack Smith is to be found this capacity to recycle artifice and cast-offs in order to create a human type, an atmosphere.

The force of the performance is held by our adhesion to such codes. We enter into the camp of pure theatricality. Playing with genres and sexual codes produces an oscillation within the genre that nevertheless has nothing to do with androgyny, but more of a constant wavering from one to the other, from one between the other, to one against the other.

Several effects: a platinum blonde wig, the movement of a leg, the linger of a kiss; in total, nothing more natural and yet artifice still rules.

A figure unfortunately little known by today's generation, Mario

Montez, like Candy Darling, was one of the first drag queens during a time when drag was not yet a fashion phenomenon, nor yet completely a way of life.

New version in French, January 1998
1st version in English:
Mix 97,11th New York Lesbian and Gay Experimental Film/Video Festival,
New York, 1997

CINEMATIC REPRESENTATION BEFORE AND SINCE THE APPEARANCE OF AIDS

The outbreak of the epidemic found in photography, film, and video its appropriate media for the elaboration of a whole series of representations of AIDS. Flexible, efficient, these media are part of a tradition deployed in the field of art and agitprop or in the field of journalism in the form of documentary or eyewitness accounts. Nevertheless, however they are used, these works bring together and articulate the notions of the public and private spheres. Because of this, since the appearance of AIDS, the treatment of sexuality on the screen has been radically transformed.

If before AIDS, the representation of gay and lesbian sexuality entered into narrative film in a metaphoric or allegorical way - Cocteau, Visconti, Paradjanov - it never invaded this domain in the way it did experimental film. In the *underground* film, the creation of a gay iconography emerged from the free portrayal of sexuality. This cinema opened a space which prefigured (while facilitating) politically-engaged filmmaking which, for its part, addressed and caused to be addressed sexuality before daring to show it. At the end of the 1960s, Rosa von Praunheim, Lionel Soukaz, Barbara Hammer and Jan Oxenburg were among the filmmakers who propelled this transition...They became the voice of a minority with all of the paradoxes which this role conferred. Several years later there would be other manifestations with the works of Isaac Julian, Pratibha Parmar, Marlon Riggs, Richard Fung, Greta Schiller and Andrea Weiss, Monika Treut and Stuart Marshall.

There is a correspondence between the eruption of a cinematography which finds itself, on the one hand, in an ambiguous position relative to traditional narrative codes and, on the other hand, asserts its difference. This freedom in the forms employed registers a protest and consequently promotes a cinema of the body. The body is no longer policed but sexualized. In fact, cinema represented what up to that time (the end of the 1950s) would not suffer representation: drugs, sex, death, etc. The cinematographic tool as a means of denouncing social norms, purveyor of an iconography which authorized every minority to master its images. Instead of submitting to representations (clichés, negation), the filmmakers created images which they would have liked to see and affirmed their desires. In this way there appeared the films of Kenneth Anger, Gregory J. Markopoulos, Jean Genet, Jack Smith, Andy Warhol, Werner Schroeter, Ulrike Ottinger...Fertile soil which permitted other generations of filmmakers to perpetuate a history by constituting the "Queer Cinema" which included Derek Jarman, Isaac Julien, Marlon Rigg, Pratibha Parmar, Tom Kalin, Todd Haynes, John Grierson.

This phenomenon of Queer developed after the appearance of AIDS. It was necessary to turn the anathema upside-down, create other images, other discourses, create a filmmaking of opposition, of protest. Instead of allowing themselves to be smothered, filmmakers and videomakers protested and made other words heard. Likewise, the appearance of AIDS brought an over-consumption of images of the body, as if to oppose the suffering, as if the pleasures of the body could be given by their representation rather than by acts. A movement towards a new sexuality which would use the image as a fundamental tool. Likewise the use of consumer video recorders made possible the home consumption of pornography, driving out the gay porno theater as a place of exchanges and pleasure. A movement which found an echo in the individual production of video-cassettes, which themselves resupplied the circuit.

From the *underground* to the sphere of the individual, by way of the eruption of activism, the cinema produced a face-off between two ways of representing homosexuality: one positive, joyously forthright, the other unhealthy, anxiety-ridden under the yoke of conventional intolerance. Simultaneously between these two poles there developed a school of documentary seeking to write (or rewrite) our history. Thus, at the end of the 1960s and at the beginning of the 1980s, documents, personal accounts of other eras proliferated while the affirmation and the demands were not possible according to contemporary norms. These films and videos addressed all aspects of life and served as models. One could cite *Black Star The Autobiography of a Close Friend* (1977) by Tom Joslin, *Race d'Ep* (1980) by Guy Hocquenghem and Lionel Soukaz, *Word is Out* (1978) by the Mariposa Film Group, *Before Stonewall* (1985) by Greta Shiller and Andrea Weiss and, in a certain way, *Taxi Zum Klo* (1980) by Frank Ripploh, or *It Is Not the Homosexual Who Is Perverse, But the Society in Which He Lives* (1971) by Rosa von Praunheim.

In most of these films, the sexual practices are shown more or less directly. Sexuality is triumphant in the sense that it has the right to be visible. Pleasure, ecstasy is no longer excluded. The screen is occupied by representations which are no longer obscured.

Nevertheless, it was rare for filmmakers to announce themselves as gay as did Fassbinder, von Praunheim or Jarman. The outbreak of the epidemic encouraged coming out and the creation of a number of documents which questioned sexual practices as much as the way they were represented. AIDS became a vast battleground of images. First-person accounts, intimate journals, documents were closely aligned with militant films which sought to create a more aggressive iconography to represent the epidemic. Thus the Gay Mens' Health Crisis group and its video and the use of the dental dam or David Wojnarowicz who blew up the barriers between genres by making images and stories collide in off-screen narration. In the same way Gregg Bordowitz with *Fast Trip, Long Drop* (1994) also made genres collide by offering his reflections on the disease and his relations with the world, history and personal history.

In the face of AIDS, one can no longer keep silent about sexuality; it is unavoidable; from now on it invades the whole realm of representation and bursts out at every moment, like desire. This affirmation of sexuality in all of contemporary creation means that its presentation today involves major struggles in the production and distribution of works both from an economic and from a moral point of view. Every manifestation (representation) of sexuality (for "sexuality" read "homosexuality") is almost never taken seriously anymore (if not denounced outright as propaganda). This encourages the outbreak of a new, even more radical, alternative.

It is in this way that the diversity of productions concerning AIDS must be understood. Filmmakers would gradually concentrate on another aspect, militancy (the Gran Fury group, etc.), first person accounts (*Sylver Lake*,1993, by Tom Joslin and Peter Friedman, *La Pudeur et l'Impudeur*, 1993, by Hervé Guibert), stories (*Zero Patience*,1993, by John Grierson, *Les Nuit fauves*, 1992, by Cyril Collard, *The Last Supper*, 1995, by Cynthia Roberts ...), essays (*Non, je ne regrette rien*, 1992, by Marlon Riggs, *The Last of England*, 1988, and *Blue*,1992, by Derek Jarman). This last category became one of the most stimulating of contemporary film because it laid out new possibilities of seeing and thinking.

2e Festival de films gays et lesbiens de Paris, Paris, American Center, 1995

KENNETH ANGER, GREGORY MARKOPOULOS, AND JEAN GENET

It is by their subjects and their treatment that these three figures can be hastily associated. Two of them are primarily filmmakers while the third made only one film. They belong to a generation of artists who found a way to create visual art touching on or dealing with the theme of homosexuality; the understanding and approach to this theme was carried out through a questioning of the medium. The affirmation of a rarely tolerated marginality was accompanied simultaneously by the creation of new forms of cinematographic storytelling which ho longer had anything to do with traditional narrative modes. They were, each in his own way, those who affirmed homosexual desire in a poetic way. Each filmmaker created a singular work which broke with the moral consensus and offered a vision of otherness and excess: affirmation of a sexuality which, by its lack of representation, invented new cinematographic forms.

IF THE FILMS of American filmmakers pre-date the one of Jean Genet, they have the particularity of works of youth which reflect desire in all of its urgency. Thus *Fireworks* (1947) by Kenneth Anger imagines the dream of a meeting with sailors and conveyed in a certain way the dreamlike influence that the films of Jean Cocteau were able to employ, principally in *Le Sang d'un poète* (1930). Made in the form of a fantasy, the film did not have to respect narrative logic. The functioning of dreams can be found in the form of superimpositions and cuts which jump from one shot to another according to patterns that have nothing to do with linearity. Sliding from one shot to another, the camera caresses bodies in a situation where the young man seals his destiny by his meeting with the sailors.

In another way Du sang, de la volupté et de la mort (1947-1948) Gregory J. Markopoulos employs his story and the filmmaker's difference as much as that of the protagonists. He uses visual strategies that radically differ from those used by Kenneth Anger. Indeed he prefers close-ups into order to make his subjects abstract, varying his shooting angles composing a kaleidoscope of shot movements that will be intertwined one after another in order to produce an economy and integrality of action. A disruptive cinema which marks its difference in the treatment of narration and whose themes themselves disrupt social norms. Here again the subject leads to the creation of new forms.

While Jean Genet made *Un chant d'amour* (1951) he was perceived as a pariah on the French film scene; his film was considered at the time as pornography. It was more in the tradition of *Fireworks* than of *The Dead Ones* (1949), the film that Markopoulos dedicated to Jean Cocteau, to the extent that he showed nude bodies embracing. Desire blossoms, in spite of fantastical signs. It is shown as being consummated and henceforth characterized as sulphurous and subversive, the definition of roles and their assignment in a prison environment, between inmates and guards tend to prefigure a particular iconography used by Kenneth Anger in *Scorpio Rising* (1963).

. . .

With this film, the domain of song gives way to a convulsive space in which an intense struggle between Eros and Thanatos is enacted. The rhythm of the film intervenes to emphasize the preparation rituals of the bikers and in particular Scorpio, for a party. The film explores the ambivalence between fascination and repulsion through provocation by painting a portrait of a gang of bikers and their sado-masochistic rites. The fascination is exerted through the recognizable codes and specific language of minority groups. This "meta-language" was favored to represent homosexuality in a kind of film which was in itself outside the norms - experimental. This affirmation of a sexual practice found its equivalent in the productions of a kind of filmmaking which could only be subversive in its forms.

Was there not a paradox in the wish to unite filmmakers under the same flag based on their sexuality, their race, or their sexual identity? Does not this understanding carry a germ of the creation of false exemplariness which, in its turn, permits the creation of other exclusions? The aesthetic of these three filmmakers is as different as the values that each of them defend. They express three modes of desire and sexuality which, because it is homosexual, should be equivalent. But it is nothing of the sort. The aesthetic advocated by Markopoulos has nothing to do with that of Genet, Anger, Warhol, or Smith. Each is about something different. Markopoulos bases a part of his aesthetic on Greek mythology and classical stories (*Swain*, 1950, *Himself as Herself*, 1967, *Twice A Man*, 1963, *Psyche*, 1947), from which he wished to fashion a new art: film. This attempt was accompanied by the singular use of the single frame (*Gamellion*, 1968, *Hagiographia*, 1st version, 1970), superimpositions in the camera (*Sorrows*, 1968, *Bliss*, 1967), the play of colors (*Du sang, de la volupté et de la mort*, *The Illiac Passion*...). The whole domain of cinema is questioned by Markopoulos who in this way over the years develops a song, a poetry, by the means of silent images and according to a wholly classical aesthetic. Nothing in his visual approach is really new; it is the subject of the film, the transgressed taboo, which brings it into the domain of experimental cinema. Anger often enacts rites: *Scorpio Rising, Invocation of My Demon Brother* (1969), or even *K.K.K.* (1964). In each he plays with the codes of the representation of desire.

THESE THREE FILMMAKERS focus on homosexual desire, but each in his own way. Without them "Queer Cinema," which questions sexual identity and gender, would not have been able to propagate itself.

DEREK JARMAN

Derek Jarman died of complications of AIDS on 19 February 1994, he was 51. The disappearance of this polyvalent artist deprived British film of one its most innovative creators. Indeed, for twenty years Derek Jarman had defied the dominant genres of experimental and industrial film of his time.

From 1963 to 1967, after studies at the Slade, he seemed destined for a brilliant future as a painter in "swinging sixties" London. He belonged to a new generation of openly homosexual artists, such as David Hockney or Patrick Proctor, who were progressively transforming British society. He had little by little become the *enfant terrible*, in the use he made of film. In fact, his palette was vast, from intimist films to independent commercial productions to music videos. It was the same for his homosexuality, moving from simple affirmation to an activism reinforced by his being seropositive which he publically declared as soon as he learned of it, in 1986.

After having designed decors for ballet and opera, he discovered film not only as the set designer for *The Devils* (1973) by Ken Russell, but also as a filmmaker, beginning with the making of Super 8 film journals initially intended just for a circle of friends. It was in 1970 that he made his first *home movies*: the quintessence of his cinema starting in 1973, for he would constantly draw new projects from this breeding tank according to the circumstances and where they were projected. His last work *Glitterbug* (1994), with a soundtrack by Brian Eno, presented an intense condensation of his journals which, over time, had become increasingly sophisticated.

With his Super 8 films, Jarman reaffirmed his affinities with *underground* film, a provocative, romantic, unconstrained cinema. This first period culminated in the film *In the Shadow of the Sun* (1974, shown publically in 1980), in which a succession of sequences drawn from earlier work, highly grainy with slow motion and jerky superimpositions. Lyrical, dream-like, sensual visions in stark contrast to the rigor and austerity of the structural and materialist British cinema dominant at the time.

With *Sebastiane* (1976) and *The Tempest* (1979) he seemed to have abandoned personal film for the sake of stories, those of the martyr Saint Sebastian, of the Shakespeare play. He finds in them an interpretation that centers on masculine sexuality and homosexual desire. The presentation of such desire encourages another way to imagine the life and work of several famous figures such as *Caravaggio* (1986), *Edward II* (1991) as seen by Christopher Marlowe, and *Wittgenstein* (1992). These more conventional films are in no way contradictory with his more intimist film work which explore other means of expression. The difficulty of finding producers for his larger scale work (it took him more than seven years to make *Caravaggio*) led him to create a cinema of "small gestures," an intimist cinema, which, after *Jubilee* (1977), enabled him to exploit the existing relations between video and Super 8, and primarily the flexibility to manipulate and rework original images once they were transferred into the other medium, as well as the relations of new technology to rock video (*Broken English*, 1979), *T.G. Psychic Rally in Heaven*, 1980). This return to intimist cinema would be well-received by a new generation of young filmmakers who shared the same affinities as Jarman for the work of Jean Cocteau, Kenneth Anger, Jack Smith, Andy Warhol and Pier Paolo Pasolini. Together they made *The Dream Machine* (1984), a rallying call for a new cinematic sensibility which would shake up the tenants of an avant-garde that had become rigid in its dogmas. The explosion of homosexual desire as reflected in the fantasies and rituals in these films with their obscure images, jerky slow motion, accompanied by new music, and which did not disguise the pleasure of seeing and showing could not but shake up Thatcher-era Britain. It was at this time that Jarman published *Dancing Ledge*, the first of an autobiographical series that mixed memories and reflections that confronted the British establishment. The same year he made *Imagine October* (1984), a major film which combined Super 8 sequences: fleeting images shot on a trip to Russia, with staged sequences in 16mm which parody the didacticism of narrative films. These sequences are linked by texts which mix personal reflections with political declarations calling for radical social change in order not to sink into apocalypse. The outburst of texts in the form of declarations and slogans, sometimes poetic, bring a new energy to these films. Jarman denounces British cinema and its false values, but also the hypocrisy of society regarding homosexuality, morality, and money. A declaration of war against a society that polices everything. A dark future is announced of which *The Last of England* (1987) will be one of the most beautiful illustrations. The film is an allegory of what England had become. Its creator serves as a link between sequences that unfold with the logic of dreams or, more exactly, nightmares. Fugitive visions in which are mixed terrorists having sex on the Union Jack with 1950s home movies, and sequences in which parody occasionally breaks through the suffocating darkness, present in the grain and tonality of the film. In this film, once again, the soundtrack has a rare richness and multiplies the layers of sound which overlap each other and facilitate their connections. The film is sculpted from photochemical grain (enlarged from Super 8 to 35mm), from voices and from background noise that is always ready to explode. The creation of a particular tension which pushes the image to damage itself with the violence of desire and which can also be shattered by the soundtrack.

His diagnosis as seropositive made him return to painting, a solitary activity whose cinematic twin was the film *The Garden* (1990). A painting of denunciation which was an echo and a critique of the homophobia around him. He joined in the militant actions of the group OutRage! and paid it homage in a scene of *Edward II*.

A public personality and one of the most visible and combative spokesman for seropositives in Great Britain, he published several books of reminiscences and reflections: *Modern Nature* in 1991, *At Your Own Risk* in 1992, *Chroma* in 1994. After *The Garden,* a bucolic antidote to the urban despair of *The Last of England,* he made a last personal film: *Blue* (1993), while he was going blind. The film is a splendid and violent audio meditation on a blue background. The absence of images immerges the viewer in a reflection on the progress of his disease and his memories associated with the color blue. The film links in a masterful way the intimacy of a perspective and thoughts without compromise to the universality of monochrome which becomes the vehicle and the basis of transcendence.

Revue et Corrigée, n°21, September-October 1994.

LOT IN SODOM

How in the 1930s, in the United States, to represent homosexuality in a film? Only one way: take a Biblical story and prioritize visual effects while preserving the story line which will slightly disguise the "scandal" of the underlying message (as the film's opening shows: the viewer is entering a strange world, the sky ripped open, breaking up to allow penetration into the territory of Sodom. The breaking up is represented by bolts of lightning that little by little are transformed, like a visible superimposition on the optical soundtrack. The breaking up of the sky emphasizes the strangeness of this city and its customs). This in a way describes *Lot in Sodom* (1933) by James Watson and Melville Webber. Homosexuality is there, quite present throughout the film. It is incarnated in the cult of the masculine body exercising nude, running, jumping, climbing, dancing, playing music, seducing, caressing and sleeping...Each of these activities more or less corresponds to a different cinematographic technique, with nevertheless a proclivity for superimposition and making the film a catalogue of the different means of technical intervention on film for visual effect.

.   .   .

IN THE LIGHTING can be felt a whole exacerbated expressionism making forbidden passions visible. Love for the masculine body will be expressed by the multiplicity of shots of a man jumping over an invisible obstacle; a multiplicity in the Futurist manner by the repetition of the same image superimposed slightly out of synchronization in space and time (anticipating a technique developed later by McLaren in *Pas de Deux*, 1967), with the image of a melancholy young man on a train. The echoes are weaker and the body, as if it was a mirage, disappears in this jump to better reappear playing a trumpet or crawling over a pile of sprawled out and listless naked bodies.

THE MALE BODY is presented here as an image of health (the Greek ideal?), the fit physique, the athletic body, the very one which would inspire a future return to figuration in painting and sculpture in the 1930s - despite the view of Parker Tyler, this has nothing to do with Surrealism - the healthy body in robust growth, thus the superimpositions...

IT WAS NO LONGER the same after the appearance of the angel (a romantic figure doubtless a reference to the aesthetics of Louis II of Bavaria), the refused body becomes monstrous, youth has fled, the make-up and the tight framing accentuate this effect.

THE WHOLE ARRAY of formal exercises will be deployed in another way in the dream sequence of *Lot* and in its production, in the manner of Abel Gance but with fewer resources, which involves another dynamic. The full force of the 1920s European avant-garde is on display: superimposed motifs, kaleidoscopic effects, slow motion, macrophotography, very tightly framed shots, moving abstract forms mutating against the background of flames, in a nod to Hans Richter.

·   ·   ·

IN THIS REPRESENTATION OF HOMOSEXUALITY, it is not astonishing to find there is no equivocal gesture, no frank portrayal of total nudity, but what is surprising is the sudden appearance of such an openly homosexual representation for its time,[1] a representation which has nothing to do with that other representation of violence and poetry to be found in *Un chant d'amour* (1950), but which is more reminiscent of the turn of the century aesthetic which dominate a great number of writers.[2]

expanded version, February 1998.
1st version, *Scratch*, n°3, November 1983.

HIROYUKI OKI

Hiroyuki Oki has a special place in contemporary Japanese cinema for several reasons. His films, up until recently, were shot in Super 8 and do not use any sophisticated techniques. They are above all the emanation of the filmmaker's expression. Notebooks of his daily life and his desires, Oki reveals his love of young men and several in particular who appear repeatedly in several films. His films are constituted by an accumulation of shots which oscillate between the improvised and the composed. In this way, in the succession of specific shots of urban spaces (suburban train stations, canal towpaths, bungalow terraces) echo the precipitation of shots of young men pursued by a camera that is an accomplice to the filmmaker's desires. The camera makes it possible for him, sometimes through the fantasy of an unfulfilled encounter, to capture homosexual desire by frequently orchestrating it. The bodies as much as the places are spaces to explore where desire can erupt at any moment. Thus time in the films is above all the time of seduction along with everything that it puts into play as expectation, languor and impatience - deferred in order to better reveal. Oki's cinema is the cinema of a lover in search of other encounters. A cinema which registers erotic desire as unsurpassable and which shows through a stretching out of time the fragility and the violence of a glance, the caress of its framing and the fascination of young men. His quest is as much that of others as it is his. Each landscape, each face, leads back to his situation to his position, in which and from which he must define himself as different: other. In this way most of his films chronicle a relatively short time: ten days for *Matsumae kun no senritsu* (1990), and two weeks for *Synjinkou* (1991). The dailiness, the familiar, are recorded in shots of small suburban train stations where the trains no longer seem to stop as in the town of Matsumae. It is in this town that he made a series of films over five years in which the street seen from his window or the terrace of his apartment and the abandoned train station become leitmotifs which scan common places over time. In *Tarch Trip* (1993) as well as in his latest films, the chronology of the sequences is no longer respected, the editing does its work; the films become more reflexive. This film draws a parallel between two periods, one light, spring-like, happy, the other dark, rainy, nostalgic. The last evokes the death of one of the protagonists. His latest films exploit sexuality more overtly, but less brutally and seem to result in a narration which distances itself from autobiography and the film journal.

THE QUALITY of Oki's work resides in the fact that a space of freedom is created. A space where desire can erupt and manifest itself on the margins of society. This difference is a reminder that Oki's films themselves reside on the margins of the Japanese film production; they are direct, raw, and do not worship the dominant technological powers. It is a cinema held close to the body which leaves time and desire yet to come.

Le Je Filmé, Paris, Centre Georges Pompidou/Scratch, 1995.

6

SOME QUESTIONS OF CINEMA

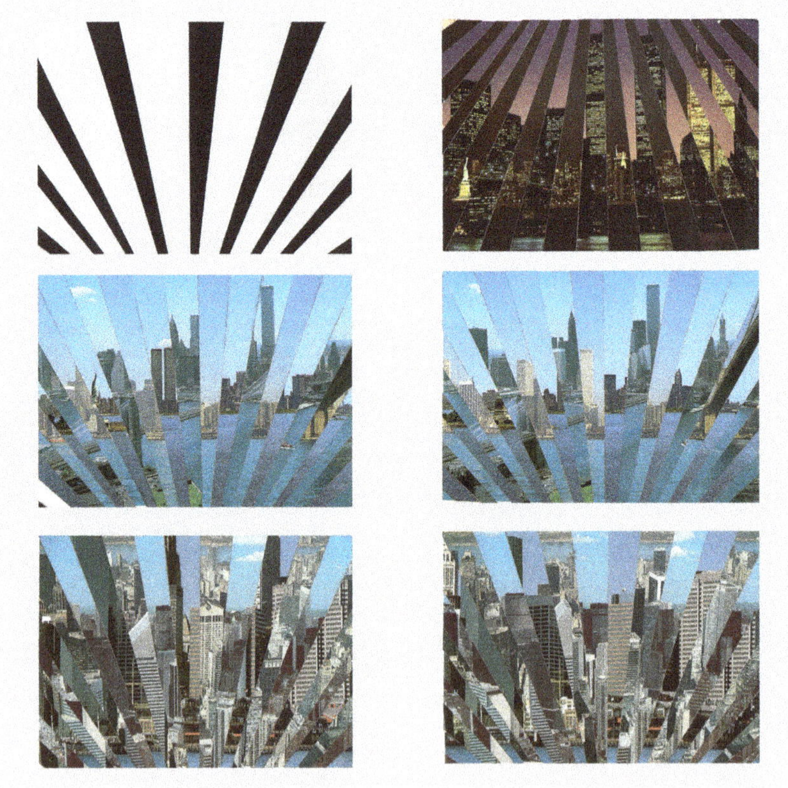

A SIMULACRUM QUESTION

The cinematographic process, even for experimental film which often avoids it, favors by its nature dramatization. It is itself a dramatization: first the dramatization of a process (24 images a second), then the use of repetition which will be more or less modified according to how its potential is exploited or the uses to which it is put. Obsession dominates, the beautiful repetition is carried out up to the end of the period of projection. Nevertheless very often, this mechanism is disguised behind the use of narrative based on a simulacrum. This is what explains the widening gap between experimental and traditional cinema. The stage, and thus the dramatization, are not the same even if it is a question of their being the same.

Since 1978, new movements have emerged in experimental film; they have in common a certain rejection of academic formalism ("Structural," or "Post-Structural," "Structural/Materialist," "Expanded")[1]. These practices rose up as a reaction against the dominant current which had been established starting in the mid-1960s. But these currents could not have led to a single type of film, the field was broader than in painting (New Figuration, Neo-Expressionism) or in music (the New Simplicity, etc.). It can however be said that there was often a return to narration, and in diverse forms.[2]

In this reevaluation of the art of the preceding decades which could indirectly support post-modernism, there can be seen the possibility of causing the emergence (or re-emergence) of meanings that up to then had been obscured. Among them, humor, irony, games and the simulacrum as fundamental ingredients of Minimalist practice. These meanings appear to the benefit of processes which put in place these arrangements, deferring pleasure, which can also sometimes be found in more traditional cinema, in the form of the Borgesian story. The dogma of the 1970s swept away, certain meanings return to the surface of the screen; the first irony: the screen is not a receptacle of depth, of relief, and of the reality of traditional cinema, it is but a surface to be activated, to take over. Up to then the tendency had been to minimize the importance that covered, for some, the brief knots of narrative, by glorifying only the processes and the repetitive chains and the differences which accompanied them, at the same time putting to the side any bitterness.

The period progressed with certitude, there was "art in order not to perish from truth," while forgetting that it was only a case of exchanging one value for another. Annihilating the meaning of Nietzsche's words, forgetting the stakes and power of appearance.[3] This, in opposition to truth, destabilized it. Interpretations needed to be revised, films too. Having emphasized the process, at its extreme, the object (here filmed) no longer had any importance. Any object could work; whatever was the most economical; interchangeability was the key. So numerous films were made from the same recipe, using it until it was worn out and the dishes no longer had any taste. It became a question more of repetition than exploration; amusement gave way to boredom. The machine ran by itself, the echo of a former utopia, a pure process, a machine that was in a sense, deliberately meaningless, thinking it had escaped any determinism, any recourse to existing dogmas. But it was obvious that this did not happen and that the institution would glorify it, analyzing the most complicated stratagems, and in doing so drying up its possibilities, including its audience. It was also that structural and procedural cinema found legitimacy in the death of mankind, proclaimed after that of God, while defending the machine, abundant in this way in the ideology of the system technician, which advocated the surrounding society.

It nevertheless happened that, beyond their topographic function, these cinematographic actions included other aspects cited above.

Tony Conrad, Hollis Frampton, George Landow, and Paul Sharits, four strategies, four uses of laughter, four attitudes: in the image, the witticism in the surrealist gangrene.

With his series of films for a dollar, Tony Conrad began to think of a different kind of film: how to make films if you are a "housewife"? The seasonings can be prepared and the film dishes simmered that combine activities that in general are totally separated, thus making "pickled" and "boiled" films, etc.: re-purposing a daily activity and reusing a specific practice from the domain of housework. All in all, the fried dishes work quite well and question in a sly way the seriousness of the business of making a film. Conrad was able, by means of this series, to renew the meaning of spectacle, the spectacle no longer being in what was made visible (although when looked at carefully these films are fairly full of spectacle) but in the approach which destabilizes the illusion of control automatically conferred on the artist. He becomes, contrary to the figure of "Brakhage the genius," an individual like any other.

With *Critical Mass* (1971) by Hollis Frampton, there can be seen a desynchronization of the soundtrack in relation to the image, a series of stutters[4] which induce a reversal of social roles between the partners during a domestic quarrel. The stuttering encourages a multiplication of meanings by producing a decomposition of words; the gestures of the protagonists seems to contradict their words and the passion they express. Here the filmmaker is playing the great manipulator, falsifying the reality of the scene to make words dysfunctional, which reveals the stereotypes of behavior.

Institutional Quality (1969), as well as many other films of George Landow,[5] introduces visual traps on the nature of representation, accompanied by all of the power games which presage the rather ironic instructions of the off-camera narrator, orchestrating fake language learning methods. The subversion of learning is repeated by the subversion of the image - the destabilization of a studious childhood.

With *3rd Degree* (1982), Paul Sharits attacks representation,[6] as he had already done in *Analytical Studies n° 2* (1971-1976). A woman's face is threatened by a burning match, the film itself catches fire and at its end the images of burning are themselves burned. There are thus three degrees of burning which create an unimaginable tension, reinforced by the refusal of the tortured woman to speak. Even though there is no narrative line, the audience (and the projectionist) are drawn into a vertiginous space, a suspense at the least abstract and at the most materialistic; a simulacrum within a simulacrum in which the viewer no longer knows what exactly is burning or not burning. The localization of reality is short-circuited, what is true for a moment becomes false, the indetermination and the floating of identity and the process of identification are at a maximum: the simulacrum rules, presented as a questioning.

Someday the link which obviously exists between Duchamp and Minimal Art will have to be acknowledged and, consequently no longer confused and separated from the different processes which organize the process as a moment of derealization of the medium employed. Perhaps not enough attention has been paid to the playful dimension to a large number of "conceptual" propositions. The critique advanced by Post-Modernism, if the reductionist interpretations of modernism can be removed, could permit a reevaluation of what is at stake in the latter.

It is in this way by using a reductivist frame of reference to their works that one of the most essential motivations for the work of these filmmakers has been overlooked. In the same way, no attention has been paid to the narrative thread of certain films and this is due to the process put in place in and by the film.[7] In their Post-Modernist reaction, the first agreement (even if it was the only one) was that of a return to fiction. Unfortunately, the return was too often only a parody of Pop Art and the "underground"...The gap was enormous, into which had to be stuffed all "post" reactions - in fact, anti-modernist.

Already in *Wavelength* (1967), a murder, a sordid history occurs while the zoom continues its conquest and control over space. The trajectory of the zoom is not so far from the general trajectory of a traditional narrative film with its pauses, resumptions, in the sense that, in both one and the other of its stages, the discontinuous process of the image creates a simulacrum of continuity: narrative in the traditional film, procedural in Michael Snow's film. What this last artistic proposition initiates is an opening up and a removal of hierarchization of the filming process in relation to the filmed action: instead of first erasing its traces in the service of the second; the two processes begin to function autonomously. The making of the film becomes hierarchically superior in relation to narrative accidents. It should not be forgotten that this zoom is only a simulacrum of continuity, a connection, perceptible by analysis, of four zooms. The viewers' expectation and perspective is booby-trapped, except in relation to the crossing of the room; it is indeed a crossing since it ends on a photograph of waves. The films escapes to other shores in the achievement of its trajectory. On the way, it questions and perturbs the zoom. Every time something seems certain, an event, the viewers' attention is deftly drawn back to the technical process, this restarts the machine and the desire to see: everything is deferred.

An analogous questioning can be found in *Doctor's Dream* (1978) by Ken Jacobs, but this time focalized on the problem of editing. Working from a found film, he reintroduces an erotic reading of the original story. What is he returning to? The banal narration is totally subverted. The film begins by a shot which, originally, was in the middle of the film, followed by the shot which had proceeded it, which, in its turn, is followed by the shot which had come just after the middle shot, and so on until the end, where the film ends with the first shot followed by the last shot broken into pieces. How can the original of a film be identified? How can the reality of a copy be determined? Is the viewer not in the quintessential universe of the simulacrum, in the sense that it is more or less a question of a copy of a copy? Cause and effect are reversed. The doctor's clinical gaze is transformed into a lascivious one... a game of meanings, the objectives of the original are sacrificed. Everything is known ahead of time, before it is even legitimized by the narration. Yet again a game, a staged action, to another degree (here in the editing) interferes with the normal course of events. By this reorganization of found footage, the narration is swept away by another logic and thus invokes other meanings. One could even wonder if there is not a supplementary game, this time with experimental cinema itself as the target.[8] With *After Lumière - L'Arroseur Arrosé,* Le Grice introduced another form of simulacrum by playing with history and the original which featured one of the very first simulacrums in the history of cinema: a comic skit.[9] Here the illusionist functioning of the simulacrum, by the repetition of the recorded action staggered over time, were to create, by the gaps between their differing points of view, the arbitrary character of the process (positive, negative, color, and then the addition of a soundtrack: *Les Morceaux en forme de poire* by Erik Satie.)

Even more directly, the game relating to the kind of story where it is impossible to judge the veracity of what is seen, in the manner of Raoul Ruiz in *Les Divisions de la Nature* (1978), Peter Greenaway plays with fiction in *A Walk Through H* (1978) by means of a soundtrack denying, confirming, thwarting, destabilizing the claims asserted earlier. It is a narration without characters. Very often, these games of calling into question are carried out by means of sound which contradicts and throws out other claims, other authorities. The sound, and thus the word, which here constitutes a part of the film, seems to be the catalyst for the simulacrum, to such a degree that the sliding into more traditional filmmaking is facilitated, the image becoming a possible medium for the message. It is thus less questionable, less enacted and documentary-like. Becoming in this way a moment in a fable, it is brought up-to-date, but not for what it represents or uncovers, but for what it masks, thus what it succeeds at deferring; it becomes evident that this delay leads to nothing tangible.

The undertaking of masking can go even further in a radical practice of cinema. It is in some ways what happens when one sees a film by Peter Gidal, in which one never knows if the film is an alibi for the theoretical argument or the opposite. In this ambiguity, the film-maker plays with the audience and their expectations.[10] The partner is silent,[11] but what is the nature of the silence? Is it possible that it is that of viewers frustrated in their expectations, deprived of their voice, condemned to emptiness? The counterfeit is at its apogee.

To not see humor and games at work in these artistic practices would be to fail to see their modernity. In this sense, a large part of the Post-Modern point of view, working from a reductivist view of the form, is lacking one of its foundational principles: a playful spirit brought to an investigation of representation.[12] Formalism is not simply attacked by parody or by the accumulation of clichés, many "punk" filmmakers have fallen into this trap, confusing a rejection of form with the multiplication of stereotypes; the reactivation is not the same. This is why the films of Erika Beckman differentiate themselves so much from all the New York trends born since 1978. Her last film *You the Better* (1983), presents a game, in the form of a game. The structure of the film is linked to a game more than the narration. But the dice are loaded, consequently even though closed - in the sense that the interactivity of the game here understood as between the casino (the authorities) and the audience (the gamblers) is impossible - the structure is undefined. Nevertheless the game most always comes first, it cannot stop, it has no end; in an infinite replay of the chain of meaning. From the game to authority, by way of profit, the viewers become participants in a game in which they do not know the rules. Escaping fatalism, the Kafkaesque world is near. Just when one almost seems to have grasped something, it escapes through the subtle slipping away of the meaning of a word, an image, or a symbol.

What then becomes of the player (the gambler) when the rules of the game are removed? He enters into the age of enigma and of the *mise en abyme*. The playing field is booby-trapped, a pure alibi, the mechanical functioning working on the excess of meaning authorized to him by the undetermined rule. In this game, nothing can be trusted or the facsimile believed. Round after round, the players are in a role in perpetual movement which ceaselessly perpetuates itself by regenerating new figures of discourse and power...

The game, the presentation of the facsimile were not absent in the previous decades. Post-Modernist criticism, blind to multiplicity, attacked only artifices; it forgot that the devices employed were not significant (nor unmarried), but that they were (too) significant. This access is always in accompaniment, below the surface, impetuous, on the sidelines, but nevertheless in the frames, not between them.[13] To see it, certain interpretative frameworks must be discarded.

Some filmmakers think that the work of undermining the facsimile (by questioning it) has been exhausted, all alibis work, to reestablish the illusionist representation, but they are doing it sideways, instituting logical systems which, by successive attempts, lead to a plurality of meanings, scenes, languages.

Alibis, Paris, Centre Georges Pompidou, 1984.

THE MUSICAL

The question of the musical haunts the cinema and in particular experimental cinema. For many filmmakers it is a preponderant question that has its sources in different periods of the history of art depending on specific criteria. Three major modes can be distinguished in references to the musical by filmmakers.

To create a music of color is an old dream that has preoccupied the medium and whose partial accomplishment has been achieved through a necessarily arbitrary synthesis. This has been conducted through an abstraction of forms.

To create and master objects which develop over time is to have recourse to musical processes and terminology. Thus music has become a paradigm of cinema.

Next to these two first modes of music-film relations, there exists a third which has been implemented since the beginning of sound film and which employs sound and music in counterpoint to the image.

The application to cinema of this synesthesia can be seen as an extension and application of ideas that 19th century artists had developed, dreaming, following Wagner, of a total art. Behind this search for correspondence between the arts lies a belief in a discernible original language which would incorporate unity, harmony, beauty. If it did not yet seem to have been attained, then it could doubtlessly be generated.

For most filmmakers having worked in this field, the spirituality of art was essential because it was inherent in the organization and development of a visual music. The fabrication of this visual music was often accomplished by means of abstract objects. As if the visual music could only present itself as long as the elements which composed it were devoid of any photographic realism, thus permitting the establishment on an elementary vocabulary from which the filmmaker could work. Thus, reviving the means used by painters at the beginning of the century (Kupka, Kandinsky, Klee), avant-garde filmmakers devoted themselves to the creation of abstract films that invoked the analogy of music, envisaging cinema as colored rhythm, visual music, visual symphony, etc. These labels imagined cinema as an art which englobed all the other arts, and in this case the musical metaphor presupposes synesthesia. Or else this musical metaphor is what permits the interrogation of the essence of this new art by freeing it of all referents in order to establish it as an autonomous art. This affirmation is necessarily accompanied by a question about the specificity of the material elements of film. The avant-garde film-makers of the 1920s oscillated between these two categorizations of cinema. Whether thinking of Henri Chomette or Germaine Dulac who advocated for the advent of a pure art or of Viking Eggeling and Hans Richter who would think of music as model for the arrange-ment and development of forms through time, or of Walter Ruttmann, Oskar Fischinger, Sandor László for whom the synes-thesia was what permitted access to the similarity between the move-ment of form and of color, sounds and emotions. Numerous exchanges between these practices took place, evoked by Germaine Dulac: "Music which provides this sort of transcendence to human feeling, which records the multiplicity of states of mind, plays with sound in movement just as we filmmakers play with images in move-ment....The integral film that we all dream of composing is a visual symphony made up of rhythmical images that only the sensations of an artist could put onto the screen."[1] By means of these flights of lyri-cism, the filmmaker displays her attachment to a spirituality of art shared by numerous artists and filmmakers at the beginning of the 20th century. This affirmation of an art close to music is what permits the simultaneous advocacy of film as an autonomous art and thus being able to make use of abstract objects (the pure painting of Léopold Survage, the absolute film of Walter Ruttmann and Oskar Fischinger, the non-objective film of Viking Eggeling) but also as what can lift the soul far above the contingencies of reality and its simple reproduction. It is in this sense that the two tendencies of that avant-garde film of the 1920s must be understood. For one, abstrac-tion manifests itself through objects while for the other it is through the creation of abstract processes out of photographic images. It is through the organization of objects according to precise speeds and rhythms that cinematographic vision can flourish.[2] Two ways of envisaging modernity can be understood here whose relation to music only emphasizes their differences. On the one hand, the metaphor of music, as a way to lift the spirit, can favor an abstract cinema which most often consists of a romantic approach and a fasci-nation for the synesthesia whose most singular examples would be the *Opus* (1919-1924) by Ruttmann and the *Filmstudies* (1929-1934) of Fischinger. While for another school, the reference to music is what permits the evocation of abstract processes, a way to articulate the intervals between images by means of editing and visual rhythm. Thus Henri Chomette and Hans Richter (whose first films were nevertheless abstract) devoted themselves to developing an art which worked above all with visual rhythm, avoiding psychological issues and any story-telling: "abandoning the logic of facts and the reality of objects, engendering a series of unknown visions."[3] Here rhythm is understood as what permits the organization of disparate visual elements; this foundational rhythm that would inspire both Eggeling and Richter would be incorporated as much into melody and harmonic effects (see Eggeling, Ruttmann, Fischinger, Dulac) as into syncopation and speed (see Richter, Chomette, Léger, Gance, Deslaw). The rhythm was a way of beating the time and the measure, what established the beat for the passage of images through time. This rhythm was in opposition to the tuning up to make melodies in the sense that it was not a transcription of musical rhythm but the application to the field of cinematography of an element of distribution (melody) of forms in time. This approach, which turns a few elements of musical discourse into a motor for an otherness, is what leads to a multiplicity of attitudes depending on what the filmmakers advocate. Working from the notion of counterpoint applied to scrolls, then to film, Eggeling and Richter generated variations in the unveiling and presentation of an initial form. If Richter rapidly abandoned the linear development of a melodic line and its variation in favor of rhythm, Eggeling made it the explicit motor of *Symphonie Diagonale* (1921). The film worked on form frontally, proposing from the starting point of a theme (a drawing) a series of variations without thickness and without volume in the shot of the black frame of the screen. It is the appearance of a few lines, the reiteration of their lengthening and retraction, their succession in the appearance of sections of diverse but nevertheless similar forms, which defines the musical aspect and make Eggeling's film a visualization of chords whose progression produces a melody which the revealing and disappearance, the inversion and rotation of forms (themes) only reinforce. The increase in the number of lines in a shot, their broadening and narrowing, introduce effects similar to those of sound intensity. The lateral movements of a form (a grid of lines), combine with other movements of curves (3 or 5) and offer a series of relations between different basic themes, alternating them and thus advancing the melody. Certain forms, or parts of the drawing act as a visual counterpart to the motion, their repetitions sweep across and pulsate the melody and are perceived as chords and rhythms when they are grouped together and alternated.[4] All of this action occurs within the shot. Eggeling's graphics are in contrast with those of Richer as well as those of Ruttmann and Fischinger in the sense that they remain on the surface and do not penetrate the depth of the spatial representation as if the accentuation (the *fortissimo*, etc.) could only be expressed in the thickness of the line and not in the depth of the screen and its illusionist space. It is this volume which Fischinger, Ruttmann and Richter exploit the most. The forms which these filmmakers use are less graphic than geometric or organic (in the case of Ruttmann and Fischinger), they appear in the case of Ruttmann as an orchestra, or a chamber music ensemble in which can be visualized the themes of each instrument according to the type of forms, colors, and rhythms.[5] In Fischinger's work the perfect synchronization of the soundtrack with the abstract imagery on the black and white films, make them perceptible as works of pure synesthesia; as if the illustration, the visualization of the music had been the essential concern of Fischinger's project, in the sense that the complex visual compositions that he sets in motion (comets, arcs, lines, circles, etc.) serve as a continuous counterpoint but are no less frequently[6] a transcription of the melody or the orchestration of a musical piece. It can be observed that the films favor sustained tempos which permit the proliferation of a multitude of swirling forms which invade all the spatial dimensions of the representation.[7]

The use of color will make it possible to amplify the relations between music and film through the color range. The apposition of an equivalence between color and the musical note, the attribution of a tonality for each color. Filmmakers will propagate the relations and attempt to present unique experiments such as those of Charles Blanc-Gatti in the 1930s, John Whitney starting in the 1940s. The production of a specific rhythmic framework of forms and backgrounds as is also the case in the direct films of Len Lye such as *Colour Box* (1935) and *Kaleidoscope* (1935) then in *Colour Cry* (1952). This rhythmic framework relates more to kineticism than synesthesia and make the white scratches and stripes in the last three films of Len Lye become a dance to music and weave relations which no longer constitute equivalence but enter, by their complementarity, into the field of counterpoint.

If music can be the common thread that facilitates the organization of visual elements, it would seem that the synesthetic work would take place primarily by using animation which after all permits limiting the elements with which the visualization is accomplished. Nevertheless, in the case of animation drawn directly on the film, the activity is closer to musical improvisation than a work of correspondence.[8] Music may serve as a model, but the interpretations and the transcriptions are more free, fidelity to a piece of music is less necessary. In addition, from the moment that photographic images are used, the musical reference is established differently; it is perhaps more a question of musicality. Music is a source of inspiration, as is the case with Dulac's *Disque 957* (1928), *Thèmes et variations* (1928) or with Marie Menken in *Eye Music in Red Major* (1961). In these cases, the music is the source for a free adaptation; catalyzing inspiration, it is not the model which permits the shaping and construction of the film. It is the source but not the motor of the film. The displacement and positioning of music as a cinematographic paradigm is carried out mainly by means of comprehension and the treatment of information (visual, aural) according to precise rhythms. It is on this note of rhythm that filmmakers have worked the most. If rhythm is understood as a beat, it in fact calls on repetition. It can be an exact repetition of the same syncopation which presupposes an alternation of sound and silence, light and dark (one could already say counterpoint). The rhythm can be calibrated, which is to say, not just the frequency of the beat (speeding up, slowing down) but also the intensity and the volume of the sound. The rhythm is the regular repetition of a sound or light event. The repetition, the beat, the rhythm, depend on time. This time is measured (if the recording of frames on the film strip is considered), or pulsed (if the regularity of the projection speed in front of the beam of light is considered; this is the starting point for the work of the filmmaker. Thus for Peter Kubelka, "film is already rhythmic at its source." All of his work will be based on defined measures equivalent to a given number of film frames. For Kubelka, cinema is metric, in other words, an art where the frame is the measure of duration, he applies to the field of film what Anton Webern did in the musical domain. Film is reduced to the space of frames and of that which separates them, bringing out in a single act the first characteristic described above regarding rhythm as alternating light and darkness. Working from a source series: 26

frames for *Adebar* (1956-1957), 16 for *Arnulf Rainer* (1958-1960), the film is composed. Either for *Adebar* as the basic sequence: a pygmy music lasting for 26 frames (in 4 phrases), from which every part of the film will be a multiple of a sub-multiple of 26 (13 and 52). The first and last image of each of the eight shot that comprise the film can be frozen according to the same multiples. All the shots are in positive or negative which produces 16 groups, corresponding to four times the base unit. Thus the total duration of *Adebar*: 1164 frames.[9] The definition of the base elements of the series (because here it is possible to speak of series in the musical sense) is what will make possible the composition of a film according to a pre-established score. A score with strict rules which structure the general organization of the film and impose on the filmmaker a rigorous application of the series which requires that one of its tones cannot be repeated until every other one has appeared. There is no - or at least no longer - a privileged element. But instead the elements of the series can appear according to four classical figures of counterpoint on the chromatic scale: the base progression, reversal (mirror), inversion (backwards), and reverse inversion.[10] It can be clearly seen how the application of these treatments to film leads to the emergence of another way of thinking about film; liberating it so to speak totally from any reference to literature, by permitting it to fashion an autonomous language out of distinct abstract elements, that the filmmaker creates. It is in this sense that the richness of the relation to music must be understood. It is not only a question of creating a new audiovisual art form as John Whitney sought to do with his digital harmony[11] which understands music as visual architecture in motion. The filmmaker can show this same architecture through graphic representation through rigorous motifs which move in time (hence the use of the computer) as in *Arabesque* (1975). For him the camera is not a recording instrument with which liquid architecture can be composed, it is in fact the particularity of music. Harmonic schemes can be applied to graphics and its elements (points, pixels, digits), in other words systems of consonance and dissonance. The resolution of the motif occurs at the point of harmonic resonance. Digital harmony consists of creating motifs evolving through time; motifs organized by expanding or contracting figures which create visual melodies, a series of harmonious forms whose development engenders new figures. Color introduces a supplementary dimension to the graphics, a textural attribute of the motif; color is the orchestration of the theme. This understanding of the relation between music and film differs from the one argued by Peter Kubelka on more than one point. If for Kubelka rhythm is at the source of music and cinema, for Whitney the specificity of music lies in the continuum of motion. In this way are produced melodies, melodious visualizations of music, whereas Kubelka composes a score, then plays it (realization by the projection of the score) he does not interpret. Kubelka works on music before the melody, Whitney makes knowledgeable bi-dimensional melodic compositions. By default film is the distribution medium of this electronic art which makes it possible to represent this digital harmony. It is an art of motifs in motion. Respecting the cadence of 24 frames per second does not, for him, allow for the subtle evolution of abstract motifs, in other words, according to a continuum of motion; there are jumps which are in contradiction to the flow of the motif and/or the music.[12] The digital harmony is what renders music visible, in this sense the concept can be considered as belonging to the domain of synesthesia and it is by that very fact that it is in contrast to all of the filmmakers for whom music is not to be transcribed, but can serve as a model to better understand the medium that they use. But the particularity of John Whitney's proposition is that it makes visible the graphic translation of musical motion in time. It can be deduced that the temporal notation by means of a computer is more effective than conventional notation, in the sense that its progression can be seen; from then on, the audiovisual composition is assisted/facilitated. A new field of application opens up, which does not come out of synesthesia and cannot be expressed without graphics.

The apparent motion of graphics contrasts with the serialization of frames such as they can be perceived in the work of Peter Kubelka, Paul Sharits, or in *Chronoma* (1977) and *Chronographies* (1982) by Jean-Michel Bouhours. In fact, when Paul Sharits attempts to create chords, harmonics, he does it by means of collusion, the fusion of pure color frames which induces dissolves, depths in the color instilled beyond the melodic lines like dominant chords. His reference to the musical is executed either according to the structure of the film or to the parts of film in which high musicality can be perceived, or by the use of multiple screens[13] and in particular in the films *Sound Strip/Film Strip* (1971), *Color Sound Frames* (1974) and *Declarative Mode* (1976). In this last film, two identical prints are projected with the exterior screen one second behind the interior one, which it contains, thus multiplying the harmonic chords and causing a great complexity by amplification in the relations developed between the two screens. It is interesting to notice that in his numerous writings (letters, memos, etc.), Paul Sharits frequently referred to music, even if it was by default[14] when he addressed issues of formalism or emotion; in the case *Declarative Mode*, it was Beethoven. All of his films are at the junction and articulation of these two fields. Nevertheless, it is not because he refers to music (often classical) that he creates similar processes to those of musicians and in particular to those of composers of Minimalist music. The use of loops, their superimpositions in phases or not can be found as much in the strips of images as in the soundtracks that he creates. The slowing down, the stretching out, the spinning of the soundtrack of *T,O,U,C,H,I,N,G* (1968) evokes the rotations, spinning, stretching out of Sharits' films or installations that uses strips of film moving vertically one over another as in *Episodic Generation* (1978). This use of loops is reminiscent of the music of Steve Reich in pieces such as *It's Gonna Rain* (1965), *Come Out* (1966), or *Piano Phase* (1967). But in contrast to Brian Eno and Malcolm Le Grice in *Berlin Horse* (1970), the music or soundtracks of Paul Sharits often use statements which are (by their very use) undermined and which by their constant repetition (the word "destroy" in *T,O,U,C,H,I,N,G*) and their superimpositions distant themselves from the images in the sense that they do not repeat them. The similarity of the processes do not create redundancy; while in *Berlin Horse* the image of the revolving horse seems to be illustrated by the soundtrack. This shift of the music of the soundtrack is perhaps what best characterizes the fundamental difference which exists in the approach to and use of music by the filmmakers who no longer understand music as an inevitable model. A musicality in the approach of filmmakers which results in their placing themselves at the border of two ways of referring to the musical. It is in this sense that the use of musical counterpoint can lead to the creation of audiovisual works in which sound is not only at the service of the image but is understood according to its own particularities. In this case music, sounds, are composed, mixed, reworked in such a way as not to paste them on just to decorate, dress up, the images: they engage in complementary relations. This complementarity can be expressed in multiple ways, of which a few can be cited here. The radicality of propositions which lead the filmmaker to offer a cinema for the ear, to use on expression of Michel Chion,[15] and the most extreme example is without a doubt *Weekend* (1930) by Walter Ruttmann. This film consists of the playing in the dark of an audio montage of the ambiance of a weekend and is a reminder by the nature of the project of the visual symphonies of the 1920s. It is almost a synesthetic inversion, here one can imagine what is heard, and viewers project their own internal cinema in the way that *El Cafetal* (1981) by David Wharry[16] invites them to do. This Ruttmann film is an exception, nevertheless: it works with collage in the same way as most films which use counterpoint in this way. The notion of counterpoint applied to film in the domain of sound seems to involve the notion of collage. The term collage evokes editing. Thus, some filmmakers such as the Lettrists use sound in a "discrepant" way, meaning without any relation to the image in order to create a disjunction between the two sources of information treated by the film. In a way reminiscent of *musique concrète* they use (particularly in the case of Lemaître) provocation as an artistic strategy in the pure Dada tradition. In the same domain, the juxtaposition of soundtracks; often the result of chance recalls certain compositions of acousticians who collect and sample sounds, and who then rework them according to their own interests.[17] This manifestation of sound as an autonomous object does not prevent other filmmakers from working with the soundtrack by manipulating it so that the sound comments on the image as is the case with most of the films of Kenneth Anger and in particular *Kustom Kar Kommandos* (1965) et *Scorpio Rising* (1963) in which 1950s pop songs give the image a feeling and meaning that they would not necessarily have had. This exemplary *camp* extravagance results in a permutation of the images that allow certain meanings to flourish. The music or, more precisely, the soundtrack is reworked and integrated according to particular methods which could go as far as an actual live musical concert, making its projection an event (as in the memorable projections by Jack Smith of his own films) in which the film is one of the elements of the performance. In the same vein can be found the performances of Jürgen Reble and Thomas Köner, as well as those of Metamkine which, each in its own way, attempts to renew the existing relations between images and sound. The randomness of the execution is more evident in Reble's work in the sense that everything depends on the reaction of the film to chemical products, while for Metamkine, the execution relies as much on musical as on cinematographic improvisation, from within an organized and repetitive framework. Here the virtuosity is not exercised so much by the manipulation of the instrument (the camera) as it is, in the case of Teo Hernandez, Jakobois, or Marcelle Thirache, but during the actual projection/concert in which the manipulations are performed live. Each time, there is a new interpretation and it is in this sense that their work belongs to the realm of performance, in which each presentation differs and is articulated in another way in time and in space.

These differences cannot but raise the problems brought out by multiple screen projections in their relation to music. In fact the multiplication of screens and thus projectors, allows the filmmaker to pass from chamber to orchestral music, from the performance of a soloist to that of an ensemble. This idea is present in several of my own works that do not specifically take music as a model, but draw from a vague idea of musicality. Each screen can be a voice in the filmmaker's composition where the transcription and the interpretation are only executed for a part of the film as in *R* (1975) et *Sans Titre*

(1984) in which the *Two Part Inventions* of Bach served as the model of the organization and distribution of the filmed objects: a panorama deconstructed into a series of angles of shots with *R* and its extensions: *RR* (1985) and *Quatr'un* (1992) of cut-up photographs of the Arc de Triomphe in the case of *Sans Titre*. It is because there is a conjugation of different attitudes in these films that the notion of musicality, despite the conceptual blurring that characterizes it, can be applied. It should first be said that the musical is what allowed me to resolve the problems of rhythmical composition. The application of musical rhythms is neither more nor less adequate than the employment of tantric, mathematical, or poetic forms. Its use permits the organization and potentially the structuring in sound of a passage or an entire film. The music, or in my case more exactly, the score which served as a model, is not played, nor heard on the soundtrack. Neither does it involve visualizing a piece of music. In *R*, a transcription of a Bach score, the addition of other screens allows not just a widening of the field of vision but also brings out the song, as if one screen was the twin, the counterpoint of the other. As if the second screen facilitated the manifestation of rhythm. In *RR* one of the screens is the mirror of the other and in the four-screen version, it is an image composed of mirrors reflected in itself. From one screen to another the tune plays with the instruments slightly out of sync: the projectors which thus permit the instruments to flee the initial theme. Its presentation as an installation, visible from both sides of the screen emphasizes even more the musical aspect of the piece, offering a series of visualizations of the forms used by Bach as the reversal, the inversion as he practices it in *The Art of the Fugue* (1751). When two screens stand next to each other, disparate events can combine horizontally synchronizing and de-synchronizing, generating the anticipation of connections from one screen to the other as is already the case with *Razor Blades* (1965-1968) by Paul Sharits with its scratches and play of texts which each screen exchanges with the other. These exchanges, these fusions, these de-synchronizations...are like the traces of a musical notation which inscribes itself differently in space. The two screens orchestrate a complex polyphony when the films develop the serialization of images. If the elements utilized are similar from one screen to another then the field of relations of editing and organization grow by simultaneously encouraging the affirmation of multiplicity. When the films on multiple screens are deployed in installations then the musical qualities can assert themselves by their spatialization which underlines the potentialities enclosed in the film. In multiples in painting and in works for keyboards can be found similar phenomena to those which are exposed on multiple screens: spinning, images-within-images, rotations, extensions of the field of resonance. The musicality can thus be understood as what in the film is connected as much to the temporal as to the harmonic without however being distorted by a particular musical model.

The musical is thus what permits the organization of defined elements by the filmmaker according to particular structures and forms, far from all narration it nevertheless enables the development of forms and emotions according to precise temporalities. For others it is the vague starting point which opens the cinema up to other horizons.

The musical is thus a concept without a fixed foundation which opens a discussion about a paradoxical cinematic quality situated at the crossroads of rhythm and cadence, of harmony and chords: a discourse to indicate the what-cannot-be-grasped which film on occasion can show.

1993 (unpublished)

THE FILM NOIR IN EXPERIMENTAL FILM

Black film leader is essential to film for several reasons which principally concern the exhibition of film. It is on the leader that the number of the reel is written and the technical instructions that define the process of duplication. At the first stage, it is on the negative where the instructions are in black on a white background. The positive print reverses all this and prints are prepared with the projectionists' leader which experimental filmmakers have used abundantly for diverse aesthetic or political reasons.

In a film theater the darkening of the room is perceived at the beginning of the screening as a signal of the beginning of the presentation. Every other appearance of darkness is a sign of of a malfunction characterized by the interruption of the continuity of images.

In traditional cinema, the black image and above all black leader is kept invisible except for the manufacture and distribution of prints or it is used to exhibit cinematographic writing of a precise stylistic form whose value depends on the meaning and the use which the filmmaker accords it.

It is in this way that lap dissolves, cuts, and pauses in black are able to establish the rhythm of a film.

Suddenly this black image, whose presence is the manifestation of an absence (but is it really an absence?), is activated, thus becoming an essential element of cinematic expression.

On the threshold of the use of the black image, there is always a reference, a question, an implication about the device or the editing. In fact, in regard to the mechanics of filmmaking, whether in shooting or in projection, there must always be a time when the shutter is closed that is equal to the time it is open to expose the film. The discrete alternation of light and darkness is a basic characteristic of the device. It is in the analysis of this function that experimental filmmakers developed the *flicker film* which reveals this function by and in the film.

The black image calls for editing in the sense that it demands a cut, the fade-out frequently signals the transition from one scene to another. Whether through a dissolve or a straight cut, the black image punctuates, sweeps across the melody of the film and permits its spatial and temporal units to be defined and follow each other in succession. It is an object of discussion: the rhythm.

The black image (understood here to mean a block of frames longer than a single frame) is what permits the very emergence of representation. In this case, their meanings are different depending on the usage and intentions of filmmakers. The black film is above all the foundation of cinematographic representation. In these films, it is the filmstrip itself that is worked on directly. In the same vein, there exists another dominant use of the black image which consists of using it as a surface on which objects can be placed: words, letters, diverse inscriptions, which can make a representation appear in an ephemeral way moving in space without the limits of the black field of the image. This use works with time. It is a play on duration and frequency that gives the black image a power to activate filmed representations or inscribed directly on the filmstrip.

Black in film is never black. It is always a qualification of light. Depending on the projection conditions (the projector, the theater), the space is more or less dark...black can be thought of as what darkens it. Black, in the context of the mechanics of cinematography itself can only be described or understood through the projection of light. The greater the intervals between light and darkness, the greater the contrast, the more black locks up and buries the room.

There are two major uses of black in film: the first is the use of black film or black leader to show or manipulate the film; while the second involves the introduction of black more during the shooting than the editing. These two uses do not in any way exhaust the diversity of approaches since they can be combined between themselves. But it is noticeable that the first category has more to do with experimental film while the second summons up traditional film (see for example the use of the black shot during the crucifixion of Christ in *The Gospel According to St. Matthew* by Pasolini, 1964). We are interested here more specifically in the use of black by experimental filmmakers.

Starting in the 1950s a new use of black in film can be identified, a use in which its fleeting insertion or, on the contrary, its persistence, confers a particular quality on the cinematographic experience. Lettrist and Situationist film made great use of black. Maurice Lemaître became one of its specialists in 1951 with *Le Film est déjà commencé ?* (1951) in which an alternation of black and white shots follow an introductory preamble (an extract from Griffith's *The Birth of a Nation*, 1915). In this example, there are black or white images without anything written on them. The alternation of shots recall an act of blinking which, as it speeds up, moves from darkness to light.[1] The systemization is not the objective of the film since its subject, as was already the case with *Traité de bave et d'éternité* (1951) by Isidore Isou, is to permit the coming of another form of filmmaking whose most important contribution lies in the use of chiseling and of "discrepance." Discrepance is the automation of the image track in relation to the soundtrack in the editing; the chiseling being the inscription on the same ribbon of anything that can denature, attack or liquidate the original views that composed the image track. The use of graphics, inscription directly on the black or white filmstrip, perpetuates this liquidation by signaling the preponderant objet. In Lemaître's film, the eruption and alternation of white or black leader, covered with signs or not, as well as the use of projectionist leader, causes a crisis of cinematographic representation by putting before our astonished eyes elements which up to now have served only to assure the smooth functioning of the film show. Thus the projectionist leader makes it possible to focus and adjust the sound level, the leader protects each reel and is cut off when the film is spooled onto a single reel. The provocative burst of everything that is usually unseen but without which the film cannot be prepared and projected correctly. Here the use of different leaders emphasizes the desire of the filmmaker to induce an insufferable tension in the viewer in order to literally blow a fuse. The leader is understood as a support for graphics or other diverse interventions which distance the images from realism and facilitate their juxtaposition with the sound, creating an ensemble of never-before-seen relations between image and sound. Nevertheless, the black leader is only one element that Maurice Lemaître employs to deconstruct the film show. One year later, Guy Debord, with *Hurlements en faveur de Sade* (1952) offered a radical experience. In this film, there is a soundtrack but no images. Each time a sound is heard, a blank image is on the screen, while during the silences, the screen is black. Dispersed dialogues throughout an hour of silence and whose total duration is less than twenty minutes, are made up of press clippings, distorted legal texts and quotes.[2] The plunge into black for long minutes made the film an object of scandal where viewers were faced with themselves and in which there was not only nothing to see but nothing to hear. They were confronted with an experience of negation and decomposition. From an avant-garde perspective, the film took the Lettrists' discoveries to an extreme and exploded them with provocative excessiveness.

If to see a film is to experience the development of forms through time, whether they are codified by a narrative framework or not, then projecting black on the screen modifies the relation the viewer has to the animated images and to the experience of time during the projection. In fact, the duration imposed by the black screen differs from that of the same screen showing images in motion. Everything depends on the nature of the film and the perceptual conditioning that the film engenders. In fact, if the black shots are followed by blocks of pure color then the progression of these shots does not change the understanding of the frame, except if the rhythm of the successive images speeds up and abruptly changes and thereby provokes secondary effects in the perception of the frame. Among these can be distinguished: the appearance of negative colors, the material movement of the floating frame as is the case with the black and white films *The Flicker* (1966) by Tony Conrad and *Arnulf Rainer* (1958-1960) by Peter Kubelka and in the color films of Paul Sharits such as *Ray Gun Virus* (1965) and *N:O:T:H:I:N:G* (1968). In *Ray Gun Virus* the fades to black are limited to three or four towards the end of the film. Their rarity reinforces the effects of the partial obliteration of the screen and the theater which is obscure to resurface ever more violently since they were submerged in the pulsation of colors. Here, the fade-out is black and strikes out the color.

When one sees a *flicker film* in which black dominates, the perception of the screen dissolves in the subjectivity of the viewer who will experience it differently depending on whether or not there is sound. In *Arnulf Rainer* and in *The Flicker* the precise composition of frames is such that the perception of the space of the screen as much as that of the room find themselves modified. The secondary effects of the lateral displacements of retinal images, the effects of persistence of vision, appear on our astonished pupils. The visual experience of these two films differs by the very nature of the structure deployed by each of these works. Both limit themselves to two visual elements: white frame, black frame; they diverge in their approach to sound for if Peter Kubelka prefers a black and white sound, this is not the case with Tony Conrad. In Conrad's work the audio continuum emphasize the development of the general composition of the film constructing an optimal crescendo in the articulation of the series of single frames according to the changes and gradual permutations of the basic unit (the black and white frames.) In Kubelka's work, the use of four basic units has to do with a modern application of a classic compositional principle. The form is not discernable during the projection of the film, it only becomes so when the filmstrips are seen laid out as a static picture. *Arnulf Rainer* produces particular visual effects which concern the perception of space: the breaks, introduced by the emergence of spans of black frames, induce extremely strong dissolutions, like blackouts. The screen, the room, disappear, evaporate at first, then reappear accompanied by parasite images; secondary effects in which slightly negative rectangles move around on the edges of the screen. These out-of-frame flickering effects are reminiscences of a recent experience of which one can only feel the diminished echoes out of which can be seen (at last) the projected black. This last is no longer black but remains extinguished, the light is reflected as an absence. It disqualifies itself by an optical aberration and makes us envisage its very disappearance.

The viewer is plunged into a waiting state, a tension is created that the explosion of images - when there is one as in *Room Film* (1973) or *Silent Partner* (1978) by Peter Gidal - does not necessarily resolve. The black influences our vision by suspending motion and its progression. Making the emergence and the nature of the representation problematic is exactly what Peter Gidal accomplishes from one film to another. Each of his films works on the conditions of cinematographic representation while at the same time denying the exploitation of the illusion on which this very representation rests.[3] Work on duration from which can be painfully extracted from obscurity several indistinct fragments, the mirage of an image. From the black grain occasionally burst shards of images which rapidly dissolve into the base. The viewer is in the domain of indetermination. This oscillation in the nature of the representation is exactly what separates most of Gidal's films like *Condition of Illusions* (1975) or *Close Up* (1983), from the Stan Brakhage film *Passage Through: A Ritual* (1990), which, as its name indicates, is a passage towards other horizons, another life. The abundance of black, rarely interrupted by images of film journals is lightened by the presence of music which offers the possibility of understanding these passages as moments of subjective elaborations. The music of Philip Corner, derived from François Couperin, is only heard at the beginning and at the end of the film, making the viewing of it an endurance test. The musical composition seems to duplicate the work of figuration: the piano chords are sprinkled throughout, arising from silence; they irresistibly evoke in their elongation certain compositions of Morton Feldman. The music codifies by its asperities and its variations the absence of an image.

When black is accompanied by a sound track, a qualified duration is understood. *A Movie* (1958) by Bruce Conner makes significant use of black by ending the shots by blackouts and thus inducing their link to the editing. In the dark, the music of Respighi permits by its continuation the understanding of each of the sequences, separated and alternated by the editing, all the while favoring open discursive effects. The black leader is time passed. This passage of time, this availability of the passage of time is remarkably deployed in the opening of *Twice a Man* (1963) by Gregory Markopoulos who, in the black of his prelude makes heard the sound of rain for around two minutes before it is dissolved into the image. In *Blonde Cobra* (1959-1962) by Ken Jacobs black emerges in an anarchic and provocative way. He records an account of a performance - namely one by Jack Smith - in his connection to improvisation. During these passages in darkness, a random radio can be heard which animates (locally) the recording. It is the imposition of a system which sets out to destabilize not the "performer" but the viewers by making the projection an experience of inadequation: bringing together fragments of autobiographical stories recounted by Jack Smith with 1930s music which floods over the sequences to slowly wreck itself in the blackness. As in the work of Markopoulos, the use of black leader is what permits the viewer to enter into and not leave the realm of dreams evoked by the film through childhood memories, proclaimed with aloofness by Smith.

This temporal flux is almost a dead time. But it is not a pause. Suddenly cinema puts us into the presence of an unfettered time, a decoded time. A free time which certain filmmakers will be able to pull back into the narrative like Christopher Maclaine in *The End* (1953) or by developing a critique of a specific film genre, like Maurice Lemaître with *The Song of Rio Jim* (1978) in which the music of Westerns colors our experience of the film, folding the absence of the image into an external presence. When the black is accompanied by a soundtrack as in *Nada le dernier film* (1978), then the eruption of this impetuousness is exactly what enables the filmmaker (materialist) to question the nature of our representations and what they leave out.

In some films, the cinematographic process is extended according to a Modernist strategy. It is an action which is analytic as much as reflective and which results in the filmmaker questioning by the means of film the very conditions of film.

Fade to black.

Pause.

When black leader is projected, the viewer is never completely in the dark. The perception of this black on the screen, and thus its dissolution, depends both on the projection conditions in a given room, the nature of the leader or film as well as the way it is used in the film: either in bunches or in blocks.

A case in point would be *Weekend* (1930) by Walter Ruttmann, which consists in listening to a soundtrack in the dark.[4] There is also *Le Rivage sanglant* (1985) by Michel Amarger in which the author harasses the audience in the dark with the soundtrack.

End of pause.

When the duration of the black is long, in other words more than a few seconds, the illusion of volume slips away to confront the flattening of an indeterminate grey surface. The opposition and the serialization of images, the tight editing and the use of flickering create particular effects which make cinema kinetic: a retinal art. Thus the perception of this black is modified by its placement in the film. Gregory Markopoulos was one of the first to exploit the tensions provoked by the bursts of black after groupings of alternating frames in which the color effects tint realistic views as in the case of *The Illiac Passion* (1964-1966), as well as in the films of Brakhage and primarily in the two series *Sincerity* (1973-1980) and *Duplicity* (1978-1980). The same is true in flicker films which assault the viewer with sheets of pure color which, by suspending the flood of colored flashes by means of pauses or dissolves in the solid blacks lead to residual effects leading to the perception of a closing in of the screen which suddenly seems to shrink and to fold in on itself, through a series of lateral displacements of often colored images which are in contrast to the suspension of the flicker of the trembling images - a sign of adaptation and adjustments which are necessary to see it.[5] Similar effects can be found in the films of Taka Iimura and particularly in *Models Reel 1* (1972) and *24 Frames per Second* (1975-1978) which bring out particular spaces reinforced by the use of sound whether in phase or not with the appearance of black leader.[6] Taka Iimura created models of exploration of space and film time by using an ensemble of basic parameters that he varies or modifies from one film to another. These films question the phenomenon of the perception of duration by intercutting sheets of black frames with the discrete appearance of light. Projected outside the theater, these installations work on our perception of time. In a gallery space, black acts differently because it no longer abolishes the space in a surge of darkness. Black becomes a particular quality of light. An extinguished light which is nevertheless still visible. The visibility of an absence.

In the tradition of direct film - meaning not the product of recording images by means of a camera and which applies to film the techniques of the rayogram (Man Ray) and the photogram (László Moholy-Nagy) - a series of films made by manipulating, scratching, or perforating black leader. It is above all in the 1950s that a large number of films were made with the animation techniques initiated by Len Lye. As already noted, the Lettrists made a specialty of chiseling directly on the filmstrip; punching holes in the original representative image allowing black to erupt in trembling streaks, zigzags of light. All of these interventions became a way of exploring light as energy. A luminous energy which revealed different aspects depending on whether the filmmaker was interested in the graphic, rhythmic or musical aspect of film. On an opaque filmstrip, Norman McLaren created in *Blinkety Blank* (1952), an intermittent animation in which objects, abstract or not, are afflicted by convulsive movements, inducing collisions resulting from their position on the filmstrip itself. In fact, McLaren spaced out his scratches by lengths of black in the manner of stroboscopic lighting which, like a shutter, blocks out phases of motion. Here (in the dark), displacement and motion can be dispensed with, snapshots are taken of the passage of the film that create the impression of a series of fixed moments telescoping into each other.[7] These jumps are all the more noticeable in that they occur against a background of figurative forms. The discontinuity, the trembling are what direct animation is most often based on: the tremors, because it is difficult to duplicate an image exactly from one frame to another, a good example being the title graphics of Brakhage's films; the discontinuity, because it is made up of blocks of frames which pulsate between blocks of black leader. Thus Diter Rot (or Dieter Roth), with *Dot* (1956-1962), works with the appearance and disappearance of perforations of every size according to a particular rhythm and frequency. This film prefigures at times the exemplary work accomplished by Len Lye with *Free Radicals* (the two versions, 1959 and 1978) and *Particles in Space* (1978) in which lines, brush strokes, points, and masses of luminous energy are put into motion and create incredible spaces, shattering by unimaginable volumes the flat black surface of the image. Successful works of the art of cinema, these films are examples in more than one way in the sense that they show that, by calibration and light, the cinema can freeze energies and distribute them according to a rhythm specific to the medium. By its scribbling, cinema makes it possible to reconnect with the primitive, unconscious rhythms that shape us, before we are regimented by aesthetics, morality, etc.[8] These scratched films are the cinematographic echo of the lacerations of Lucio Fontana and the "zips" of Barnett Newman. Despite the apparent poverty of the elements employed these films are extremely rich. This economy of means inherent in computer-assisted animation can be found in the work of Larry Cuba in *3/78* (1978) and in *Calculated Movement* (1985), as developed in a different way by John and James Whitney in which a small number of forms constituted by hundreds of white luminous points against a black background create, by successive transformations and permutations, magnificently choreographed arabesques. *Scratch* (1966-1967) by Robert Huot and *Parallel* (1974) by Taka Iimura use white scratches and imagine film as a privileged space of varia-tion. And so does *Black and Light* (1975) by Pierre Rovère in which a visual music can be heard from perforated paper. The rotations and displacements of perforations display the primordial role of the opening and closing of the camera shutter. The lighting up and extinction of white circles reinforce the idea that, to be seen, black leader must be exposed, open, therefore filled with holes. These utilizations of film as a black canvas on which can be inscribed auto-matic writing, drawings and texts, make the film, the black leader, that surface which film had always been, namely a light-sensitive surface ready to be printed on, ready to say something. The film, the black leader, like the blank page for the writer. This blank page, in fact black, is the place which makes all expression possible. It is for this reason that numerous filmmakers devote themselves to this aspect of cinematography: from graphics to the graph through the photography of texts, words.[9] Black leader can thus be understood as the equivalent of the white painting of Kazimir Malevitch; a space in which everything is possible: a space of potential and absolute virtuality.

Thus films of text occupy the symbolic domain that is the black screen, the black frame subject to every modification possible. The diversity of approaches makes each film a unique proposition. The word-by-word of *So is This* (1982) by Michael Snow differs radically from my *Vo/Id* (1987) in the sense that the former explores the varia-tions of size between white letters on a black background, while the latter plays with the possible inversions of negatives and positives, blacks and whites, in order to syncopate the reading of texts adjacent to each other on a double screen. The black pauses in the film func-tion as respiration, they become what gives body to the text. It is no longer word-by-word but bunches of words which are worked out according to rhythmic schemes in *Sid A Ids* (1992) or *Still Life* (1997). In *Still Life* there is a supplementary detail, induced as much by the bilingualism as by the use of the discursive form: the manifesto. A strategy that was already employed with *Vo/Id*. By putting aside the word-by-word, a graphic dimension emerges through the positioning of words on the screen and at the same time working with the distinct rhythm of the two languages used by varying the duration and appearance of each block of words.

In *Secondary Currents* (1984) Peter Rose plays with the notion of black film and the multiplicity of meanings that can be given to black film. From a police investigation to a loss of language, there is not a single step that the black screen does not succeed at wearing down, despite subtitles which do not translate language that goes beyond the image. Plays on words which recall the generative power of virtuality, that encloses the black depths of all these text-based films. Does the black function as a support that makes understanding possible or does it abolish it? The image of a white word on a black background indicates this otherness of language. When the words become signs moving around on the surface of the screen they distort themselves into nonsense and become like the concrete poetry practiced by Marc Adrian in *Wo-Da-Vor-Bei* (1958) or in *Text 1* (1963). *White Calligraphy* (1967) by Taka Iimura plays on this unreadability and this nonsense by means of calligrams scratched directly onto black leader and go past with such speed that the readability dissolves into a "chorecalligraphy." Taka Iimura scratched the calligrams of one of the oldest collections of Japanese stories, *Kojiki*, only the first pages of which he transcribed. Iimura does not seek to identify the story except in terms of the motion of light. A shift in meaning which refers back to the sign as a graphic element and makes the surface receptive as a space to be occupied. A space which Anthony McCall sculpts in black in *Line Describing a Cone* (1973) by means of a line of light. The film only exists as the incision of a luminous line in the black of the screen. The elaboration of a circle of light on the screen to produce a triangle outside the screen: a beautiful externality revealed.[10] The same can be said of *Remote Control* (1972) by Hollis Frampton where a frame is drawn in the form of a white dotted line. The filmmaker struggles mightily to maintain this fixed frame within the viewfinder of his camera and consequently on the screen. To be revealed, the frame must be obscured. Similarly, film must be hidden to be exposed. This obscuring was primarily exploited in three films: *Fire of Waters* (1965) by Brakhage, *Nocturne* (1980-1990) by Phil Solomon and *34, les ciels* (1993) by Jean-Claude Mocik. In these films, night plays an essential role. In *Fire of Waters*, lightening from a storm tears holes in the night and momentarily restores sight to the viewer. In *Nocturne*, the burst of the light of a torch in a room creates a climate of strangeness by calling up memories of war and aerial bombardment, restoring to children's games all their violence. In *34, les ciels*, night falls and so the image disappears, to let dawn break into a new day. The domain of night blossoms with shards of moonlight which dissolve the opacity of a night without dreams; fade to black? But is this fade an artifice of editing or the trace of a stretching out, a pause, or does it indeed foster the eruption of other images, another scene, another voice? Is it necessarily what dissolves, could it not also be what excludes, differs like an uncontrolled proliferation of the line separating frames on the filmstrip acting like leader which announces the return and the restarting of the image? So in the films of Martine Rousset, *Mansfield K* (1989) and *Kleist* (1993) the black image has a particular place in the attribution of off-camera voices and the images. Black is not the absence of an image, because it can be seen, it is both a respite which fosters the birth of the image and the other way around. This same attribution of black can be found in the film by Marie Craven *Pale Black* (1922), in which the creation of a subjectivity can only be identified by its gaps: the subject is constituted in those zones in which it disappears. A paradoxical function which has been adopted above all by women: Marguerite Duras with *L'Homme atlantique* (1981); Su Friedrich in *Gently Down the Stream* (1981), which recounts a series of dreams scratched directly on the filmstrip; Jennifer Burford in *Cortex* (1988), which summons words according to a series of variations and permutations of syllable, all the while extracting them by layers of black. The use of black leader by this filmmaker permits her to assemble sequential fragments in micro-units from which she establishes chromatic permutations and inversions. The subjects dissolve in ambiguity, genres become fuzzy according to an alternation which prevents the precise reconstitution of a body in *In/Side/Out I-IV* (1980-1984) as much as in *Eccentrics* (1986-1987). Very often, the affirmation of an individual is effectuated in the silence of images, which is to say, in the dark, in a place where it cannot subtract itself from the voice. Damaging itself in the dark so that the voice can be held back one last time: the silence of the screen. As if what is fragmentary, the explosion of representation, its dissolution into black, could permit the sketching of an emerging subject that cannot be frozen into a solid representation.[11] Constantly differed, the word and representation always return, in the form of a perpetual becoming whose potentiality is recorded directly on the screen in the dark of a not yet codified or decodified emulsion as Jeanne Liotta does in *Ceci n'est pas* (1996) in which the death of a loved one is evoked.

A dissolution in the medium. The surface which up to then fostered the optical resolution fractures and opens to the pure matter. An alchemy from which Jürgen Reble could orchestrate effects still to come.

Fade to black

3rd version revised and expanded, February 1998.

2nd version: *L'Armateur*, n°12, June 1994.

1st version in Flemish: *Andere Sinema*, n° 115, May-June 1993.

SPEED READING

If cinema didn't exist, visual artists would have invented it. Indeed, its appearance galvanized the literary and artistic scene. Immediately it stood forth as one of this century's essential elements: a startling purveyor of new representations of the world. It rapidly influenced artists and intellectuals after pulling free of its fairground origins, and despite industrialization, it claimed its place as a full-fledged art, offering major works which have transformed our way of seeing.

The redefinition of the world envisaged by Modernism took cinema as one of its strongest allies. The trepidation of modern life and the cult of the machine found an equivalent in the variety and multiplication of viewpoints, in the rhythm and inter-connection of images produced by editing techniques. Cinema was understood as a form of art that threatened to abolish all the others, to the extent that it could embrace them all. It partook of painting no less than music, its relations with poetry and dance were clear. It emerged as a new language, freeing itself from dramaturgy and literature. Visual artists and theorists of the first avant-garde upheld it as abstract, pure, integral, and absolute.[1] It offered a dynamic way to conceive man's relation to the machine. In this sense, it is one of the privileged tools in the production of new definitions of art and of art's manifestations.

The possibilities of visually inscribing the development of forms in time, independently of narrative constraints, suggested new forms of cinematographic expression which fashioned the first avant-garde. The filmmakers and cinema theorists of the early avant-garde shared with plastic artists certain formal concerns which revealed the identity crisis of the subjects of representation and at the same time sought to fashion a new world, with the transition to abstraction resolving, to some degree, the subjective crisis. When painters like Viking Eggeling, Walter Ruttmann, and Fernand Léger, or visual artists like Marcel Duchamp, Man Ray, and László Moholy-Nagy threw themselves into the adventure of cinema, it was not in order to resolve pictorial problems; it was not a matter of doing painting or photography in cinema. It was a matter of offering cinematographic practices the benefit of the advances that had been achieved in abstract painting as well as in atonal music and poetry, in order to set the newly born art apart from the controlling forces of narrative and naturalism, with their specific codes of representation. Painters wanted to know the constituents of this new medium which had not been totally broken by rules, asphyxiated by tradition. It was young, and full of the future, it brought the questions of energy, movement, light, and speed into play, and these elements formed the core of reflection for artists fascinated by the medium. This is how we should understand the interest shown by the painters. Narration and representation were very rapidly subverted. Such subversion was an essential contribution from the artists of the time to what would later be designated as experimental cinema. The subversion was only possible because it emanated from artists who were not filmmakers. Subsequently, this would less frequently be the case, even though the contribution of visual artists was to remain important in the domain of experimental cinema. The first generation of artist-filmmakers (Léger, Richter, Ray, etc.) disappeared with the advent of sound films, excepting a few rare individuals such as Len Lye, Oskar Fischinger, Jean Cocteau, and Luis Buñuel, and a renewal on the West Coast of the United States in the 1940s.

An effervescence similar to that of the first avant-gardes, with respect to cinema, cannot be found again until the early 1950s in France, with Lettrism,[2] or with the Beat Generation in America in the late 1950s, or with the Actionists in Austria in the 1960s. These latter manifestations echo the emergence of happenings and performances which, beginning in the late 1950s, would de-compartmentalize artistic practices as well as the conditions of delivery and reception of the work, and this, without failing to take the spectators into account.[3] Experimental cinema in the 1960s is American above all.[4] For political and aesthetic reasons it was conceived as a subversive practice (the qualifier was coined by Amos Vogel to speak of cinema as a breakaway art). It was inscribed in the field of revolutionary demands and became a central object of the period's artistic production and reflection. Emancipating itself from economic contingencies, it came back into touch with its public, as in the 1920s. The creation of the Film-Makers' Cooperative in 1962 played a preponderant role in the distribution of experimental cinema. The existence of this organization favored the emergence of an independent circuit of distribution, a veritable parallel network, fed and energized by the work of new filmmakers no longer encumbered by the criteria of profitability governing industrial cinema and its codes. Filmmakers no longer faced any limits either on what could be shown on the screen or how it was made. Projections were organized by Jonas Mekas; in 1964 the Film-Makers' Cinematheque was founded.[5] The field of the production and distribution of cinema saw highly individual practices come to the fore (this was the moment when the notion of "personal cinema" was conceived), alongside communal endeavors, almost familial or tribal, running counter to the division of labor in traditional production. A space of freedom opened with the constitution of the New American Cinema.[6] This advance toward the autonomy of cinema echoed the upsurgent representation and affirmation of alternatives breaking away from mass production. The emergence of a counter-culture which found its models in the movements of liberation, and particularly the Afro-American movement, promoted the idea of a community. Cinema could no more avoid this ideal than the plastic arts; together they became the privileged conduits of the transformation. By creating new projection contexts, by constituting a group and elaborating a history, experimental cinema built itself up as an avant-garde space, with a contradictory dynamic stressing both liberation and community spirit. It redistributed the new forms of art and encouraged cross-overs and de-compartmentalization. Plastic artists such as Robert Rauschenberg, Andy Warhol, Yoko Ono, Carolee Schneemann, Bruce Nauman, Richard Serra, Jan Dibbets, Jack Chambers, and Ben began using film. Their production drew on and pillaged the experimental cinema of the 1960s and 1970s.

In 1963, the art world in the United States underwent considerable change. Pop art dominated the artistic scene. Wolf Vostell's first video installations were exhibited in New York, while Nam June Paik showed his first sculptures involving TV sets in Germany. Fluxus gave performances mixing poetry, music, dance, film... Artists were becoming more and more interested in experimental cinema, and Andy Warhol declared that he was giving up painting in favor of film. The medium played a preponderant role in Warhol's art. It generated the paintings by the quotation and recycling of a few emblems such as the Hollywood stars. It encouraged the proliferation of clichés. The Factory saw itself as a place for the production and reception of images, before even considering the question of the material supports. These only moderately effected the treatment and the characteristics of the shot and the pose.

The Factory was at once a workshop for the serial production of silk-screened, photographic, cinematographic, and video portraits, but also a parody of Hollywood studios. If cinema fascinated Warhol, it was both through its capacity to produce stars and to contaminate our gaze on the world, mediated above all by the gaze of the stars.

The cinematographic treatment of banal actions renders them spectacular, whether by the extension in time with *Sleep, Blow Job, Fat* (all 1963), and *Empire* (1964), or by the reiteration of an action with *Kiss* (1963), or by the series of portraits in *Screen Tests* (1964-1967).[7] The actions are reduced, almost minimal; the framing is not totalizing but fragmentary, as in *Blow Job* or *Empire*. This last film, eight hours long, shares the Pop technique of objectifying daily life, through recourse to common objects or consumer goods. Indeed, what could be more banal for New Yorkers than the Empire State building? There it is; but you always move on, you never spend eight hours in front of it, unless while working or making a film. By stretching out the projection, objects are turned away from their habitual significance, while viewing itself is turned into an endurance test. The screening becomes a performance, and the filmed object trips us up by its persistence. With *Sleep* and *Empire*, Warhol slammed the door on cinematographic spectacle by multiplying the images. This representation of everyday life attested its ties to Pop art, while the representation of a seamy and scandalous world (drugs and homosexuality) aligned the films with experimental cinema's affirmations of life on the fringes. Where Hollywood embodied the bright side of cinema, the underground stressed its freedom-seeking and "camp" aspects. "Baudelairean cinema"[8] was of prime importance for Warhol since his very first film, *Tarzan and Jane Regained... Sort Of* (1963), which inscribed this influence both in the acting (Taylor Mead) and in the incorporation of numerous random events, most fervently promoted by Jack Smith, Ken Jacobs, and Ron Rice. This film, *Tarzan...*, takes its place in a tradition inaugurated by Alfred Leslie and Robert Frank with the film *Pull My Daisy* (1959), which celebrated a day in the life of a band of poets. The spontaneity of the film became a characteristic of underground cinema, even though everything was already played out in this inaugural work. The liberty of tone and the quality of the recording conferred an apparent freedom on the document, something which crops up consistently thereafter. All the accidents that singularize the film are included in its unfolding, a little like a happening which includes the participants, eliminating the sacrosanct separation between spectators and actors, amateurs and professionals. The influence of John Cage[9] can be felt over a wide range of practices running from dance to music by way of cinema. Though Cage did not directly influence Warhol, he did so indirectly, through Allan Kaprow's happenings and actions in the street, through the environments of

Claes Oldenberg and the choreographies of Yvonne Rainer and Trisha Brown.

Alongside this Pop experience of cinema, there exists another attitude which emerged from everyday life and inscribed the circulation of images quite differently, through recycling and detournement (twisting away from normal use or conception). Instead of making the proliferation of images into the object of the work, it is the selection of diverse elements and their redistribution in new wholes (sculptures, photographs, films) which generates the piece. The idea of "found footage,"[10] as employed by Maurice Lemaître and Bruce Conner in the cinematographic domain, is central here. It allows the filmmaker to work on and to transform objects and clichés which he has not produced. The assemblage of disparate objects offers an interpretation of society which is most often critical, to the extent that the work is constituted of salvaged objects which society has cast aside. Like Joseph Cornell with his boxes and his films, Bruce Conner and, to a somewhat lesser degree, Maurice Lemaître, play with the images of a time which still believed them innocent. Lemaître's work openly calls for social transformation and revolt. In the films of these artists, narratives are built up using clichés and quotations. They take possession of a history that is beyond us; they steal images by breaking into the flux of history. This displacement of the signifier by distorting it prefigures the massive use of "found footage" by the cinema of the 1980s. Post-modernism, with its propensity for the recycling of styles, would make cinema one of its tools of choice. However, in distinction from Warhol's work, it is not the proliferation of images that predominates, but on the contrary, the use of montage as an extension of collage. This means the juxtaposition of shots according to multiple criteria. What matters is their redistribution and their capacity to be reinjected into new circuits, risking the notion of the author and of the work.

This multiplicity of shots and sequences contrasts with the minimalism of Fluxus and Warhol. Fluxus shared with Warhol a similar minimalism of the objects or actions being filmed, as well as related strategies of stretching out certain actions.[11] The filmed actions run from the appearance of a smile or the striking of a match in extreme slow-motion, to extreme close-up shots of a pair of wandering buttocks. Each film, like the performances of Fluxus, is reduced to an idea, an action, a joke, using this deliberate simplicity to criticize the avant-garde, often judged too serious. But unlike Warhol, *Fluxfilms* make use of ultra-fast recording speeds, with the effect of making an action of a few second's duration last for several minutes; while in Warhol's work it is the extremely slow speed of projection that produces the long duration. This slowed-down projection provokes an intensely scintillating light that irradiates the grain of the emulsion, evoking the grain of press photography as well as that of the silk screens. The experience of duration refers both to the understanding of time in Eric Satie's *Vexations*[12] and to pieces by La Monte Young. The experience also depends on what is represented, and it can be said that Pop art's iconography of everyday objects is complemented here by the influence of the Judson Dance Theater's performances and of Yvonne Rainer's choreography, which stage such commonplace actions as running, walking, etc.[13]

The representation of the body is handled differently by filmmakers and performers. Its involvement leads to opposed modes of filming which also crop up in the use of film by artists recording their performances. Indeed, when Carolee Schneemann films her actions she goes beyond the simple recording of the act, mixing in double-exposure effects and graphic manipulations of the film base. In this sense she is in tune with the gestural approach of Stan Brakhage and Jack Smith. Even though the subjects treated by Schneemann and Barbara Rubin are quite different from those of Warhol, they share the affirmation of sexuality and an evident taste for provocation. However, Warhol's distanced aesthetic is opposed to the lyricism, sensuality, and subjectivity of Brakhage. The Vienna Actionists also privileged cinema as a means of recording. It was the memory of an action or an event, as photography was for land art. But many artists replaced this documentary use of cinema with a more dynamic conception of the medium, closer to experimental cinema. Thus along with Carolee Schneemann, artists such as Günter Brus, Otto

Mühl, Hermann Nitsch, and VALIE EXPORT were able to find radical manners of filming, their performances, no longer seeking realism but using editing techniques, framings, camera treatments and movements to link up with the emotive and affective dimensions of the performance, translating its violence into film. These artists are in debt to the filmmakers Kurt Kren, Hans Scheugl, and Ernest Schmidt.[14] All three took a similar path, moving from close collaborations with artists (Günter Brus and Otto Mühl with Kurt Kren) to metric or structural cinema as it had been defined by Peter Kubelka. The action conceived formally with the filmmaker thus becomes a work in its own right. A similar attitude comes up again in the late 1960s in France, with Christian Boltanski, Gina Pane, and various people working in body art.[15] Among the latter group, the spiritual dimension is developed through sacrificial practices borrowing heavily from Catholicism. In Michel Journiac's work during the 1960s, this attitude is found in the films of his rites of communion and of offering. The cinema becomes the privileged catalyst for a special type of action. Action is conceived for the cinema, as is the case with Vito Acconci's Super-8 films. In these, the sparsity of means is perfectly in synch with the action being depicted, as in Ben's performances, whose best testimony is constituted by their cinematographic traces. In the same way, Boltanski's early films illustrate this capacity to propose and to realize scenes from which narration is absent, scenes without any progression, just the unfolding of an event, without any beginning or end. This absence of resolution is what differentiates them from the filmic proposals of Robert Filliou and Daniel Buren, which always end with some kind of final scene, often a pun or a reference to art history. Depending on the artist in question, the formalism of the film takes more or less precedence over the performance; but in every case, it is the performative aspect of cinema that is exploited. On the one hand, the accent falls on the action being filmed, whether conceived for the medium or not; on the other, the mode of presentation comes to the fore, in such a way that the projection unsettles the norms. There is a much greater production of films in the first register, where the reflexivity is not directed toward the medium but reflects an attitude toward the artist's environment or history. The artist's involvement is more or less violent, according to the stress laid on the body and its manifestations. Thus the relations to religious rites are more pronounced in the work of the Viennese, who explore, for other ends, the energy and the affects in the phenomena of trance and possession. A spectacular dimension is inscribed in the action, which is often marked by unusual cruelty: the bodies suffer, or at times take pleasure, always being pushed to their furthest reaches. Underground cinema became one of the great purveyors of this experience of extremes. By means of film, the performance is affirmed beyond its brevity: it becomes timeless through recording. It attains reproduction without the risks of live experience. Once filmed, it becomes a performance forever fixed in its unalterable unfolding, somewhat like legendary concerts: a paradoxical manifestation of eternity, when it was initially a question of the pure moment. These problems of temporality are concomitant to those of spatialization as approached by the exponents of modernist aesthetics. The links are slighter but they are also more clearly recognized, favoring the primacy of a reading of art from the formal viewpoint.

In this sense the relations that experimental cinema maintains with minimal and conceptual art are primordial, for their similar attitudes underscore processes and intersections that facilitate the movement from one medium to the next, as is the case with Eric Andersen. This can be easily grasped if one draws the parallel between the processes deployed by repetitive music and structural cinema. The isolation of basic sequences or structures as cells whose elements are progressively varied is common to both practices. Unlike in the 1920s, the question of cinema is conceived in terms which always reveal a way of thinking, an artist behind or beyond the medium. However, this does not preclude a relatively traditional use of cinema by plastic artists such as Robert Morris and Martial Raysse, who pay homage to Hollywood cinema even while parodying it, or by Robert Smithson, who cites and refers to it with *Spiral Jetty* (1970). The technological tool disappears into the validity of the proposal. These attitudes permit overlapping and cross-references, as in the work of emblematic figures such as Paul Sharits, Michael Snow, Anthony McCall, Gordon Matta-Clark, Richard Serra, Jean-Pierre Bertrand, and Marcel Broodthaers. The cross-references run from painting, photography, and sculpture toward cinema, and vice versa. The questions being posed aim to reduce the medium to its constituents, on the basis of which the production of a work can be envisaged; they are questions concerning the nature of cinematographic representation and the processes of perception that it brings into play. The definition of the constituents encourages the emergence of analytic works ranging over all the dimensions of cinema. These investigations lead to different models of presentation, breaking away from the standardized screening: multiple projections, installations, environments. It may be recalled that as early as 1912, Bruno Corra sought to create colored environments.[16] The installation using cinema inscribes a will to plunge cinema into the world of the plastic arts. Such installations analyzing the conditions of a film's projection refer to primitive cinematographic systems. These became an inexhaustible source for numerous filmmakers and artists like Ken Jacobs and Werner Nekes, who modified the projection devices to produce pieces exploring stereoscopy, relief, or color. These investigations simultaneously nourished the plastic works of Alfons Schilling and Paolo Gioli. Multiple projection moved away from performance as soon as the problem of continuous projection was resolved. By proposing works that enlarged the field of perception through the use of particular devices - loops, multi-projections, environments - artists could totally occupy galleries or museums, in a practice of which Documenta 6 in 1977[17] represented both the consecration and the burial. It is easily understood that recourse to the less fragile medium of video led to the near disappearance of these same film installations in the 1980s. In an obligatory return of the repressed, cinema has been invading the field of contemporary art in an unavoidable way for several years now.[18] In 1987, Paul Sharits admitted to me that he could no longer devote his time to such installations because they require too much technical follow-up. With implacable rigor, Sharits had conceived and shown cinema as "Location Pieces" and "Frozen Film Frames."[19] A theatricalization, a dramatization of the projection experience immerses the viewer in specific conditions; he is no longer seated, there are no more precise temporal limits. The installation gives itself over all at once: there is no narrative development or introduction of new elements, instead the work deploys variations and articulations which one grasps almost immediately upon entering the space. The temporal experience of the piece allows us to deepen our perception of it, as in the experience of painting or sculpture. Of course, all film installations do not answer to these same criteria but they are certainly found in the work of Taka Iimura and Chris Welsby, both of whom employ multi-projections. Cinema installations are the logical extension of expanded cinema with its multi-screen projections. But unlike these, their duration is extendable, in contrast to the duration of a performance or an action. There is something like an opposition of projects here, which certain contemporary experimental film-makers will use to their advantage, playing on the articulation of these two directions. Jürgen Reble's installations deploy a dematerialization of the support over time; it can be seen but cannot be totally grasped. The process and the action are clear; their development transcends our attention span, as was already the case with *Empire*. The installation is a unique event which undergoes constant transformation, and it can just as well cease to function entirely. Like a land art proposal, it can freeze at a given point in its evolution; a random event can shatter its beautiful machinery. It is always a matter of "seeing how forms and colors are subject to perpetual movement."[20]

Today the installation has become a full-fledged genre, a category, where it was initially the sign of a crossing of media. It seems to be privileged by the market for its spectacular aspects. However, all such proposals do not necessarily involve this spectacularization. When Anthony McCall created *Line Describing a Cone* (1973), he brought out the sculptural dimension of any film projection. It was above all a matter of modeling and modulating a beam of light outside of any receiving support: an architecture of fragile, ephemeral light, whose experience is more closely related to meditation than to the incessant consumption of images. Such consumption and circulation of images is encountered in contemporary proposals which apply their disparate montage to the installation components, according to an organization and an aesthetics close to "found footage." This is the reign of salvage and recycling, in a supermarket of the image. Henceforth it will be pointless to produce one's own images, only the retreatment of the image holds meaning, in a veritable fulfillment of Postmodernism. This appropriation is applied as much to the arrangement of shots as to their presentation in space; compare the installations of Stan Douglas, Peter Fischli and David Weiss, Sylvia Bossu, and Douglas Gordon. Thus cinema itself is recycled, becoming an object of quotation no less than of fetishization; to many it seems to have no more future. And yet from the moment when cinema is recognized as obsolete by the exponents of interactivity - preferably digitalized - it demonstrates a prodigious capacity to transform our ways of seeing, by incorporating and playing with everything that endangers it, showing how fleeting and fragile the medium of film really is. Paul Sharits worked on just this fragility and vulnerability when he used scratches and burns in various installations and films, as though he were trying to destroy cinema. A similar perspective appears with Jürgen Reble when he declares: "We didn't do that to mistreat the material. What we wanted was to discover our own limits, and establish those beyond which a filmic object can no longer be projected."[21] To push cinema to the extreme, all the way to its destruction, so as to confirm its necessity in the face of the all-devouring media which see it as no more than a nostalgic pastime: such remains the only possible attitude for filmmakers today."

3e Biennale d'art contemporain, Lyon, Réunion des Musées Nationaux,
1995
Translated from the French by Brian Holmes

FROM ONE WORLD TO ANOTHER

Experimental cinema was not always concerned with narration. In certain periods of its development the emphasis shifted to other aspects of the medium, as it is shown by experimental works of the German and French avant-garde in the 1920s, as well as by Structural Film and Underground Cinema during the 1960s and 1970s. On the basis of its separate components those filmmakers question the preconditions for the special characteristics of the medium. These analyses and filmic discourses sometimes completely disregard the notion of authorship, meaning that the filmic means themselves take on the function of the author. It is in this way that the devices put forward by these films prefigure the role of the author becoming the generator of possibilities for the elaboration of a story that viewers dives into and transforms as they wish according to more or less predetermined modalities.

This article will restrict itself to pointing out the relationship that experimental cinema bears to the non-linear modes of narration and how has it been able to develop or set up devices that break up classical techniques of narration while creating space for other technologies to fashion a new language.

Let us first make it clear that we are not interested in the form of mimetic cinema that handles film material according to a series of codes based on notions of resemblance and conformity to reality. We shall give preference to an experimental cinema that has questioned the modalities and potentialities of the basic plot within or beyond the scope of narration. These questions often arise when the film project is carried out using a large quantity of images - shot either by the filmmaker himself or someone else. In this respect the approach is related to that of documentary film, film diary and found footage films. In each of these categories the question of meaning and especially of making sense of a collection of disparate materials arises. This organizational problem also raises an underlying question on the nature of montage and its importance, a question that the Soviet filmmakers, above all Eisenstein and Vertov, tackled in an exemplary fashion. For Vertov, the interval is the essential link for creating meaning in a juxtaposition of shots: "It is the intervals, which lead the action to a cinematic denouement. The organization of movement is a matter of organizing its elements, that is, of the intervals in the phrase."[1] Vertov is thus also able to say: "Montage means organizing the pieces of film (the images) in a film, 'writing' the film by means of the filmed images; it does not mean selecting pieces of film to make 'scenes' (as in theatre) or stories (as in literature)." In the light of these statements one understands that it is necessary to see cinema as a practice that distances itself from literature. This opinion is shared by the entire avant-garde cinema from the moment when cinema is envisaged as a separate practice, and the more so, the more the film-makers try to find, to account for, or to categorize the logic that determines the combination of different elements (sensations, images) in a film. What are the determining aspects in the elaboration of a form? A similar argumentation is found in the case of Maya Deren when, alluding to the structure of her films, she sees them as being nearest to poetry: "These films stand in relation to most films as poetry does to literature. Actually, in a sense, their structure is closest to music. One of the habits that we bring with us is the anticipation that there will be a narrative in the film and that that narrative will give the film form. In this case there is no narrative, any more than there is narrative in musical composition. To say there is no narrative is not to say it is anarchic, but according to another logic. My effort is directed toward discovering what would be the logic of film form as constructed to the logic of narrative form: to discover this logic - as a poet discovers the logic of one tone following another - and in which we recognize a melody, although it is not a narrative."[2] This expectation of narration was called into question by the avant-garde, whether by Dadaist and Surrealist filmmakers like Man Ray or Luis Buñuel upsetting the linearity of narration by means of intertitles,[3] or by Stan Brakhage, who, by means of the elaboration/affirmation of a subjective vision, disencumbered himself of the parasite of narration to the benefit of subjective expressiveness, thus declaring the advent of "Personal Cinema". Malcolm Le Grice condemns this anchoring of an artist's work in a romantic subjectivity as promoted by American filmmakers. He gives preference to an anonymity of cinematographic devices from which he develops virtual processes.

Similar strategies have often been employed by the filmmakers of the avant-garde when they were trying to undermine a linear development to let the structural and processual framework emerge within the space of the film. In this context films like *Histoire de détective*, (1929) by Charles Dekeukeleire,[4] Hollis Frampton, Peter Rose come to mind, each of whom in their own way worked outside the usual fields of language. Wordplay that has the images cross on different planes and causes a suspension of the film's action, nearly a standstill.

A suspension that always means the outburst of a memory by means of an image. Here, the experience described by Proust (but not by him alone) comes to mind, where a whole piece of his past comes back to him upon his tasting a madeleine. Simultaneous expression of two temporal levels within a single experience, experienced in the cinema through an intersection of processes that expresses a temporal plurality. Thus in diary films, the presentation of an event is sometimes accompanied by images that blur and interfere with the experience in relation to the perception of the present moment. Thus, in the case of Jonas Mekas,[5] the role played by intertitles and off-screen voices allows the diverse elements involved to be introduced into the perception. The same is the case with Matthias Müller, where one finds overlapping experiences that show both the act of memorization and the structure of this perception (primarily in *Memobook - Aus der Ferne*, 1989).

These processes of memorization convey sets of variations that can become in their turn the subject of a film, thus undermining the narration in favor of the pure process and its exploitation. Structural film was one of the champions of these methods in its examination of the components, thus determining the basic elements of cinematographic technique. Here the work of Ken Jacobs comes to mind with *Tom, Tom, the Piper's Son* (1969), in which burlesque comedy is analyzed and examined in such a way that, when the final recapitulation comes, the narrative frame yields up its place to the potentialities that it contains, of which the film has been the exposition. This secondary elaboration is what allows the reintroduction of multiplicity in the course of a domestic scene, if one thinks of *Critical Mass* (1971) by Hollis Frampton, who, by manipulating the soundtrack, letting the woman's voice gradually slide into the place of the voice of the man and vice versa, calls the role distribution within a partnership into question. This reversal questions both the concept of genre and the assignment of roles, and the conformity of what is recorded to the action that is played. What part of truth is at stake in that fictional reality? The whole illusion of cinema as a means of faithfully reproducing reality is revealed by the employment of such processes. This criticism becomes more radical in the case of Peter Gidal, who condemns all representation as a form of enslavement of the images. According to him they resemble a particular ideological affirmation that gives the preference above all to the experience of the (re-)recognition and thus expresses in a certain way the perpetuation of the power of illusion.

But to regard cinema as a procurer of exterior potentialities or virtualities does not restrict us to a meta-linguistic approach to film, in which the language expresses a distance to and a comment on the object that determines the action, as can be seen in *Who Do You Think You Are?* (1987) by Mary Filippo, or in *L'appartement de la rue de Vaugi-*

rard (1970) or even *Nostalgia* (1970) by Hollis Frampton. Cinema regarded as something that works with possibilities; virtuality is already hinted at in Gregory Markopoulos suggestions regarding a new form of film narration. In a famous text written in 1963, he suggests that we turn our attention to the photogram; in this sense he indirectly connects up to certain preoccupations of the filmmakers of structural cinema: "The film frame which creates each shot composition has been neglected; it has been understood only as a photographic necessity. I propose a new narrative form through the fusion of the classic montage technique with a more abstract system. This system involves the use of short film phrases which evoke thought-images. Each film phrase is composed of certain select frames that are similar to the harmonic units in musical composition. The film phrases establish ulterior relationships among themselves; in classic montage technique there is a constant reference to the continuing shot: in my abstract system there is a complex of different frames being repeated."[6] The affirmation of the autonomy of visual processes is not foreign to Markopoulos' radicalization of cinematography, whose advent is marked by *The Illiac Passion* (1964-1967). This film turns narration into a distant icon, into a specter that no longer belongs here below. This "evacuation," this rejection of narration in all its forms is related to some proposals to make films an event, so to speak a performance. Those peculiar moments then come to mind, where the cinematographic concept is elaborated in a diversity of shots that includes the audience by "compelling" them to take an active role. A new relationship is built up between the filmmaker, the filmed subject and the audience. *La vache qui rumine* (1969) displays this tendency and has this challenge as its favorite theme. Playing on our irrepressible anthropomorphic desires, the cow seems to apostrophize us and engage in a dialogue whose burlesque character is not the least of its qualities. The aspect of play makes it possible to undermine the cult of linearity if the game does not obey the rules that lead to a reinstatement of the linearity of traditional fictional films; these solve a more or less hackneyed riddle again and again.

In the undefined space of a game whose rules we have not

mastered, an exchange arises between the protagonist and his potential audience. George Rey and Ericka Beckman in *You The Better* (1983), and Robert Nelson in *Bleu Shut* (1970) work on such spaces. These films open up territory that will then be developed by technologies that connect real time with the moment in which one passes through it.

Avant-garde films have worked towards developing other usages of time which escape in the progress of continuous time. This notion of time is rejected by philosophy, which cannot cope with states of flux and the present moment, and desperately holds fast to the concept of chronology. From the moment when simultaneity is introduced, the structuring of narration and the development of a narrative or musical form is again called into question. These questionings have been and continue to be a source of stimulation for experimental cinema. At the same time, they are blueprints of a possible intervention for other techniques, whose most recent manifestations are the virtual worlds.

43 *Internationale Kurzfilmtage*, Oberhausen, 1997.
Published simultaneously in English and German under the same title.

THE CITY REVISITED

For quite some time I have been thinking about filming cities as a particular form of cinematographic activity. The filmed cities which I have inhabited or traversed reflect a complex sensory experience. Indeed, as with most of the filmmakers in this series, the relation we have to space reflects our way of being in this world, our living in this world at any time - we concur, despite the multiplicity of our imagery. The city in film is never an anonymous space. It always confirms a subjectivity that develops from looking at this private and public space as well as from one's dealing with it.

Being in this world means, above all, measuring out a personal space vis-a-vis a public space. This measuring is based on the relationship we have to history - our own history as well as that of places and spaces which, on the one hand, turn us into what and who we are and which we, on the other hand, produce ourselves. In this respect, film proves to be a privileged tool in the forming and shaping of such (private and public) mental spaces.

Filming space is somewhat like desiring to halt time or, more precisely, the flow of a river. In this sense, the Gardens of the Villa d'Este filmed by Kenneth Anger in *Eaux d'Artifice* (1953) are exemplary. These water gardens play with the different organic aspects in order to solidify the water in bubbling, quivering sculptures, similar to the wind and the crazy race of a twirling chimera. What seemed solid a moment ago becomes liquid before turning into luminous blue dust. When filming cities one always lets oneself be swept away by parasitic images, by phantoms which come to interfere with or take possession of the portrayed space. One should not assume that such phantom images are always to be judged negatively - that would be a mistake; there are sometimes reminiscences of childhood or of times passed which we may experience solely via these images. One need only think of the New York of Jonas Mekas (*Walden*, 1969) in which nature and childhood are so present that one sometimes comes to ask oneself whether it is actually about New York and not perhaps about some section of Lithuania transplanted to Manhattan. This representation of the city is paradoxical since it occurs precisely at that moment in which devotion to this city (is it a belief?) is at its slackest, virtually suspended in the breath of a soul.

There are no virginal spaces; there are no places which have not yet been spoilt by clichés and various, more or less conscious, illusions.

At other times, the spaces are so replete with history that it is impossible not to see it, the concentration camps as described by Alain Resnais (*Nuit et Brouillard,* 1955) or Daniel Eisenberg's *Cooperation of Parts* (1987). The scarred bodies in Alain Fleischer's films are also readable on the pavements of the city. However, these scars are not only part of the past - that is what Alain Resnais, Jean-Luc Godard, Jean-Marie Straub or Chantal Akerman have demonstrated to us unequivocally in some of their films.

Layers of images cut the cities up according to elusive architectures; series of travelling shots interlock with each other in *Chicago Loops* (1976) by James Benning, *Non, je ne regrette rien* (1984) by Gustav Deutsch, *Seeing in the Rain* (1981) by Chris Gallagher, *Nichtsehennichtsehen* (1993) by Jan Peters or *Highway* (1958) by Hilary Harris. This spatial syncopation contrasts with another kind of camera-travelling which stretches time until it dissolves, as one can witness in *Eureka*

(1977) by Ernie Gehr or *Chicago* (1996) by Jürgen Reble. The city becomes an emulsive substance.

Italian cities or also New York hold an unbelievable aura for numerous film makers. But for each one of them, filming such cities amounts to, knowingly or unknowingly, looking into the history of the representation of the city by means of the given medium. Thus, in the shadow of each new vision others can arise which carry us towards other shores, faces or landscapes. Filmmakers searching for a remembrance of things past or of lost characters are particularly fond of falling back on an allusion which is not a quotation. Marjorie Keller's *Heiress* (1991) and Christian Boltanski's *L'Appartement de la rue de Vaugirard* (1975) particularly come to mind. Similarly, the recurrent use of motifs, such as the bridge, is to be understood as a homage to a master: it is in this sense that the film by Jakobois about the bridges of Asnières (*Les ponts d'Asnières*, 1987) is a homage to Van Gogh.

In the same way, the Impressionist vision of Paul Strand in *Manhatta* (1921) is reflected in a number of shots of *News from Home* (1977) by Chantal Akerman, that reach across the successive transformations of Manhattan: the fascination with the Meatpacking District, the Staten Island Ferry pier...

Places that have already been filmed are revisited. In *Amoroso* (1983), I refilmed the gardens of Tivoli, but to record a supplementary difference: the water displays and other subjects are seen in tones of red and the visions of Rome evoke those of *Home Movies - Rome, Florence, Venice* (1965) by Taylor Mead.

In the same way the filmed space can permit us to remember and, in this sense, the fiction of representation, so its interpretation becomes the trace of a beyond that we convoke while simultaneously confronting the experiences of the moment when one of them occurs: it is in this way that *Son nom de Venise dans Calcutta désert* (1976) is like the reverse of the decor of *India Song* (1974-1975). The latter film allows the memory to arise out of its dazzling fragility. A pure event, if there can be one, the film makes use of our memory in order to bring to bloom through the palace ruins what it means to be under the spell of amorous passion. Renunciation and abandonment are engraved in the deserted places, almost as a terrain to be deciphered as much as cleared out.

The city as a tomb of images presents surface concretions in which the first shots flourish at the moment of their dissolution. Cemeteries as a place where time is suspended enable the past, the distant memory, to be evoked more easily. They are also urban spaces that are particularly rich for letting the imagination wander. Purveyors of emotions, they are the catalysts of images, witness *The Dead* (1960) by Stan Brakhage in *The Fallen World* (1983) by Marjorie Keller as well as the films of the MétroBarbèsRochechou Art group made in Père Lachaise cemetery.

At the bend of a street history emerges, as much by the traces of submerged monuments, preserved or restored, as by their disappearance. Here the films *Premonition* (1995) by Dominic Angerame, *Les Antiquités de Rome* (1989) by Jean-Claude Rousseau, *Verlussen; Verlore; Einsam, Kalt (Missa Solemnis)* (1990) by Klaus Wyborny are exemplary of such disappearances or the unease which they provoke in our being in the world. But these places themselves are inseparable from the events which took place there. Commonplace daily events such as in the films of Alain Fleischer, as much as dramatic stories. This boiling over of history is such that certain cities are haunted by the memory of images that end up signifying them. The city robbed by its very images becomes a source of contempt and of wandering, in search of a neutral space.

But one does not have to go far, it is enough to film a room, an apartment, a square, in any city to summon an indescribable otherness, the welling up of another time which comes to life on the surface of the screen. I am thinking of *One Second in Montreal* (1969) by Michael Snow, *Spacy* (1980) by Takasha Ito, *Maas Observation* (1997) by Karel Doing and Greg Pope.

The wandering of filmmakers as much as viewers who only see cities through the piling up of images: *De Maasbruggen* (1938) by Paul Schuitema, *U.S.S.A.* (1987) by Vivian Ostrovsky and *Dreaming in Yellow While Searching For Carpaccio's Gold* (1990) by Andrea Kirsch function as catalyzers: they impact shots, sequences.

The city falls apart. Memory plays tricks on us and makes us wander through cities which we are in but to which we will never go, although we nevertheless know them so well, as is the case with *Weit Weit Weg* (1995) by Björn Melhus. On their side, filmmakers fabricate cities which we are always eager to walk through eyes closed, with delight or horror. Are not the most beautiful voyages those taken without traveling, in the manner of the tourist without baggage whose guide would be Joseph Cornell?

And yet I will never stop filming certain cities (New York, Paris or Venice) in order to discover them and tirelessly lose myself in them. To bring back the city always takes us back to the moment in the past that we have not yet experienced.

3rd Biennale Film + Arc, Graz, 1997
published simultaneously in German and English

ACKNOWLEDGEMENTS (1998 EDITION)

Éditions du Centre Georges Pompidou; Éditions Jean-Michel Place; Film+Arc Graz (Charlotte Pochhacker); Galerie nationale du Jeu de Paume (Françoise Bonnefoy et Danièle Hibon); Internationale Kurzfilmtage Oberhausen (Angela Haardt); Ma Dai (Catia Riccaboni); Mix (Rajandra Roy); Musée national d'art moderne (Jean-Michel Bouhours); Project 180; Réunion des Musées Nationaux (Anne de Margerie).

ART PRESS; *L'Armateur*; *Limelight*; *Revue et Corrigée*; *Vertigo*.

IRENE BOCCHETTA; Pip Chodorov; Christian Janicot; Coralie Le Van Van; Miles McKane; Giovanna Puggioni; Leesa Wang.

NOTES

Resistance Cinema

1. On this subject the recent article in *Art Press* in July 1997 is edifying to say the least in its exemplary misunderstanding of the uses of film. In the desire to over-defend and over-promote a history of moving images to guarantee a definitive role for video installation, it exhibits an extraordinary inability to analyze the medium of film.

2. Examples would include: *Passages de l'image*, Centre Georges Pompidou, Paris 1992, *Hall of Mirrors*, MOCA, Los Angeles, 1995, Biennale de Lyon 1995, *Spellbound*, Hayward Gallery, London 1996, Printemps de Cahors 1997, Venice Biennale 1997, to cite just a few. On another note, Documenta X paid homage to other aspects of the filmic image by favoring an auteurist approach.

3. *Leap Frog* is composed of found footage discovered in the trash bins of the Jardin des Plantes in Paris in the summer of 1992. It consists of positive color films which Miles McKane printed as if it were color negative, which gives it its particular quality and its undefined background on a color base. Nicole Brenez described this color in her "Couleur critique" in *La Couleur en cinéma*, edited by Jacques Aumont, Paris, Cinémathèque française/Mazzota, 1995.

4. *Alchemy* (1994) and *Tabula Smaragdina* (1997), shown at the Louvre on the occasion of a colloquium on 3-D, shares this principal of using sound to neither repeat nor anticipate the work on the image but to accompany it according to its own modalities of distension and loss, following the repetition of pulsating but not syncopated loops. As if its rhythm had just ceded its place in favor of the dynamic progression.

5. This notion of recycling intersects more broadly with that of found footage, see *The Harder They Fall* in this collection. Recycling is a more global notion which can include quotation, the appropriation of sequences both shot for the occasion and found. In this sense the concept permits the development of another way of viewing contemporary film and video.

6. Numerous films on the subject of AIDS have had to resolve this question of nostalgia. This question, concurrent with the one of how to portray persons with AIDS, is impossible to resolve. These problems have engendered the development of activism in film and video of Queer Cinema; an emblematic figure in this regard is Gregg Bordowitz. His film *Fast Trip, Long Drop* (1994) magnificently articulated what should be public and what private. On Queer Cinema see: *How Do I Look? Queer Film and Video,* edited by Bad Object Choices, Bay Press, Seattle, 1991; *Queer Looks: Perspectives on Lesbian and Gay Film and Video,* by Martha Gever, John Greyson and Pratibha Parmar, Routledge, New York and London, 1993 and *Les Gais savoirs,* edited by Patrick Mauriès, Le Promeneur, Paris,1998.

7. Sadie Benning, Joe Gibbons, and many others have made remarkable use of the Fisher-Price camera. They have created mini-accounts of coming out as gay in the case of Sadie Benning, and in the case of Joe Gibbons, parodies in the tradition of Tony Oursler and Tony Conrad with whom he has frequently worked.

A Minor Cinema, A Cinema of Customs, A Cinema of Moods

1. This trilogy has never been easy to accept in the history of film. One has only to think of, among others, Germaine Dulac.
2. The text of the film has been published in *Cinematograph, vol. 4. A Journal of Film and Media Art*, by the Foundation of Art in Cinema, San Francisco.
3. On *Memo Book*, see the interview with Matthias Müller by Mike Hoolboom "Germany: Over the Wall" in the special issue of *Independent Eye*, vol. II, n°2-3, Toronto, 1990.
4. The archivist Peter Delpeut has made two films from partially decomposed nitrate film: Lyrisch Nitraat (1991) and *The Forbidden Quest* (1993), as if seeking to stop the loss of images. On the theme of the fragility of the medium, Paul Sharits has built an important body of work by burning and scratching directly on the film.
5. On the importance of found footage in contemporary film, see four exhibition catalogues: *Found Footage Filme aus gefundenem Material*, edited by Peter Tscherkassy, *Blimp*, n° 16, Graz, 1991; *Found Footage Film*, edited by Cécilia Hausheer and Christoph Settele, Lucerne, Viper/Zyklop, 1992; *Desmontage: Film, Video/Apropracion, Reciclage*, edited by Eugeni Bonet, Valencia, IVAM Centre Julio Gonzales,1993, as well as my text "Plus dure sera la chute," Paris, Galerie nationale du Jeu de Paume, 1995, translated and included in this book as "The Harder They Fall."
6. On Jakobois, see Alain-Alcide Sudre: "Cueillir l'instant : piéger l'éphémère," a brochure of the *Cinéma du Musée*, Paris, Centre Pompidou, 1988.
7. On Hiroyuki Oki, see the article in this book.

Reminiscences...

1. On film as an abstract model of Warhol's artistic practice, see Patrick de Haas: "Vider la vue" in *Andy Warhol Cinéma*, Paris, Centre Georges Pompidou, Carré, 1990.
2. Mekas's first years in the United States are covered by both *I Had Nowhere to Go*, his written journal from 1944 to 1954 and *Lost, Lost, Lost* (1976), his film journal of the years 1949 to 1963.
3. Shot in 1958, the film would win first prize in the Porretta-Terme Festival in Italy in 1962.
4. In fact, the model used by the New York Cooperative would be applied from 1966 on by filmmakers' cooperatives founded in Britain, then in Italy and in

France.

5. A talk on *Reminiscences of a Journey to Lithuania* (1950-71/72) given by Jonas Mekas in 1972: first published in French in *Scratch* n°3, Paris, 1983, translated by Thierry Jacquemin; a second translation by Dominique Noguez, 1992 ,in *Jonas Mekas*, Paris, Galerie nationale du Jeu de Paume.

6. *In Praise of Marie Menken, The Film Poet, January 4, 1962,* in *Movie Journal, The Rise of a New American Cinema, 1959-1971*, New York, Macmillan, 1972.

7. *Notebook* (1962-1963), *Glimpse of the Garden* (1957) and *Arabesque* (1961) were certainly essential films for Mekas. In *Notebook* can be found a prefiguration of Mekas's use of intertitles to create another dimension of expression.

8. *Paradise Not Yet Lost* (1977-1979) presents a second return to Lithuania by Mekas to celebrate his mother's ninetieth birthday.

9. In this 1964 film, Mekas uses a fixed shot which stretches out in time as he films a scene of Warhol receiving a prize at a *Film Culture* awards ceremony. A film homage which, nevertheless, differs from Warhol's films by the addition of a soundtrack of 1960s music.

10. With *Notes for Jerome* (1966-67, 74-78) Mekas began his series of portraits paying homage to departed friends. He devoted one to Andy Warhol and another to George Maciunas. In 1990, he assembled an unfinished film by Jerome Hill on Carl G. Jung.

11. On this point, see Andy Warhol and Pat Hackett: *Popism. The Warhol Sixties*, New York, Harcourt Brace Jovanovich, 1980, pp. 31-32. On Jack Smith and his influence on the American theatrical scene, see J. Hoberman; "The Theater of Jack Smith" in *The Drama Review*, vol. 23, n°1, March 1979.

12. See the Warhol interview with David Ehrenstein in *Film Culture, n°40*, New York, 1966.

13. For a detailed description of Warhol's films see my article: "Fixer des images en mouvement" in *Andy Warhol Cinema,* op.cit.

Gregory J. Markopoulos

1. This is why one can never speak of the adaptation of a book in the films of Markopoulos, where the literary basis is a source of inspiration. There is no faithfulness in the adaptation, even less the outline of a story, although *Serenity* may be an exception.

2. Could the title of this film be a reference to the expression "double mâle" which pops from Mignon's mouth in Jean Genet's *Notre Dame des Fleurs*?

3. Friedrich Nietzsche, *Human, All Too Human* (posthumous fragments) 16 (22). Complete Philosophical Works. Tome III, Volume I, Paris 1968.

The Harder They Fall

1. Adrian Brunel, *A.B. Film Craft*, London, George Newnes Ltd, 1933, p. 114.
2. Ibid.
3. Eisenstein too used stock shots in *Potemkin* to emphasize the isolation of Potemkin faced with the huge Czarist fleet; the images were in fact taken from newsreel footage of the British Royal Navy fleet.
4. Adrian Brunel, "Experiments," in the issue of *Close Up*, London, 1930. On Brunel, see Rachel Low, *The History of the British Cinema*, vol. 3 (1919-1929), London, George Allen & Unwin, Ltd., 1952.
5. On compilation films, see Jay Leyda, *Films Beget Films, A Study of the Compilation Film*, London, George Allen & Unwin, Ltd., 1964.
6. Cited by Raymond Borde in *"Le Cinéma au service de l'histoire* (1935) : Un film retrouvé de Germaine Dulac," *Archives*, nos. 44-45, Institut Jean Vigo, Cinémathèque de Toulouse, November-December 1991.
7. René Viénet, "Les situationnistes et les nouvelles formes d'action contre la politique et l'art, *Internationale situationniste*, Paris n°11, 1967.
8. On the montage of attractions, see Eisenstein's definition (1923), French translation published in "Au-delà des étoiles," *Œuvres*, tome 1, Paris, 1974.
9. On the montage of blocks of images, see Artavazd Peleshian, "Le montage à contrepoint, ou la théorie de la distance," Paris, *Trafic*, n°2, 1992.
10. See the descriptive text in the *Light Cone* catalogue, Paris, 1994.
11. A detailed description can be found in an article by Paul Marris, "Politics and 'Independent' Film in the Decade of Defeat," *British Cinema Traditions of Independence*, London, Don McPherson, B.F.I., 1980.
12. On discrepant sound and the specificities of Lettrist cinema, see the book by Frédérique Devaux, *Le Cinéma lettriste*, Paris, Paris Expérimental, 1992. On the different aspects of Lettrism, see Jean-Paul Curtay, *Lettrism and Hypergraphism, the Unknown Avant Garde*, catalogue, New York, Franklin Furnace, 1985; and Roland Sabatier, *Le Lettrisme*, Nice, Z' Editions, 1989.
13. On Bruce Conner, see Warren Bass, The Past Restructured; Bruce Conner and Others, *Journal of the University Film Association*, Carbondale, Volume 33, n° 2, Spring 1981, as well as the chapter later in this book.
14. For a description of this film, see the publication of the same name, Maurice Lemaître, *Le Film est déjà commencé ? Séance de cinéma*, Paris, André Bonne, 1952.
15. *Paolo Gioli, Cinéma du Musée* brochure, Paris, Centre Georges Pompidou, 1983.
16. See the interview of Leslie Thornton by William C. Wees in *Recycled Images*, New York, Anthology Films Archives, 1993.
17. On the techniques of Cécile Fontaine, see yann beauvais, "Cécile Fontaine," *Blimp*, Vienne, n°16, 1991: as well as *Le Cinéma décolle*, Paris, *Cinéma du Musée* brochure, Centre Georges Pompidou, 1994, the complete text of which is included in this book.
18. "Le cinéma comme alchimie : interview de Jürgen Reble," *Revue et Corrigée*, Grenoble, n°12, 1992.
19. Thanks to Jean-Damien Collin for identifying the location.

Relations Between Len Lye and László Moholy-Nagy

1. See "Interview of Len Lye by Wystan Curnow" published in *Art New Zealand* n° 17, Auckland, 1980.
2. In *Malerei, Fotografie, Film,* Bauhausbücher, n°8, Munich, Albert Langen, 1925. English translation by Janet Seligman; London, Lund Humphries, 1966.
3. "An Open Letter to the Film Industry," *Sight and Sound,* Summer 1934, Vol 3. No. 10, *Vision in Motion* Chicago: Paul Theobald, 1947.

László Moholy-Nagy

1. On this point, see Terence Senter, "Moholy-Nagy's English Photography" in *The Burlington Magazine*, November 1981
2. This same slow rhythm can be found in *Manhatta* (1921) the film of Paul Strand and Charles Sheeler, as if the migration from photography to film necessitated a slowing-down of movement.
3. An explanation of this phenomenon can be found in a work written by Hans Richter from 1937 to 1939 but nevertheless never published in his lifetime: *The Struggle for Film*, in which Richter argues for a creative documentary cinema, explaining the transition from the first avant-garde to the second by perception of film as an agitprop tool. Hans Richter, *The struggle for Film*, Aldershot: Wildwood House Ltd, 1986.
4. Moholy-Nagy: a letter to Frantisek Kalikoda, June 1934, an extract from *Telehor* (Brno) Cahier 1-2, 1936 p. 117, reprinted in the catalogue *Moholy-Nagy,* Paris, CCI Centre Georges Pompidou, 1976.
5. In *Telehor* (Brno), Cahier 1-2, 1936, p. 126, then reprinted in *Vision in Motion*, p. 271, Chicago, Paul Theobald, 1947.
6. Barbara Rose, "Kinetic Solutions to Pictorial Problems: the Films of Man Ray and Moholy-Nagy," *Art Forum*, September 1971.

Len Lye

1. On the genesis of *Tusalava*, see Len Lye, *No Trouble*, Majorca, Seizin Press, 1930. Extracts from this work were republished in *Cantrills Filmnotes*, n° 29-30, February, 1979, pages 41-42. "Len Lye's Films" by Roger Horrocks, catalogue of the exhibition: *Len Lye, A Personal Mythology*, Auckland City Art Gallery, 1980.
2. On these points see Len Lye: "The Tusalava Model," an extract from an autobiographical manuscript in *Experimental Animation* by Robert Russett and Cecile Starr, New York, Van Nostrand Reinhold, 1976.
3. On the relations between music and film in Len Lye's work, see the transcription of his appearance at the Cinémathèque française in *Film Culture*, n° 44, New York, Spring 1967.

4. Ibid., p. 50; a description of the sequence can be found in "Len Lye, The Career
    of an Independent Filmmaker" by Roger Horrocks in *Film Quarterly*, vol. 14, n° 3-
    4, New York, 1981.
5. For a description of the main color processes in *Rainbow Dance*, see *Figures of
    Motion: Len Lye's Selected Writings*, edited by Wystan Curnow and Roger
    Horrocks, Auckland University Press, 1984.
6. Text from 1959 republished in *Figures of Motion, op.cit.*

Lot in Sodom

1. *Lot in Sodom* was not the first film with homosexual content. For more historical
    details on the subject, see Vito Russo, *The Celluloid Closet*, New York, Harper &
    Row, 1980.
2. Barbara Hammer proposed a way to look at *Lot in Sodom* in her film *Nitrate
    Kisses* (1992). Questioning the historical representations of gay and lesbian sexu-
    ality, she seeks to show, by incorporating sequences from Watson and Webber's
    film, that the invisibility of gays and lesbians cannot be measured by the atti-
    tudes and behavior of today, thus the necessity to explore and re-use images to
    rescue them from an imposed oblivion. This wish to establish a history that is
    no longer asexualized is characteristic of a liberation movement. It began to play
    a meaningful role with the rise of *queer studies* and found its preferred place in
    documentaries that were close to experimental work: *Race d'Ep* (1980) by Lionel
    Soukaz, *Black Is...Black Ain't* (1995) by Marlon Riggs, *Oh Happy Day* (1996) by
    Charles Lofton, *Paris Was a Woman* (1996) by Greta Schiller and *The Female
    Closet* (1998) by Barbara Hammer.

A Simulacrum Question

1. "Structural," a term first employed by P. Adams Sitney in 1969 to designate a new
    tendency of American film starting in 1960s, in *Film Culture*, New York, n°47.
    "Structural/Materialist," a notion formulated by Peter Gidal in 1974, refuting the
    analysis of Sitney, in Studio International, London, February 1974, and again in
    Structural Film Anthology, London, B.F.I., 1976. "Expanded," work principally
    developed by the British avant-garde around the years 1972-1976. "Post-Structur-
    al," work seeking to go beyond American structural film after 1976, principally in
    France and Europe.
2. Narration came back in different ways, returning to classical themes, by paro-
    dying the underground or, in the case of contemporary British production, in
    becoming didactic, by explaining what it was about, lest it would be forgotten
    that it was about a simulacrum. Or, in the case of American and German
    production, by becoming "weakly" political. See.*The Anti-Aesthetic: Essays on Post-
    modern Culture*, edited by Hal Foster, Bay Press 1983, as well as the commentary
    on this work by Deke Dusinberre: "Ceci n'est pas une théorie (or How I Became

a Post-Critic)," in *Scratch*, Paris, n°4, April 1984. See also *Cinema off e videoarte a New York*, edited by Ester de Miro, Germano Celant, Genoa, Bonini, 1981.

3. Appearance seen as illusion (simulacrum), this conceptual approach was championed by Malcolm Le Grice in *Abstract Film and Beyond*, London, Studio Vista, 1977, as well as by Peter Gidal, *op.cit.*

4. A similar use of stuttering can be found in *Passion* (1982) by Jean-Luc Godard.

5. For example *On the Marriage Broker Joke as Cited by Sigmund Freud in Wit and its Relation to the Unconscious, or Can the Avant-Garde Artist be Wholed?* (1980), a film in which language plays a preponderant role as does the history of art in general (Henri Rousseau, Duchamp, etc.).

6. Paul Sharits worked and played a great deal with the different elements of film: the subject (for example, in *T,O,U,C,H,I,N,G*, 1968, the representation of blood with sequins) or with the physical medium (in his installations, it is impossible to determine the exact placement of scratches, they being the result of refilming scratched film; and more recently the later refinements consisting of accompanying the projection of the film with a supplementary scratch made directly, totally blotting out in this way the nature of the image).

7. In traditional cinema, Ruiz and Hitchcock played with this processes of image-within-image where the story line is lost and then resumed.

8. After all, it is found footage and the importance of this type of discovery to the history of avant-garde film is well-known: Lemaître, Gehr, Conner, Jacobs... A kind of "ready-made," which like any good ready-made is removed from its context to be placed in another.

9. In fact, Lumière almost certainly did not invent it himself because this skit was very probably based on the scenario of a "comic book" of the time.

10. There is not enough space here to study the ambiguous role that theoretical arguments play in film production and to wonder in what way one does not mask the other in a sort of theoretical bidding war, or by visual concentration.

11. The silent partner is a reference to Peter Gidal's film *Silent Partner* (1977).

12. *La Vache qui rumine* by Georges Rey can be understood in this way, a simple fixed shot permitting any interpretation depending on one's mood at the moment, or *La Petite fille* (1978) by Pascal Auger which, through jerky repetitions, breaks the model, or *Face* (1971) by Jean-Pierre Bertrand playing on representation through means of certain devices of capturing it: photographs and film.

13. See the theory advanced by Peter Kubelka.

The Musical

1. Germaine Dulac, "The Essence of Cinema - the Visual Idea" in *Writings on Cinema (1919 - 1937)* edited by Prosper Hillairet, translated from the French by Scott Hammen, Paris, Eyewash Books Collection/Paris Expérimental, 2021.

2. Raoul Hausmann: "De l'enregistrement cinématographique à la vision filmée" in *L'Âge du cinéma*, n°6, 1951.

3. Henri Chomette in *Les Cahiers du mois* 1925, quoted by René Clair in *Cinéma d'hier, cinéma d'aujourd'hui*, Paris, 1970.

4. A detailed analysis of the film is given by Louise O'Konor in *Viking Eggeling (1880-1925) Artist and Filmmaker, Life and Work*. Acta universatis Stockholmiensis Stockholm, Studies in History of Art 23, Stockholm 1971.

5. On Ruttmann's *Opus* series see the filmography commentary in *Walter Ruttmann Eine Dokumentaion*, edited by Jeanpaul Goergen, Berlin, Freunde der Deutschen Kinematek, 1988.

6. In fact, few of Fischinger's films visually orchestrate music: *Studie 7* (1931) uses Brahms' *Hungarian Dance n°5*, *An American March* (1941) uses *Stars and Stripes*, while it is a question of visual music for other films such as *Liebspiel* (1931) and *Allegretto* (1936).

7. On Oskar Fischinger see "The Films of Oskar Fischinger" by William Moritz in *Film Culture*, n° 58-59-60, New York, 1974.

8. The improvisation of Len Lye, which presents the painted film synchronized with jazz. It is at this stage of the synchronization that the synesthesia occurs.

9. A detailed analysis of Kubelka's films was made by Stefano Masi in "Peter Kubelka, Sculptor of Time" in *Peter Kubelka*, edited by Christian Lebrat, Paris, Paris Expérimental 1990. On the relations between Webern and Kubelka, see Peter Weibel: "The Viennese Formal Film," in *Film als Film, 1910 Bus Heute*, edited by Birgit Hein and Wulf Herzogenrath, Cologne, Kölnischer Kunstverein 1977.

10. These are exactly the forms of development which I used in *Quatr'un* (1993), but by multiplying them because these processes apply to the entire film. It is a four-screen film. Each screen is the mirror-image of the one next to it or above it. Here it is more a case of double reversal than of inversion.

11. *Digital Harmony* is the title of the book by John Whitney in which he presents a collection of his reflections on the relations which music maintains with the art of motion; Peterborough, McGraw Hill, 1982. On this book, see yann beauvais: "Sur les propositions de John Whitney," *Scratch*, n°3, Paris 1980.

12. Whitney, John, "Audio Visual Music, Color Music - Abstract Film in Digital Harmony, 1944. In *Digital Harmony: On the Complementarity of Music and Visual Art*, Peterborough, N.H.: Byte Books, 1980. p. 138-4.

13. On this point see: "Hearing: Seeing" in *Film Culture*, n° 65-66, New York, 1978.

14. On these relations between music and cinema, see "Interview de Paul Sharits" by yann beauvais, *Scratch*, n°1, October 1982.

15. The title of a chapter in a work by Michel Chion:"L'art des sons fixés ou la musique concrètement," Rives, Metamkine, 1991.

16. *El Cafetal* by David Wharry is a color adaptation of a zarzuela, a traditional Spanish form of musical comedy, where only pure colors are seen, a veritable synesthesia which calls on the imagination to furnish the images.

17. It brings to mind all the films which use radio recordings, or those which rely on the presence of a radio turned on during projection, such as *Blonde Cobra* (1959-1963) by Ken Jacobs.

The Film Noir in Experimental Film

1. For a detailed description of the shots and sound of the film, see *Le Film est déjà commencé ?* by Maurice Lemaître, Paris, André Bonne, 1952.
2. A description of the film can be found in *Contre le cinéma* by Guy Debord, Bibliothèque d'Alexandrie Collection, Éditions de l'institut scandinave de Vandalisme Comparé, 1964; reprinted in *Œuvres cinématographiques complètes*, Paris, Champ Libre, 1978.
3. On the specificity of the work on film as it is conceived and advocated by Peter Gidal, see "Theory and Definition of Structural/Materialist Film" in *Structural Film Anthology*. B.F.I., London, 1976, at *Materialist Film*, Routledge, London, 1989.
4. A breakdown of the sound editing of this film can be found in *Walter Ruttmann Eine Dokumentation*, edited by Jeanpaul Goergen, op.cit.
5. For a description of the functioning of vision and its possible restitution in experimental film, see *Light Moving in Time, Studies in the Visual Aethetics of Avant-Garde Film* by William Wees, Berkeley, University of California Press, 1992.
6. For a description of the films of Iimura, see Scott MacDonald, "The Films of Takahiko Iimura" in *Takahiko Film and Video*, New York, Anthology Film Archives, 1990.
7. For a precise technical description of this film, see the special issue of the magazine *Sequences*, n° 82, Montreal, October 1975.
8. On Len Lye's notions of these primitive rhythms, see Chapter 4 on Len Lye in this book.
9. On the use of the word in experimental film see *Mot: dites, Images*, edited by yann beauvais, Paris, Scratch/Musée national d'art moderne, 1987.
10. A description of Anthony McCall's film can be found in the catalogue *Exprmtl5*, Knokke-Le-Zoute, Brussels, Centre expérimental de la cinématographie, 1975.
11. This dissolution of representation in darkness has been extraordinarily well treated in films whose dominate nature is photographic: see the sequence on the face and body of a woman in *Cartoon Le Mousse* (1979) by Chick Strand. In this vein, there is still to be done a study of films which use black background to isolate the filmed body: I am thinking of *L'Enfant qui a pissé des paillettes* (1975) by Maria Klonaris and Katerina Thomadaki, a number of films by Ed Emshwiller including *Thantopsis* (1962) and *Relativity* (1966), as well as certain films by Teo Hernandez. Likewise, the use of masks is a way to work on the surface of black in the foreground or in the background: *Film numéro deux* (1976) by Christian Lebrat, *Scaling* (1988) by Mike Hoolboom...

Speed Reading

1. For the cinema of this period, see Patrick de Haas, *Cinéma intégral, de la peinture au cinéma dans les années vingt*, Paris, Transéditions, 1986.
2. On the various protagonists of Lettrist cinema, see Frédérique Devaux, *Le Cinéma lettriste 1951-1991*, Paris, Paris Expérimental, 1992 and Jean-Michel

Bouhours, *Maurice Lemaître*, Paris, Centre Georges Pompidou, 1995.

3. A history of provocation toward the spectators would run from film projections at the Dada soirées, via the ideal screening of Maurice Lemaître's *Le film est déjà commencé ?* (1950), to the expanded cinema projections in Britain in the 1970s.

4. See Dominique Noguez, *Une Renaissance du cinéma: le cinéma "underground" américain* Paris, Klincksieck, 1985; John Hanhardt, *A History of The American Avant-Garde Cinema*, New York, The American Federation of Arts, 1976; David James, *Allegories of Cinema: American Film in the Sixties*, Princeton: University of Princeton Press, 1989.

5. On the many activities of Jonas Mekas, see David James, *To Free the Cinema: Jonas Mekas & the New York Underground,* Princeton, Princeton University Press, 1992, and Jonas Mekas, exhibition catalogue, Paris, Jeu de Paume, Réunion des Musées Nationaux, 1992.

6. The New American Cinema could not have existed without the filmmakers who came before it, such as Maya Deren, Gregory Markopoulos, Kenneth Anger, and Stan Brakhage. On the relations between the underground and censorship, see J. Hoberman, "License for License: Underground Movies and Obscenity in the Cities," in Steve Seid, *Banned in the USA, America and Film Censorship*, Berkeley, Pacific Film Archives,1993.

7. For several years Callie Angell has been working on the establishment of a filmography of Andy Warhol; so far she has tallied over five hundred "Screen Tests." See Callie Angell, *The Films of Andy Warhol Part II*, New York, Whitney Museum, 1994, and *Something Secret: Portraiture in Warhol's Films*, Sydney, Museum of Contemporary Art, 1994.

8. "Baudelairean cinema" is an expression first used by Jonas Mekas in May 1963, in an article in the Village Voice, to designate the films of four filmmakers: Ron Rice, Ken Jacobs, Bob Fleischner, and Jack Smith. See *Movie Journal, The Rise of a New American Cinema 1959-1971*, New York, Collier Books, 1972. A study on this kind of cinema and its relations with "camp" has been written by Carol Rowe, *The Baudelairean Cinema: a Trend within the American Avant-Garde*, Ann Arbor, UMI Research Press, 1982). On "camp", see Susan Sontag, *Against Interpretations and Other Essays*, New York, Dell, 1966.

9. See Jean-Michel Bouhours, "Au-delà de l'écran... L'invisible et le hors-champ," in *Hors Limites*, Paris, Centre Georges Pompidou, 1994.

10. For this notion see yann beauvais, *Found Footage*, Paris, Jeu de Paume, 1995.

11. For this question of similar actions, see the film project by Jackson Mac Low, *Tree* (1961), in which a tree was to be filmed in a still shot lasting several hours. George Maciunas complains that *Sleep* (1963-1964)... is a cinematographic plagiarism of *Tree Movie* (1961) by Jackson Mac Low, just as *Eat* (1964) is a plagiarism of *Invocation of Canyons and Borders for Stan Brakhage* (1963) by Dick Higgins in "Some Comments on Structural Film," by P. Adams Sitney, *Film Culture* n° 47, New York, 1969. Only in 1992 was a Fluxfilms anthology established by Jonas Mekas; it was presented for the first time in France at the preceding Lyon Biennial.

12. Warhol attended the presentation of this piece in New York.

13. Concerning Yvonne Rainer, see *Works 1961-1973*, New York, The Press of Nova Scotia, 1974, and Sally Banes, *Greenwich Village 1963*, Durham, North Carolina, Duke University Press, 1993.

14. For a chronology of Vienna Actionism, see *Von der Aktionmalerei zum Aktionismus 1960-1965*, Vienna, Ritter Verlag, 1988, and *Wiener Aktionismus 1960-1971*, Vienna, Ritter Verlag, 1989.

15. This notion of body art and its cinematographic extensions has been studied particularly well by Dominique Noguez in *Trente ans de cinéma expérimental en France (1950-1980)*, Paris, Arcef, 1982.

16. See Bruno Corra, "Musique Chromatique," in *La Poétique de la couleur,* an anthology edited by Nicole Brenez and Miles McKane, Paris, Musée du Louvre/Institut de l'image, 1995.

17. "Film fiber Film," in *Ausstellungskatalog*, vol. III, *Portraits & Signatures: 81 Kiinstler der Documenta 6*, Kassel, 1977.

18. Cinema serves as a major reference for Cindy Sherman, Jean Le Gac, and Alain Fleischer.

19. See the special edition of *Film Culture* n° 65-66, devoted to Paul Sharits, New York, 1978, in particular the text "Exhibition/Frozen Frames."

20. Jürgen Reble, "Alchimie des couleurs" in *La Poétique de la couleur,* op. cit.

21. Idem.

From One World to Another

1. "Nous," published by Vertov in the review *Kinophot* N°1, 1922, republished in *Articles, journaux, projets, Cahiers du cinéma*, Paris 1972.

2. Maya Deren: "The Cleveland Lecture" in *Film Culture* N° 29, New York, Summer 1963, p.66.

3. In *L'Âge d'or* (1930), eighth intertitle: "Quelques heures après," fourteenth intertitle: "Parfois le dimanche". There was already a similar use of intertitles in *Un Chien andalou* (1929) by means of which the logic of the narrative was destroyed by breaking up its sequential effect. The same thing happens in Man Ray's *L'Étoile de mer* (1928), in which the title links suggest another register of discourse that is neither illustrated nor explained by the images, a register that underlines both the poetic aspect of cinema as much as its non linearity.

4. In this film it is a matter of the incorporation of the camera as a story generator that causes cinema itself to be understood as the subject to the extent in which it makes an appearance through its relationship to the events it shows.

5. It is in *Lost, Lost, Lost* (1976) that the work on the acquisition of memories and its reprocessing in the course of shooting is most remarkably revealed.

6. "Towards a Narrative Film Form," Gregory Markopoulos, *Film Culture* No. 31, Winter 1963-64, New York.